EVERYDAY MEN
Living In A Climate of Unbelief

STUDIEN ZUR INTERKULTURELLEN GESCHICHTE DES CHRISTENTUMS
ETUDES D'HISTOIRE INTERCULTURELLE DU CHRISTIANISME
STUDIES IN THE INTERCULTURAL HISTORY OF CHRISTIANITY

begründet von / fondé par / founded by
Hans Jochen Margull †, Hamburg

herausgegeben von / édité par / edited by

Richard Friedli   Walter J. Hollenweger   Theo Sundermeier
Université de Fribourg   University of Birmingham   Universität Heidelberg

Band 46

Verlag Peter Lang
Frankfurt am Main · Bern · New York · Paris

Roger B. Edrington

EVERYDAY MEN

Living in A Climate
of Unbelief

Verlag Peter Lang

Frankfurt am Main · Bern · New York · Paris

BV
4593
.E37
1987

CIP-Kurztitelaufnahme der Deutschen Bibliothek

Edrington, Roger B.:

Everyday men : living in a climate of unbelief /
Roger B. Edrington. - Frankfurt am Main ; Bern ;
New York ; Paris : Lang, 1987.
(Sudies in the intercultural history of Christianity
; Vol. 46)
ISBN 3-8204-9875-3

NE: Studien zur interkulturellen Geschichte des
Christentums

Library of Congress Cataloging-in-Publication Data

Edrington, Roger B.
Everyday men.

(Studies in the intercultural history of Christianity ;
46 = Studien zur interkulturellen Geschichte des
Christentums ; Bd. 46 - Etudes d'histoire interculturelle
du christianisme ; 46)
Bibliography: p.
1. Labor and laboring classes--England--Birmingham
(West Midlands)--Religious life--Public opinion.
2. Birmingham (West Midlands, England)--Religious life
and customs--Public opinion. 3. Public opinion--
England--Birmingham (West Midlands) 4. Faith.
5. Skepticism. I. Title. II. Series. Studien zur
interkulturellen Geschichte des Christentums ;

Bd. 46.
BV4593.E37 1987   208'.80623   87-3127
ISBN 3-8204-9875-3

ISSN 0170-9240
ISBN 3-8204-9875-3

© Verlag Peter Lang GmbH, Frankfurt am Main 1987
Druck und Bindung: Weihert-Druck GmbH, Darmstadt

ABSTRACT

This study is about everyday men. They are approached through a unique marriage of biblical theology and empirical research which gives birth to a missionary challenge.

Part One attempts to build a theological foundation for looking at people from the aspect of belief and unbelief. It sees this distinction as a crucial theme in the biblical material which remains relevant to men everywhere. The author discovers five elements of Christian belief in the biblical material while unbelief spans the five elements by its void, denial, or choice of an alternative.

Part Two starts with a random sample, in-depth interview of fifty men in a "working-class" area of Birmingham. The interviews attempt to discover the nature and saliency of the men's belief and unbelief in the Christian faith. The analysis stresses the qualitative response with the emphasis on listening to the men describe their lives, values, beliefs, and lack of beliefs in their own words. The findings are also compared to other related studies, prompting some conclusions regarding the meaning of these findings. Chapter Eight attempts to bring the biblical material to bear on the findings about ordinary people and asks whether they can be described as believers or unbelievers. From this starting point, it becomes obvious that the scope of unbelief is very broad.

Part Three takes the understanding of God's Word and men's words and moves toward a missiological purpose of approaching unbelievers with a gospel for today. It sees both the content and context of the gospel as important. The cultural problem is briefly considered and specific approaches are suggested in relation to "working-class" English culture.

TABLE OF CONTENTS

PART ONE

FOUNDATION: TOWARDS USABLE BIBLICAL DESCRIPTIONS OF BELIEF AND UNBELIEF

III

PART TWO

APPLICATION: BELIEVERS AND UNBELIEVERS IN BIRMINGHAM

PART THREE

COMMUNICATION: RELATING THE GOSPEL IN A CLIMATE OF UNBELIEF

FOREWORD:

RELIGION IN A SILENCED CULTURE

It is not often that a piece of research can be described as moving. Roger Edrington's dissertation is one, because he has the charisma of listening. That is why the fifty men whom he interviewed on belief and unbelief for his research work told him what many of them have told nobody else, not even their own wives. They were astonished that somebody was actually interested in their ideas and their lives.

Almost all of these men have never been to church since Sunday School days--i.e. since the age of about ten--except of course on the social occasions such as weddings, christenings and funerals.

Anyone familiar with the religious scene in Europe would expect the usual results from this research: mistrust of church and clergy, arguments from science and science-fiction against Christian beliefs. All this is contained in Edrington's research, but not as prominently as one would expect. What comes through as more important and with unambiguous clarity is the genuine modesty, honesty and lostness of these men. These are three great words which need some explanation.

Modesty is shown in the way the men confess their ignorance on vital issues of their lives. They neither know what they believe nor what they disbelieve. They are almost equally critical in relation to the atheistic slogans as in relation to the tenets of the Christian faith. And if they have some convictions or some knowledge they phrase it in a very cautious language. Very little propaganda, much pain in grappling with the issue, and many times a resigned confession: "I would say that I was a Christian and an agnostic". They term themselves "a not sure religious Christian", "a don't know believer". Sometimes a mild criticism of the official spokesmen of religion comes through: "It's alright for these blokes who write books, but they don't tell you, they don't put it plain enough for you to understand because I don't think they know theirselves."

God is to many of them--as one told Dr. Edrington--like that "Captain in the Gurkha rifles" who "carried me across the paddy fields and the Japs were shelling over him and he was ill himself. He was rotten with dysentery. I've never seen him since and I don't know his name, but I think of him".

Many of the men have had a religious experience once or several times in their lives which has made a deep impression on them. But they cannot articulate this experience. They do not know the names of the one who saved them but they "think of him".

Honesty comes through in the way both believers and unbelievers volunteer their experiences of prayer. But it is a very private prayer. "Don't tell the Missus that I am praying." The best place to pray is the (water-)closet.

They never talk to anybody about religion. It is a taboo. Yet they let Edrington tape their visions, the answers to their prayers in war and peace, their anger of the years lost in the war. They express their criticism of the misuse of God's name by the military:

> You take the Falkland Islands. Our lot blessing our boys going out there and their priest blessing their men, instead of as the Bible says . . . . It's stupid! You're going out to kill each other and you don't even own an ounce of the land and you don't own nothing here. Most of the people at home, they've got nothing. They haven't even got control over their rent. They've got nothing and they're going out to massacre each other. And there's priests on the dock blessing them, you know. Fellows carrying the picture of the Virgin Mary on his gun. Poor old Argentinian, he's dead now, you know. Okay, he might have had a belief, but is that belief going to keep your family? It's not. So as far as beliefs are concerned, I'm afraid it's a no-no with me. Never convince me.

Asked which is the most important concern in their lives, they say: health and family. Money seems to be very secondary.

Lostness. "Our opinion don't count for much. We don't have any opinion any more, we just live from day to day." It appears that not only do they not talk about religion amongst themselves but they "do not have any opinion any more". People whose language does not count, lose the will and the ability to communicate--except in those places where it still matters, namely in the family.

The Bible as grammar and word-book for testing, articulating and shaping opinions (theological, existential, and political) is absent and replaced by nothing. The church as community which creates, tests and inspires language about the meaning of life and death is also absent and replaced by nothing. The family certainly cannot replace it and the place of work does not provide a language and thinking context for these working men.

In the opinion of these men the church must be there, but not for them to take part. The church must also not change its language and organisation, although they do not understand it. It would be a foreign thought to them that the church has something vital to offer to them and that--more importantly--their insights and religious or non-religious experiences are vital for the survival of a church which takes its intercultural ministry seriously.

In fact the two cultures are almost totally divided: the ever-speaking proclaiming church and the almost silenced workers. The cultural elements which could build a bridge over the abyss of the two cultures (prayer, doing the faith, dialogue in small groups) are absent in the church or do not reach them. So, the cultural gap in Birmingham between those who have a say and those who lack a generally acceptable language to express their feelings and concerns, is mirrored by the churched and unchurched. Although nowadays there are many people outside the church who have a say, they are not workers and so far they have been as unable as the church to enter into genuine dialogue with the workers.

When Roger Edrington had finished his research he emerged a changed man, as he describes in his introduction. He wants to be an evangelist. He wants to pass on the good news. That is why he came from the USA to Great Britain.

The fifty interviewees have introduced him to the alien culture of working people. They have shown him that certain Christian concepts can only be misunderstood in this culture, that the individualistic concepts of his evangelical commitment do not really meet the sad lostness of "his men". But listening, patient listening, is a first step at communicating the Gospel.

So we have to think again, and think hard and think together with these men, what shape and form the Gospel could take in a working class culture.

There is, of course, a flourishing working class church in Birmingham. But it is black. In spite of slavery and repression they are not silenced. They have created their own vigorous language of faith. It may be that they could show us the way.

If it is part of "intercultural theology" that people are not only carried through the paddy fields of life's danger but that we also know the names of the one who carries us, then we must dig deep into our memories to find these names. If knowing the names is important, we must meet with the others who were also carried through the shell-fire and ask them, compare our memories and visions. This search for names is called theology. If it is done across cultures it is called intercultural theology. And if it is done across the social and cultural divides it becomes a tool for recognising the body of Christ.

Dr. Walter J. Hollenweger
Professor of Mission
University of Birmingham
England

PREFACE

It is almost a universal condition of mankind to feel (and probably be) misunderstood. There is so much noise and no one is listening. Everyday men feel the same way. Many are surprised when someone comes to listen to them rather than to speak or sell. This study has attempted to ask questions before it speaks.

Yet the church is truly a speaking institution: proclamation, dialogue, witness, discussion, negotiation, sermons, testimonies, prayers, pronouncements, and so on. Speaking is part of the very nature of the church, yet perhaps the church has also forgotten to listen. It seems she has rarely listened to everyday man. This study is a tiny part of the church listening to a small, but important, part of the world.

The fifty men who participated with me in this study have been my informants. They told me what it was like to be an everyday man, from their perspective. These men have become "my men"--not that I possess them, far from it. Most will have forgotten a researcher from the University of Birmingham, but I have not forgotten them. I have lived with them not only in the hour or so which I spent with them, but nearly every day since as I listened to the tapes, transcribed them, read, re-read and read again the transcriptions, collated the results and contemplated their meaning, wrote about them, and then read it all again.

The influence of these men on me has far exceeded the work on this volume. They live with me. As I talk to other men and women, they consider with me the way of belief and unbelief in my own life. They are "my men" because they live with me as family. For some, I have great affection, others I only pity; some give me great stimulation, others only exasperate me. But I have respect for them all as men, "my men". They are all in the family and would not go away even if I wished them to.

This is a study of ordinary people, so I often use plain rather than academic language. I use "I" whenever it seems stilted to use the third person, which hopefully makes it more readable. Whenever possible, especially in part two, I use the words of the men themselves. I have retained the broken sentences, incorrect grammar, and occasional swear words to retain the colour of the original, everyday men's own picturesque language. The quotations are very selective, as in any research, so I can only give snapshots rather than video presentations of the men. The numbers in brackets [00] are the number of the interview, so that if you want to, you can piece together some of the necessarily fragmented interviews. The only way around this is

for you to read for yourself the 440 single-spaced pages of
transcripts or listen to the fifty tapes. You may find different
snapshots, but I have tried to present the men as authentically
as I am able.

As the writing is finished, I can now relate--at least
partially--to George Orwell's *Why I Write*:

> All writers are vain, selfish, and lazy, and at the very
> bottom of their motives there lies a mystery. Writing a book
> is a horrible, exhausting struggle, like a long bout of some
> painful illness. One would never undertake such a thing if
> one were not driven on by some demon whom one can neither
> resist nor understand. For all one knows that demon is
> simply the same instinct that makes a baby squall for atten-
> tion. And yet it is also true that one can write nothing
> readable unless one constantly struggles to efface one's own
> personality. Good prose is like a window pane.

As an everyday man myself, you will see a great deal of me in
what follows but my desire is that you see more of my everyday
men and the Everyday Man than you do of me.

                                              Roger Edrington

Birmingham, England

CHAPTER ONE

INTRODUCTION

This research is not about everyman's unbelief (and belief), but about the unbelief (and belief) of everyday men, ordinary people in one location in Birmingham. They are not big people with big ideas. Their concerns are concrete and their language is plain but colourful; they are honest but private all the same. They are decent and respectable, but not highly respected or even widely known. Their world is limited mainly within the confines of home, work, and social meeting places.

One is, however, struck by their lostness--both in an ordinary and theological usage of the word. Their lives have little direction except to follow the meandering path of raising a family, working for a living, and relieving their misery through social and leisure activities. They suspect, increasingly so with age, that the path leads nowhere. They pass on their hopes without conviction, their beliefs without certainty, their faiths without sight, their prejudices without thought, and their lifestyles without option. Despair is obvious in some, although more often hidden by the necessity of coping with life. If the government, no matter what its colour, cannot save them, still less can the church or God. Even God or the gods appear in trouble. Perhaps the unbelievers among them feel the same sort of pity toward the church that Christians feel toward them.

With relation to beliefs, they know neither what they believe nor what they do not believe. The results of a vast increase in the volume of knowledge leaves them without usable knowledge even in the trade for which they trained. A shift in epistemology itself leaves them with no basis to even gain knowledge. They remain reasonably contented, unrevolutionary, and irreligious, somehow holding on to a hope against hope that there is a better day for them in this world or the next (but not another) world of their children.

What can we call the beliefs of these everyday men? Are they Christian faith, unbelief, "a kind of believing"[1] or something else? Colin Campbell expresses his dilemma regarding the problem of "the boundary between irreligion and religious commitment." He sees the "no-man's-land" as occupied by "the religiously sympathising unbeliever", which is a variety of irreligion. This unbeliever

is a person who neither possesses commitment to a religious
position nor regards religion with hostility or indifference,
but on the contrary is favourably disposed toward it. Such a
person is not easily fitted in to the sphere of irreligion as
we have outlined it above, but is equally unamenable to
inclusion in the category of the religious.[2]

It is relatively easy to categorize some people as believers and
others as unbelievers: "Where a person defines his own behaviour, and it is defined by others, as constituting the rejection
of religion, then he is clearly irreligious. Where these two
criteria do not overlap, then the problems mentioned become very
real."[3] But many of the men in this sample did not even know
whether to define themselves as believers or not and their usage
of the word was much less than precise. In order to find out
what believers and unbelievers there are among these everyday
men, we will need categories from which to begin. This we have
attempted to supply in part one as a fairly precise and usable
description of belief and unbelief.

The Scope of Unbelief

Our contention is that the scope of unbelief today is
very wide indeed, despite those who attempt to deny its existence
at all (discussed in chapter two).

The question of unbelief is undergoing a special transpo-
sition in present-day theological thought. It is passing
from being a borderline question within an apologetical
defence of belief or within a confrontation with other philosophical views of life to being a central question of theology itself where the importance and seriousness of its problematic can become manifest. The reason why this question of
unbelief is being seen as the more basic question of belief
itself and as a theological question is not without reason
due to the embarrassment encountered by the direct apologetic
of belief when faced with present-day unbelief, because this
unbelief has not only ceased to be the esoteric privilege of
the sophisticated, but it has become the spiritual attitude
of many people.[4]

Yet even though the unbelief is widespread, as we shall
show later, there is very little hard data available, so little
that Rocco Caporale records in 1969 that there is the realization
of an "appalling lack of empirical data on unbelief and the
supreme ignorance of what really obtains in the world of the
proverbial man in the street."[5] J. Russell Hale points out that
even the institutions of irreligion have been studied, but the
unchurched and the unbelievers have been left out. From a North
American perspective, "They have been treated as if, as a residual category--those left after the others have been counted--they
were one homogeneous whole. Obviously, logic tells us, this is
not the case."[6] A Latin American also sees the necessity for
study in a related area:

One of the many "sociologists" who are studying the "fabulous
growth of the Church in the Third Word" could render an
invaluable service to the study of missions, by including a

survey, not only of those who enter the Church, but also of those who leave.[7]

Whether this research helps give some data about ordinary men, or is too limited or specific, will have to be judged by others. I make no claims to universality. My limited use of percentages speaks only of the everyday men who I encountered. What follows is what everyday men revealed to me, yet I would not be surprised if they strike notes of similarity with other everyday men throughout England.

Theological, Missiological, Sociological

This study is a strange marriage, then, of biblical theology and empirical study which gives birth to a missionary challenge. It is theological and missiological, but not truly sociological. It uses the interviewing tools which sociology lends, but only to ask theological questions with missiological goals. It makes no attempt at sociological analysis although there is scope for someone to use the empirical data from that perspective. The study touches sociology, but is not a full participant in it.

Peter Berger says that the theologian's

encounter with serious sociology is very likely to be something of a let-down. Not only do the theologians discover that sociologists are in great disagreement among themselves, but that the disagreement extends to fundamental questions of method and of the validity of alleged empirical findings about contemporary society. . . .
If exaggerated fears concerning sociology on the part of theologians are misplaced, so are exaggerated hopes.[8]

He further adds:

Liberal or progressive theologians (again, this is true in both confessions) tend rather to an exaggerated view of what sociology may be able to do for them. Such theologians tend to look toward sociology for authoritative insights into the reality of the modern world, if not indeed for authoritative programs on how to reform or revolutionize this world. What makes this worse is that "culture-prophets" and "critic-intellectuals" of every description have an inclination today to envelop their pronouncements in the jargon of sociology, thus obfuscating the line between ideology and science--with the result that the former is as often enhanced as the latter is discredited with different audiences.[9]

This study of men looks for its authority to biblical revelation--looking to God as it looks at man. The lessons of sociology will also have something to say to us about how to approach man, but it will always be in the context of the Man who is the Revealer and Knower of all men.

Caporale notes that "a discussion on unbelief cannot be conducted with equal ease by the theologian and by the social scientist." He sees the theologian's position as "restricted".

The social scientist, on the other hand, is permitted to
move about more freely, may formulate alternative
explanatory schemes, and, far from experiencing any threat
to his discipline, may find in the study of unbelief a
challenging area of investigation.[10]

It is true that the theologian has a self-imposed, or
Theos-imposed, restriction, but this can be a helpful restriction
because he has a more firm place on which to stand. Because the
social scientist often has no precise theoretical definition of
the phenomena, he is subjected to theoretical examination of the
possibilities rather than scrutiny of the subject (as was
revealed in the symposium on unbelief discussed in chapter two).
There is, however, a place for phenomena to be examined with no
prior imposition of external criteria, but as Professor of Sociology at the University of Lille, Francois Isambert has said,
"Eventually we end up with the same conclusion, namely, that
unbelief can only be defined with reference to a given belief."[11]

Value-Free?

This study does not claim to be value-free, objective
research. In fact, it questions with a number of scholars (e.g.
Kuhn, Popper, etc. pace Weber) whether this sort of neutrality
can be achieved. E. Vogt questions the classical solution to the
problem of bias in sociology, i.e. the *wertfreie* sociology:

To separate the factual content of a phenomenon from its
value content is to separate it from reality. This is particularly true in the case of religious phenomena. By putting himself in a completely disinterested frame of mind with
no standard of value to guide his thought and the direction
of his research, the sociologist can do no more than record
passively an endless series of trivial and insignificant data
from the purely phenomenological world. To provide a realistic answer to the problem of objectivity in the sociology of
religion we must first recognize the existence of and the
need for values both as elements in the subject matter of the
discipline and as factors in the activity of the sociologist.

Vogt concludes that the final solution to the problem of
bias in the sociology of religion must be a philosophical one:

We must search outside our own discipline for the Archi-
mediean point from which to start bringing order to the
present confusion. The fields of philosophy of immediate
interest are the philosophy of value and more particularly,
the philosophy of religion. As sociologists of religion it
is only here that we will find the ultimate criteria for the
significance of religion generally and, in particular, of the
various types of religious phenomena.
    This view does not imply that the sociology of religion
is not an independent scientific discipline. *All* empirical
sciences have their sets of philosophical suppositions. The
sociology of religion, the most difficult of disciplines,
should least of all try to make do with a few elementary
philosophical commonplaces in the way more technical disciplines can.

This does not mean that philosophical argument should or
could be substituted for research. Scholastic philosophers
have adopted a formula which we might well adapt for the
sociology of religion. We should make philosophy the hand-
maid of our discipline, assigning to her certain basic prepa-
tory tasks, so that we may become free to devote ourselves to
our own task of empirical research.[12]

Some sociologists go so far as to claim that a subjective
involvement gets better results in interviews than objective involvement. Robert A. Stebbins contends that "validity is increased, not by pursuing objectivity, but by pursuing subjectiv-
ity": "The sooner we recognize that the goal of objectivity is
misplaced when studying personal meanings, the sooner we can
begin to generate situationally based, and hence more valid, data
in this area."[13]

Although attempting to be as objective as possible, we
found in our empirical research that the interaction process
itself was important since the men who were interviewed saw
someone not only who asked questions, but who caused them to
think and who even possibly cared about their views. This interaction is also important in learning about the communication
process, which we discuss further in part three.

This study, then, neither claims nor desires to be completely value-free. There is a bias toward biblical revelation
as normative for the description of biblical belief and even more
specifically, a personalistic bias. A starting presupposition is
that faith is personal, although not private, and has social and
faith-community consequences. It is hoped, however, that as
liberation theology uses its conscious biases positively, we can
also use our biases in a manner helpful to the mission of the
church.

Keith Dixon's statements, however, caution us not to be
too content with a simple subjective value orientation:

The dictum "expose your value judgements to public view
and proceed happily with your analysis" has a tendency to
reduce sociology to propaganda. What I wish to insist upon
is that necessary to sociological and anthropological investigation and explanation is some non-arbitrary and certainly
discussable concept of rationality and human worth. If I
hold dogmatically that religion is both irrational and worth-
less as a possible moral, metaphysical and explanatory system, then my approach as a sociologist of religion must be
social or psychologically reductionist. If I hold religion
to be intellectually wrongheaded and of ambiguous worth I may
prove to be more sensitive to claims to the possible autonomy
of the discourse. If I hold religion to be a worthy,
rational, and humane activity, then I am likely to suggest
counter-explanations to reductionist sociological interpretations. Each of these options seems to me to be worthy of
open-minded debate in the sense say that astrological interpretations of human life are not.[14]

Our view is to maintain a strong foothold in objectivity while
realizing that our "objectivity" also has subjective elements.

We seek to relate to the objective revelation of God while realizing that our perception of it is limited, as is our perception
of the men with whom we speak.

The Functions of Unbelief

Even from a believer's view, unbelief has its functions,
some which are judged more positively than others. From the
perspective of irreligion, Colin Campbell lists several functions:

1. The best-known function is to "purify" or strengthen
religious belief itself by: a) reminding the believer of his own
commitment, b) providing a rallying point for the faithful, in
its extreme, against the Muslim "infidels" in the Crusades, and
c) helping to advance more factional interests, especially
against the more radical fellow believers.

2. Irreligion may have beneficial consequences for the
psychological health of the individual, since religion sometimes
produces guilt or neurosis.

3. Secularism provided an ideology which was radical
enough to use in attacking the *status quo* above those on the
lower social and economic scale.

4. Irreligion helped to create a more secular state and
made education, social welfare, and private morality autonomous,
outside of religious control. This is seen as a benefit even in
some of the most "Christian" nations.

5. Irreligion has diverted expressions of discontent and
frustration away from the religious toward more socio-political
channels of expression.

6. Irreligious movements help to transform mildly a-
political people into radical protestors, or sometimes the opposite, they divert attention from pressing social and economic
problems into the "sterile" field of theological controversy.

7. Irreligion, for some, is one stage in the necessary
shift from religion to economics and politics, from a state of a
dominant religion to one where modern socialism or nationalism
takes over.[15]

Listening

This study is about listening: listening to God and
listening to men. Listening--and the care that lies behind it--
may be one of the most important things anyone can do.
Part one attempts to listen to God through the biblical writers.
It seeks to answer the question, "How does God view belief and
unbelief?" Blessed are those who have ears to hear **God**.

The empirical study (part two) reveals that many men had
no listening ear. They cried, confessed, told stories they had
never told before, tried to puzzle out their beliefs, felt

guilty, and were self-righteous--some of the very same things one does when one has God for a listening ear.   Believers need to hear the stories of unbelievers.   They need more than abstractions from mental assessments of the general situation.   It is essential for them to listen to unbelievers speak in their own language, for the sake of the believers themselves as well as the unbelievers.   Blessed are those who have ears to hear **men**.

Based on listening to the Word of God and the words of men, part three desires to listen to the Holy Spirit as the one who "goes between"[16] God and men.   He is the director of mission. Blessed are those who have ears to hear the **Holy Spirit**.

PART ONE

FOUNDATION:

TOWARDS USABLE BIBLICAL DESCRIPTIONS OF

BELIEF AND UNBELIEF

CHAPTER TWO

BEYOND BELIEF AND UNBELIEF?

> The real, the deepest,
> the sole theme of the world and of history
> to which all other themes are subordinated,
> remains, the conflict of belief and unbelief.[1]
>
> --Goethe

It is to this conflict, or at least distinction, to which we turn. But is it a genuine distinction? Is it not deemed socially or rationally irrelevant in a pluralistic culture? Is it possible to go beyond belief and unbelief by synthesis or by redefinition?

Atheism Beyond Belief and Unbelief

Much of today's atheism sees itself beyond the problem of belief and unbelief and even beyond the problem of God:

> To many [atheists] it now seems as ridiculous to attempt to prove the non-existence as the existence of God. In the nineteenth century atheism passed from the intellectual to the existential plane; in Proudhon's terms it became anti-theism. But the struggle against God springs from and presupposes belief in God. Anti-apologetics presupposes apologetics; anti-theology, theology. For this very reason the most vital and the deepest currents in contemporary atheism tend to place themselves beyond the problem of God. And if we are to understand it, we must study it in this paradoxical situation.[2]

For many atheism is a way of life, rather than a nega-tion. Atheists simply take it for granted that there is no God. "When Marx wrote that atheism would be transcended, he meant that communism would be able to consider the non-existence of God as granted, and so be free to take the existence of man as its starting point."[3] Or as in Arthur Rich's analysis,

> Marx doesn't bother NEG-ating God, he POS-its man. History is man, man is the sum of all his production and social being. He is object and subject. This is (not psychological but) historical, and (not Idealistic but in contrast) material: Historical Materialism.[4]

Johannes Baptist Metz explains,

> Above all, it has ceased more or less to be "direct unbelief" involving the explicit negation of belief. It is no longer a world view or a philosophy of life *in opposition to God*, but rather the presentation of a positive possibility of existence *without God*. Today, this thematic atheism is not really the object of unbelief, but rather its presupposition.[5]

Magno and Lamotte also stress "the positive aspect" of the atheist's "disbelief, the conviction that with the total exclusion of God from the cosmic picture, man is at last free to devote his efforts to the one thing that really does exist: the world."[6]

In the atheist's view, then, we live not only in a post-Christian culture, but also in a post-atheistic culture where man is the beginning, judge, goal, and conclusion of existence. To even speak about God becomes nonsense at a popular level and "non-sense" at a philosophical level. Lacrois sees that "the problem of God can be pronounced unreal and mythical, for it no longer divides men."[7]

Milan Machovec, representative of a unique breed of Marxists who are more open to Christianity, explains:

> As there is a Christian dogma--"credo in unum Deum," the belief in one God--so most people think that atheists must have a dogma of God's nonexistence. This is not true; we doubt all these dogmas. But we do not necessarily possess any cosmic experience; we therefore have to remain open also toward the deepest secrets of the cosmos, the same experiences that moved Teilhard de Chardin.[8]

An Irrelevant and Superfluous God

Following on from an atheism which does not have to ask the questions of God's existence is a world which finds God irrelevant and superfluous. Martin Marty quotes

> Eric Hoffer who said that, at some point in history, God and the priest seemed to become superfluous while the world kept going anyhow. I think that this is the fundamental experience in the culture of Western man's unbelief; not that God was to be raged against, but that he seemed superfluous; he no longer explained processes.[9]

This became true not only on a personal level, but on a societal level. Bryan Wilson puts the stress on unbelief in the structures of society:

> I want to suggest that belief systems do not in fact inhere only in individuals but that cultures carry belief systems and unbelief systems. It may be that, in the modern world with its highly integrated role performances at high levels of specialization, what individuals actually believe as private persons becomes scarcely relevant to many of the social involvements in which they find themselves. The fact that freedom of choice is emphasized especially in America,

but increasingly through the Western world, suggests to me
that freedom is in fact of very little importance for the
vital and continuing processes of society. The choices men
make do not in the main affect the social performances in
which they find themselves involved. Except for extremists,
the differences of belief and unbelief become relatively
trivial and relatively inconsequential for the ongoing social
process. This of course is an oblique comment on the process
of privatization of religion.[10]

Thomas Luckmann sees that unbelief "is about to disappear
entirely as a social fact." Unbelief, then, becomes a "non-
category".[11]

Belief is Universal

One of the ways in which some transcend the problem of
belief and unbelief is by denying the very existence of unbelief.
In an international symposium on the culture of unbelief, con-
vened by the Vatican Secretariat for Non-believers, sociologists
and theologians from around the globe tried to come to terms with
unbelief. The chairman, Peter Berger, makes his descriptive
comment: "What is rather remarkable, though is that the theoretical position papers, each in its own way, tend to deny the very
existence of the phenomenon under scrutiny."[12] He further
delineates:

Thomas Luckmann, using the very broad concept of religion
he derives from an intriguing marriage between Husserl and
Durkheim, says, in effect, that religion is a universal
attribute of the human condition, that unbelief in the sense
of some sort of irreligion is anthropologically and
sociologically impossible, and that consequently we must
shift our attention from this unrewarding focus to an
investigation of the new forms of "invisible religion" in the
modern world.[13]

Luckmann sees that

the only way to study the socio-psychological phenomena that
were traditionally designated by the concept of unbelief will
be by a technically and theoretically very difficult analysis
of various kinds of highly privatized subjective *belief* systems. The notion of unbelief may be heuristically unproductive even today.[14]

"The Objectivist Fallacy". Robert Bellah, on the other
hand, suggests that, "Unbelief, like theology, is a product of
the Greek mind, one might almost say, of the mind of Plato." He
sees that it is a notion quite alien to the Bible and stresses
that belief is "belief in" as opposed to "belief that". He sees
that this cognitive view of belief, which he calls "the objectivist fallacy," is found only in the religious traditions deeply
influenced by Greek thought--Christianity and Islam.[15]

Harvey Cox posits even more strongly that

Christianity is perhaps the only religion with the idea of belief; it is perhaps the only religion in the world where one can equate adherents or followers with believers. In most other religions, the outsiders are not thought of as nonbelievers. It may very well be the case that we are guilty of a certain amount of Western provincialism, and that there is something far more basic and essential to our faith than what we have called belief and nonbelief.[16]

In a very different context, Brunner observes that "it is only in Christianity, not in the other world religions, that faith has so central a significance. Neither in Islam nor in Hinduism nor in Buddhism is the relation to the divine conceived of as faith."[17]

In his own book, *Beyond Belief: Essays on Religion in a Post-Traditional World*, Bellah states that,

The modern world is as alive with religious possibility as any epoch in human history. It is no longer possible to divide mankind into believers and unbelievers. All believe something and the lukewarm and those of little faith are to be found inside as well as outside the churches. The spirit bloweth where it listeth and men of passionate integrity are found in strange places. If we have outgrown the idea of mission, we have probably also to outgrow the idea of dialogue, as though separated human groups must talk across a chasm. Christians along with other men are called on to build the boundaryless community, the body of man identified with the body of Christ, though men are free to symbolize it in their own way.[18]

Berger summarizes that Talcott Parsons,

in his interventions during the symposium and in his extended observations published in this volume, tends to strengthen doubt about the empirical reality of unbelief, which he sees in the context of a global institutional differentiation in modern society. Somewhat like Bellah, though (I think) with less enthusiasm, Parsons points to new religious formations in the making specifically to a new "religion of love" that, in historical perspective may be seen as a "Christianization of the world."[19]

"Other" Believers. Machovec wonders whether "the so-called unbelievers, are not really 'other' believers or believers in something different."[20] Luckmann's similar suggestion that "one man's belief is another's unbelief"[21] is true, but only when belief is not defined carefully enough. D. Gerard speaking of Luckmann and Parsons in another context, points out that using belief so widely "empties the term of content."[22]

The Mixture of Belief and Unbelief. It is also noted by many that unbelief exists in believers and belief exists in unbelievers. Paul Pruyser uses this to caution the way we use our terms:

It is a shabby business to compare a group of believers with a group of unbelievers when we know that within each group, individuals are tormented by questions of belief and unbelief. We can no longer indulge in the game of calling unbelievers all those who do not share our particular posture, whether of self-confessed unbelief, doubt, skepticism, agnosticism, or atheism.[23]

This is, of course, an important point, but it does not negate the fact that the terms can have real meaning and relevance when specified by a particular belief. David Martin clarifies the contrast:

In his paper, Professor Bellah defines Christianity as a moving dynamism, not necessarily continuous, in any important sense, with its past, even with respect to its name. Therefore, there is not even within Christianity the possibility of defining unbelief, because there is neither a definable core nor a locatable continuity. I hold, on the contrary, that there is ultimately a continuity and a core, that this involves some degree of exclusiveness, and that in terms of such a definition the problem of unbelief is precisely the breakdown of those exclusive acceptancies and historical affirmations, if that has in fact happened.
Otherwise the moving center creates a new crisis of unbelief with every generation.[24]

Berger pointed out that those views which denied the very existence of unbelief, particularly Luckmann's and Bellah's had an ambivalent impact on the participants in the symposium. Berger clarifies the ambivalence in his inimitable way, "The ambivalence was one of initial relief and subsequent new alarm--a little like the reactions of a man told not to worry about his ulcer, since he does not have an ulcer, but rather has cancer."[25]

N. J. Demerath III, in a different 1969 conference in Rome, suggests from a sociological perspective that theologians denying the existence of unbelief produce only a semantic victory. He could have also included some of his sociological colleagues when he said:

There are many theologians of the Tillichian variety who tend to define religion in the broadest possible terms so that it is difficult, if not impossible, to conceive of irreligion at all. Whether one uses such phrases as "the courage to be," "faith in the transcendent," "ultimate commitment," or even Karl Barth's nicely enigmatic, "religion as unbelief," one must conclude that everyman is religious and perhaps none more than the atheist himself. From my sociological perspective, this is a form of territorial aggression that produces only a semantic victory. . . .
Insofar as believers and non-believers feel themselves to be different, the distinction is sociologically real regardless of its theological status.[26]

This moves us to the next method which attempts to overcome the belief/unbelief dichotomy.

Redefining Belief

Demerath has suggested above a number of possible ways of broadening the scope of belief, so that there is little room left for irreligion. It may be more accurate, however, to suggest that these are ways of changing the dividing lines. Harvey Cox questions whether "the category of nonbelievers is really a useful one": "How can we use the label of unbelievers or nonbelievers for people whose search for the transcendent is somehow more serious and sometimes more ardent than the search of people who can be called traditionally religious?"[27] Jean Danielou agrees with Cox

> that the distinction between believers and nonbelievers does not correspond at all to the actual state of affairs, and that in fact it is very difficult to determine what could be called "the borderline" of faith, if we define belief precisely as signifying a search for the ultimate meaning of existence, which constitutes for me, essentially, the religious attitude.[28]

Bellah appears to see "men of passionate integrity" as his definition of the people in whom the spirit blows in his "boundaryless community."[29]

A slightly different touch is presented by Milan Machovec, who suggests that desire for *metanoia* is the standard for extracting believers from unbelievers, rather than the content of belief. In this sense, secularisation could represent a contemporary way of believing, a modern expression of dealing with the most profound and enduring human questions.

> I am sure that if we look to the Evangelists, "to believe" did not just mean "I think that something is true." Belief was no gnostic statement; but it meant, rather, that Christians converted with all their souls, with all their personalities, that they had turned towards something great, something to be expected. It was an ardent desire for *metanoia*. Belief was a desire for conversion, for turning towards the new world. From this point of view, Marx and his movement are not a movement of nonbelievers, but the movement of those who seek the new belief, the new conviction, the new *metanoia*, the new great conversion, the new and deeper humanity.[30]

If decision itself were the only distinctive characteristic of a believer (discussed in chapter three), Machovec's suggestion might be taken up. However, a non-Christological belief misses the heart of Christian belief and becomes something other than Christian faith. The other four elements of Christian belief (also discussed later) assume a turning point to a new world, but the object of the turn must be found in the person of Jesus. *Metanoia*, as a biblical term, is not just turning, but turning *to*. "Repent and believe *the good news*" (Mark 1:15), in which "the good news" is not an undefined content, but a content wrapped up in the identity of the Person of Jesus Christ.

The suggestions of Tillich, Cox, Danielou, and Bellah are also non-Christological while emphasizing the integrity side of belief. These attempts to redefine belief miss the mark by limiting belief to less than its multi-dimensional quality (as delineated in chapter three).

Redefining God

Machovec asserts that were he asked whether Marxists are basically atheists or not, he would "answer that it has become difficult to know any longer whether one is an atheist or not; but that is not our business; it may be the business of the theologians, who are struggling to define God."[31]

Popular media theologian Don Cupitt is one of those theologians whose radical redefinition of God alters the whole nature of biblical belief:

> God, on my account, is non-factual. It's a transcendent ideal which gives worth to our lives, but God is not factual. My idea of God is something with which I confront the world, it's not something that I read off the world. I don't think in terms of the existence of God at all because to think in those terms is to make God one being among others. God is more like an ideal or the sum of our values or the aim of our lives, a goal that we live by. The idea of existence is inappropriate, if you like. It would be better to say that God is eternal, timeless, not in the world of fact at all.

He still maintains a distinction between believer and unbeliever, but its object makes it very different from the biblical distinction:

> The difference between a person who believes in God and a person who does not believe in God, is that in the case of the believer his idea of God plays a part in shaping his *life*, is powerful in his life. Whereas the person who doesn't believe in God can't see how to use the idea of God; it has no power for him.
> Remember, in ancient thought, the question about gods was never their existence; it was their *power*. The Bible compares *the power* of different gods *not their existence*. So, the question of the reality of god is the question of his power in your life not the question of whether he exists *as a being*. Because the God who exists *as a being* would be an idol, a graven image.[32]

Cupitt, however, ignores the fact that the Bible *assumes* the existence of a factual God. That is its beginning point. It would be totally alien indeed for a single Old Testament or New Testament theology to think of either Yahweh or the Father of Jesus Christ as an idol. Cupitt makes an existential distinction between believer and unbeliever, but his redefinition of God denies any biblical foundation for the existential. In Christian thinking, Paul would term this futile faith, baseless belief (1 Cor. 15:17).

"Anonymous Christians"

Karl Rahner sees that atheists can be candidates for salvation by being "anonymous Christians". One is an anonymous Christian when he accepts the "supernatural existential" of the human spirit. He receives grace

> whenever he really accepts *himself completely*, for it already speaks *in* him.
> In the acceptance of himself man is accepting Christ as the absolute perfection and guarantee of his own anonymous movement towards God by grace, and the acceptance of this belief is again not an act of man alone but the work of God's grace which is the grace of Christ.
> Anyone who in his basic decision were really to deny and to reject his being ordered to God, who were to place himself decisively in opposition to his own concrete being, should not be designated a "theist," even an anonymous theist. . . .
> Therefore no matter what a man states in his conceptual, theoretical and religious reflection, anyone who does not say in his *heart*, "there is no God" but testifies to him by the radical acceptance of his being, is a believer.[33]

Empirically, however, atheists are in no way flattered by being referred to as "anonymous Christians". It is an odd form of Christian patronizing which insists that everyone to be considered one of us even though they do not wish to be. Roger Vaillant wrote some years ago of Catholics much less sophisticated than Rahner:

> For a Catholic nothing worthwhile can be foreign to God. If an honorable man is an atheist, it is because he seeks God and to seek God is already to have found Him. If he protests that he does not seek God, then that is because he seeks Him without knowing it: Providence has hidden ways. The violence of his protest is itself a proof of the intensity of his secret need, for why would he be so violent if he did not feel the goad of the divine shepherd? Is he insulting? Still another proof, for God is more concerned with one stray sheep than with the rest of the flock. God is a vicious circle from which we cannot escape. . . . The truth is, it is impossible to argue with a Catholic.[34]

Another catholic theologian, Hans Küng disagrees with Rahner:

> Neither may atheism be theologically appropriated as hidden "belief in God." The atheist's conviction must be respected and not played down speculatively. As if their atheism were not genuine, as if their unbelief were belief, as if atheists were "secret" believers in God. As if Feuerbach, Marx and Freud, together with atheists of today, were simply "anonymous Christians"--an idea that would seem to them, if not arrogant, then at least comic.[35]

Conclusions

We fall back on the rather simple conclusion: "Both denial and affirmation of God are possible."[36] And they are quite different conclusions. We cannot ignore Goethe's conflict between unbelief and faith. It will not go away no matter what intellectual, definitional, psychological, or synthetic methods we use to attempt to squelch it. It is indeed "the one true deepest theme of the history of the world and mankind to which all other themes are subordinate."[37]

Brunner is also unwilling to give up the distinction of this important theme which he views from a believer's perspective:

Only in the encounter with Jesus Christ can the unbeliever recognize himself as such, since outside this encounter he uses religion or morals to protect him against the judgment of God and "makes his boast" of it. Only when Christ is known, can man really understand that the final choice is between faith and unbelief, and why it should be so.[38]

CHAPTER THREE

BIBLICAL ELEMENTS OF BELIEF AND UNBELIEF

This study is mainly concerned with unbelief, but unbelief has no life of its own apart from belief. Unbelief or
nonbelief is dependent on the qualities of belief in the same
sense that Paul Tillich sees nonbeing dependent on being:

> The ontological status of nonbeing as nonbeing is dependent
> on being. Secondly, nonbeing is dependent on the special
> qualities of being. In itself nonbeing has no quality and no
> difference of qualities. But it gets them in relation to
> being. The character of the negation of being is determined
> by that in being which is negated.[1]

In order to develop usable categories of belief and
unbelief, it is necessary to return to the earliest documents
available. Our study is not so much based on systematic theology, although it perhaps becomes that, as it is grounded in the
biblical records themselves, regarding the nature of belief as
revealed there in its varieties of expression:

> To develop a truly theological understanding of unbelief,
> it is necessary to treat it not merely psychologically or
> sociologically, but within the theological dimension of faith
> itself. Psychology, sociology and philosophy will contribute
> to this understanding, but always within the comprehension of
> man which Revelation alone can furnish. It will be an in-
> sight into unbelief as intrinsic to the man of faith, the
> believer. Accordingly, it will be derived from an explora-
> tion of the properties of faith which make it vulnerable and
> open to deviations as well as from a probing of the existen-
> tial situation of man the believer to uncover the tension
> that is disclosed in the lived dialectic of belief-unbelief.[2]

THE ELEMENTS OF BELIEF

Christian belief/faith derives its original meaning from the usages of the double word grouping πειθ- and πιστ- , both which derive from the same verbal stem. They originally denoted the relationship of partners in an agreement and the faithfulness on which their promises were based.[3] In the New Testament, πιστ- has a greater theological significance in the relationship between man and God and is used much more predominantly. The πειθ- stem, however, gains significance when the the subject of unbelief in raised.

An Overview of the Elements of Belief

From the various biblical records, one can glean at least five inherent elements of Christian belief:

1. **choice**   to believe
2. **confession**   belief that
3. **trust**   belief in
4. **obedience**   belief for
5. **hope**   belief until

Of these, trust could be said to be the central element. At times, one or the other of the elements will be consciously emphasized or will unconsciously protrude, yet trust is intentionally both the focus (but not the focal point) of the believer himself. Thus, in many cases, it becomes the most essentially visible quality of Christian belief.

choice
confession

T R U S T

obedience
hope

Seen from the perspective of trust's centrality, the elements are:

Trust Chosen
Trust Affirmed
Trust Received
Trust Lived
Trust Assured

Trust is the glue that holds the other elements together. As a largely subjective element, it is not able to stand alone. Rather it is objectified by decision and confession and issues in obedience and hope. Confession and obedience are essentially objective elements while trust and hope are largely subjective. Decision has both subjective and objective qualities. Tyrrell describes faith as

> first and essentially inter-subjective, involving attitudes
> of trust, confidence, love, obedience, respect and all those
> factors that comprise free self-giving and acceptance of the
> other in inter-personal relations.[4]

He also sees that faith has an intellectual dimension:

> It has to do with what we believe as distinguished from the
> one we believe in. It is subsidiary to the personal
> dimension inasmuch as we have faith-in-an-assertion because
> we have faith-in-a-Thou who makes the assertion.[5]

In practice the elements of belief are so intertwined
that belief is nearly impossible to dissect. Theoretically, one
might consider several chronologies. One might give this appearance:

    1. To
        B E L I E V E
                2. That
                    3. In
                        4. For
                            5. Until

In reality, it rarely works in any set order. True belief as an
entity tends to bring all of the elements together at once, now
emphasizing one, later emphasizing another, dependent partially
upon the person and upon the emphasis of the presenting church.
Brunner writes of the chronological problem of needing to
"believe that" first:

> There can thus be no question of his having *first* to
> believe in a fact, and then on the strength of that being
> able to believe in the sense of *fiducia*. He does not owe his
> Jesus, the Christ, to the historian, but to the man who bore
> witness to him about Jesus as the Christ, so that in peni-
> tence and faith he recognized Jesus as such through the same
> Spirit in which He had been preached to him. Therefore his
> faith is not first a faith in facts, but, from the beginning,
> vital faith in Christ. The believer knows nothing of a faith
> in facts which would have to precede his genuine faith. It
> was the same Spirit of God that created the witness of the
> evangelist, that authenticated Himself to him, the hearer of
> this witness, when the witness created in him the saving
> faith which caused the *pro vobis*--the "for you" of the wit-
> ness--to become the *in nobis*--the "in us"--of faith. The
> Jesus of the historian is unknown to him, the believer, for
> the Jesus whom he knows is none other than the Christ, his
> Saviour.[6]

B. B. Warfield sees the outlines of the biblical conception of faith thrown into very high relief "by means of the
providentially mediated diversity of emphasis of the NT writers
on the several aspects of faith":

> Of its *subjective nature* we have what is almost a formal
> definition in the description of it as an "assurance of

things hoped for, a conviction of things not seen" (He 11:1). It obviously contains in it, therefore, an element of knowledge (He 11:6), and it as obviously issues in conduct (He 11:8, cf. 5:9, 1 P 1:22). But it consists neither in assent nor in obedience, but in a reliant trust in the invisible Author of all good (He 11:27), in which the mind is set upon the things that are above and not on the things that are upon the earth (Col 3:2, cf. 2 Co 4:16-18, Mt 6:25, 16:33). The examples cited in He 11 are themselves enough to show that the faith there commended is not a mere belief in God's existence and justice and goodness, or crediting of His word and promises, but a practical counting of Him faithful (11:11), with a trust so profound that no trial can shake it (11:35), and so absolute that it survives the loss of even its own pledge (11:17). So little is faith in its biblical conception merely a conviction of the understanding, that, when that is called faith, the true idea of faith needs to be built up above this word (Ja 2:14ff.). It is a movement of the whole inner man (Ro 10:9.10), and is set in contrast with an unbelief that is akin, not to ignorance but to disobedience (He 3:18.19, Jn 3:36, Ro 11:20.30, 15:31, 1 Th 1:8, He 4:6.2, 1 P 1:7.8, 3:1.20, 4:18, Ac 14:2.1, 19:9), and that grows out of, not lack of information, but that aversion of the heart from God (He 3:12) which takes pleasure in unrighteousness (2 Th 2:12, and is so unsparingly exposed by our Lord (Jn 3:19, 5:44, 8:47, 10:26).[7]

Bultmann sees the specifically Christian usages of πίστις and πιστεύω under these headings:

a. Acceptance of the Kerygma. . . . It is thus the saving faith which recognises and appropriates God's saving work in Christ. Here too, of course, πίστις contains the element of believing. Obedience, trust, hope and faithfulness are also implied.[8]

b. The Content of Faith. . . . Paul in R. 10:9 states the content of Christian faith in a sentence in which he does not simply give his own view but is saying what is obviously self-evident to every Christian preacher . . . it is apparent that acknowledgement of Jesus as Lord is intrinsic to Christian faith along with acknowledgment of the miracle of His resurrection, i.e., acceptance of this miracle as true.[9]

c. Faith as a Personal Relation to Christ.[10]

d. Believing. . . . πίστις is to be understood as acceptance of the Christian message.[11]

e. πίστις as *fides quae creditur*. . . . The message itself, then can be called πίστις.[12]

O. Michel sees that for Jesus, in the synoptics, faith in God means being open to the possibilities that God presents. He adds further:

But it must not be forgotten that every summons and statement of Jesus contained the elements of faith, trust, knowledge, decision, obedience and self-direction. The preaching of

Jesus cannot be understood apart from the many-sided aspects of faith (Heb. '^{e}munah) and trust (Heb. bittahon). The faith of Jesus was directed towards reality. It was deeply involved in the act of living, and was on a completely different plane from hypothetical abstractions.[13]

Theologians have given a variety of approaches to the elements of biblical belief, some emphasizing one element more than another, as some of the biblical writers themselves seem to do. However, we suggest that these five elements of biblical belief stand as a firm foundation upon which to base our study. A brief survey of some of the relevant biblical material for each element follows:

1. Choice: To Believe

Choice is one of the root ideas in the word grouping πειθ-/πιστ-. From a believer's perspective, he sees himself both as having been chosen by God (John 15:16,19; Ephesians 1:3-14; 2 Thessalonians 2:13-14) and choosing God. There can be no argument over the fact that the initiative in faith is always from God. The choice element of biblical belief, which encompasses aspects of persuasion/decision/conversion, is *only* man's response to God's initiative. Of course, it is a significant "only" since it is crucial to the existence of belief.

God's Grace and Man's Freedom

The existence of choice (or lack of it) necessitates discussion of the classic problem of God's sovereignty and man's freedom. There are believers who explain their belief exclusively in terms of being chosen while others explain the origin and existence of their belief only in terms of their own choice. These two experiential stances and the various combinations are usually linked with similar theological or historical denominational ties. Christian belief pays its dues to both God's sovereignty and man's freedom. As human relationships are usually both gift and choice, Christian belief must take account of the paradoxical truth that faith is jointly a gift of God and the result of man's decision. Francis M. Tyrrell attempts to reconcile them:

> Faith is not some "thing" that is given to man and held on to as a possession. It is rather a saving relationship of man with God, ever proceeding from and dependent on the initiative of God, even while it is the human individual's most profoundly personal response to that divine call. Like any other inter-personal relationship, it cannot be taken for granted, for that very attitude is not only a menace to it's well-being, it is a sign of its deterioration.
>
> Supremely beyond all other relations, man's relation with God is not at his own disposal. Faith is God's gracious free gift to man, not only initially, but always. It comes to him as a summons, ever fresh and new, totally unearned, from the incomprehensible abyss of God's infinite goodness and love.

Man's faith can only be a response to this unfailing yet undeserved invitation, fittingly as diffident as it is grateful. As a consequence, he must acknowledge its ultimately precarious and imperilled status, delicately balanced as it is at the meeting point of God's free grace and man's freedom.[14]

Another Roman Catholic, Hans Küng, sees faith as both deed and gift:

Belief in God is man's confident decision, it is my deed. This has nothing to do with rationalism or Pelagianism. For, as already indicated, it is not in advance--in virtue of a proof or demonstration--but only when I confidently commit myself to it, that reality itself lays open to me its primary ground, deepest support, its ultimate goal. That is why it is right to say that without preparedness for confident acknowledgement of God (with its practical consequences), there is no rationally meaningful knowledge of God. As with fundamental trust, so also with trust in God, I am expected to make an advance, to venture, to take a risk.
But also like fundamental trust, trust in God cannot simply be decided on, willed, extorted or produced. I cannot simply create or produce ultimate certainty, security, stability, for myself. . . .
* *Belief in God is a gift. Reality exists before me. If I do not cut myself off, but open myself entirely to reality as it opens out to me, then I can accept in faith its primary ground, its deepest support, its ultimate goal: God, who reveals himself as primal source, primal meaning and primal value.*[15]

Deed, however, is an unhelpful way of expressing what choice is, leading to its relegation to the sphere of works. The biblical idea of choice is not a contribution to God's grace but simply the empty hand which opens to God's giving. Without the opening, there is no existential appropriation of faith. Without God's gift, there is no substance of faith at all.[16]

Changing the image, Brunner's words help us to see faith as the ear which listens to God:

When we hear the message of Christ and let it be told to us, and told in such a fashion that we have no longer anything more to say to it, but have simply become listeners--when we hear thus--we believe. This hearing and faith are one and the same thing. But we can hear this message only through the witnessing Word of the witnesses. Thus the Word which creates faith is at the same time God's Word and man's word, Word of the Spirit, and *paradosis*, tradition.[17]

Persuasion

The πειθ- stem also reveals the experience of persuasion. The classical Greek usage of the active πείθειν from the time of Homer, "to convince", "to persuade", "to seduce (by persuasion)", "to corrupt", is not always sharply differentiated from New Testament usages.[18]

Paul is perhaps the most vocal advocate (2 Cor. 5:11) and practitioner (Acts 18:4; 19:8; 28:23) of persuading men about the kingdom of God and about Jesus. All persuasion in this sense leads ultimately to the necessity of personal choice. The perfect of πείθω denotes a situation in which the act of examining and weighing up has been concluded and a firm conviction has been reached.[19] In the Pauline corpus, it comes to express strong, personal conviction often using the first person, singular pronoun (e.g. Rom. 8:38ff.; 2 Tim. 1:5,12) and can also be used in a secular way.

Persuasion and Confidence

In relation to the first element of Christian belief, persuasion is what happens *to* the potential believer; confidence or conviction is what happens *within* the believer. Confidence, however, does not arise on the grounds of human argument. Rather, it renounces human certainty and by doing so, it acquires the distinction of faith, i.e. confident assurance of God's action in Jesus Christ (past, present, and future).

Bultmann points out that it is surprising and significant that there are so few New Testament references to confidence in God, in contrast to the many references in the Old Testament, especially in the Psalms:

> If there is so little reference to confidence in God in the NT this is because the concern of the NT, as distinct from the Psalms, is not with the individual destiny and need of the worshipper, in face of which the righteous sets his trust in God, but rather with the common distress of mankind and with eschatological salvation. With this reference, however, confidence takes the form of faith. The confidence in God which characterises the relation to Him is subsumed under faith. This also means, however, that confidence in God is taken in the radical sense in which it includes absolute surrender of one's own assurance. It is thus united with obedience, which is free from all autonomy. That πεποιθέναι in the sense of radical relying on God is now caught up in πιστεύειν may be seen from the fact the new relationship to God in faith can be described as the rejection of false πεποιθέναι, cf. esp. Phil. 3:3f., where πεποιθέναι ἐν σαρκί characterises the Jewish confidence which is grounded in the privileges mentioned in vv. 4-5 and which forms the antithesis of the πίστις Χριστοῦ of v. 9.[20]

This false Jewish confidence results in the fact that even the people of God's covenant are unbelievers (Rom. 11:20ff.) unless they are persuaded not to persist in their unbelief (vs. 23) and begin to live in the fulfilment of God's covenant through the Messiah.

The πειθ-/πιστ- double word grouping is mainly concerned with that personal relationship to a person or thing which is established by trust or trustworthiness. If it is being emphasized that the relationship has come about through persuasion or conviction, the verb πείθομαι is often used.[21]

Becoming a Believer

The usage of the aorist of πιστεύω confirms the decision point of *becoming* a believer. "He believed" means the same
as, "He followed the Lord", "He was saved", or today's, "He
became a Christian."

The synoptic gospels never use the aorist, preferring
instead the noun πιστός , while John's gospel records thirteen
times people who believed (ἐπίστευσαν) in Jesus. Acts is the
only other book where the aorist is used (seven times) while the
aorist participle (with nearly identical meaning) is used twice.
These concentrated usages are not surprising given the purposes
of the writers: John's stated purpose was to move his readers to
become believers (20:31) while Luke was recording the creation of
God's new church where many became believers. In the same pattern as the synoptics, Paul emphasizes the noun, which sometimes
has the meaning of a decisive moment when a person believes the
gospel (e.g. Eph. 2:8, "For it is by grace that you have been
saved through faith."). He uses the verb (as aorist participle)
only once.

Repentance and Belief

Repentance is inherent in this first distinguishing mark
of faith. Jesus inseparably links repentance with believing the
good news (Mark 1:15). When hearing the good news of Jesus and
it is judged to be both true and relevant (or more correctly, the
word judges the hearer), a decision to allow the experience of
μετάνοια happens and a decisive reversal begins. Yet it could
also be said that there must be a sort of turning around before
the good news can properly be heard, i.e. one must become (or be)
one of "those who has ears to hear". Μετάνοια is both caused by
and causes a decisive commitment. In the joint experience of
repentance and belief, an entirely fresh perspective and a whole
new standard of values is created. Life and truth are viewed
through discipleship to Jesus rather than through alien or autonomous structures and values. As the decision to believe has
thorough consequences, repentance leaves nothing in the
believer's life untouched.

James D. G. Dunn sees Acts 2:38 as Luke's attempt to
establish the pattern and norm for Christian conversion-initia-
tion including "the three most important elements in conversion-
initiation: repentance, water-baptism, and the gift of the
Spirit." He sees repentance and faith as being the opposite
sides of the same coin:

> The three principal words used by Luke to describe man's
> act of faith are μετανοεῖν, ἐπιστρέφειν and πιστεύειν. Each
> describe the act from a different angle: μετανοεῖν always has
> the sense of turning away from (ἀπό) sin; ἐπιστρέφειν always
> has the sense of turning to (ἐπί) Christ. They can be used
> singly, when they may have a fuller sense (e.g. 2.38; 9.35;
> 11.18; 16.31), or they may be used in pairs (e.g. 3.19;
> 26.20; 2.38 with 2.44; 20.21; 11.21; 26.18). In the former
> cases they obviously often comprehend the whole act of faith;
> in the latter, their sense is more restricted in the way

already suggested. $(\mathring{\alpha}\pi o)\delta\acute{\epsilon}\chi\epsilon\sigma\vartheta\alpha\iota$ (2.41; 8.14; 11.1; 17.11)
and $\pi\rho o\sigma\acute{\epsilon}\chi\epsilon\iota\nu$ (8.6, 11; 16.14) also describe the response to
the preached word ($\lambda\acute{o}\gamma o\varsigma$).[22]

The new object of the turn around of repentance, the
motivator of the decision, and the essence of the good news to
which one turns in belief must be Jesus Christ himself.

Existentialist Choices

The existentialists make choice even more significant
than Pelagius and Celestius, although in a different way. For
Kierkegaard, choice is everything. The passionate concern of the
individual is subjective truth--truth for me--which is only found
in faith and in decision. H. Richard Niebuhr quotes Kierkegaard's Johannes Climacus and adds a word of explanation: "'The
decision lies in the subject . . . The thing of being a Christian
is not determined by the *what* of Christianity but by the *how* of
of the Christian.' This *how* is faith."[23] Niebuhr welcomes the
necessity to decide in the presence of Christ and our culture,
but he also criticizes Kierkegaard from that perspective:

> Our decisions are individual, that is true; they are not
> individualistic--as though we made them for ourselves and by
> ourselves as well as in ourselves. They are not
> individualistic in the Kierkegaardian sense, first of all,
> because what is at stake is not simply or primarily our own
> eternal happiness. . . . We raise our existential questions
> individually, doubtless, and we do not forget our personal,
> individual selves. But the existentialist question is not
> individualistic; it arises in its most passionate form not in
> our solitariness but in our fellowship. It is the existen-
> tial question of social men who have no selfhood apart from
> their relations to other human selves. . . .
> Our individual Christian decisions are not individualis-
> tic, in the second place, because they cannot be made in
> solitariness on the basis of a truth that is "true for me."
> We do not confront an isolated Christ known to us apart from
> a company of witnesses who surround him, point to him, inter-
> pret this and that feature of his presence, explain to us the
> meaning of his words, direct our attention to his relations
> with the Father and the Spirit. . . . The more important our
> knowledge the more important is not only directness of meet-
> ing but also the companionship of fellow knowers. . . . The
> Christ who speaks to me without authorities and witnesses is
> not an actual Christ; he is no Jesus Christ of history. He
> may be nothing more than the projection of my wish or my
> compulsion; as, on the other hand, the Christ about whom I
> hear only through witnesses and never meet in my personal
> history is never Christ for me.[24]

Niebuhr also values the contribution of existentialism in
emphasizing "the reality of decision and its free, individual
character [which] has also made us aware of the significance of
the moment. . . . As a man he must make decisions; and the time
of decision is neither past nor future, but the present."[25]

Niebuhr sees Bultmann's existentialist Jesus as

more Kantian than Markan or Pauline or Johannine. Bultmann can find no real content in the gospel idea of obedience. . . . although God is mentioned as the one whose will is to be obeyed, the idea of God ascribed to Jesus is as empty and formal as the idea of obedience. Just as for liberalism God is the counterpart of human love, so in this existentialism He becomes the mere counterpart of moral decision. He is "the Power which constrains man to decision," the one whom man can find "only in actual comprehension of his own existence"; "God Himself must vanish for the man who does not know that the essence of his own life consists in the full freedom of his decision."[26]

Summary

The biblical element of choice is apparent enough to be overemphasized. But choice is not everything, it is only an initial step in belief. The choice for belief is individual without being individualistic; it is personal but neither solitary nor private; it is both subjective and objective, the how and the what; it may come in a moment but has enduring (even eternal) results; and it is a regular part of the life of the believer. Brunner emphasizes faith's decisive consequences:

Faith or unbelief is the decisive question of human existence, both of the individual man and of the peoples, i.e. of humanity. Man *lives* either in faith or in unbelief, and whether he is the one or the other is decisive for the healthy or unhealthy character of his life.[27]

When John describes a group of people who have come to a firm conviction about their response to Jesus, he writes, "They believed" (ἐπίστευσαν). When a group of believers describes its present state, they express, "We believe" (πιστεύομεν). There is a decisive moment when belief takes its first shape, but the continual state of the Christian is described as present believing. It is difficult to comprehend Christian belief without some kind of personal choice or decision, but choice is only one of the biblical elements of belief.

2. Confession: Belief That

Christian belief based on the biblical records cannot avoid "belief that" as one of its aspects. The New Testament's almost formal definition of faith as an "assurance of *things* hoped for, a conviction of *things* not seen" (Heb. 11:1, RSV) makes us aware that there is something--and also someone--that believers believe.

The saying of Jesus ἀμήν λέγω ὑμῖν (truly I say to you) is found seventy-five times in the gospels, emphasizing Jesus' stress on truth. The noun πιστός sometimes has the article (ὁ πιστός) which refers to the whole body of Christian teaching.

The message of Christianity itself can then be called ὁ πιστός, that which the Christian is to believe.

The Fourth Gospel

The verb πιστεύω is used with ὅτι at least twenty-three times in the New Testament; it is especially emphasized in the gospel of John, where all the references are confessionally Christological and are phrased as the words of Jesus or his disciples. Martha gives classic expression to the content of belief when she says, "I *believe that* you are the Christ, the Son of God who has come into the world" (11:27). She anticipates, in response to the person of the historical Jesus, precisely what John wants his readers to do in their encounter with the post-Easter Christ through the written gospel: "But these are written that you may *believe that* Jesus is the Christ, the Son of God" (20:31).

Other passages where John's gospel records πιστεύω ὅτι phrases refer to the relation between the Father and the Son, either that Jesus came from the Father (16:27; 17:8 and the reference where the disciples confirm this, 16:30) or conversely, that the Father sent Jesus (11:42; 17:21); another reference is that Jesus is in the Father and the Father is in him (14:11).

The Fourth Gospel declares that the object of cognitive belief is God revealed in human life, *viz.*, the historical Jesus Christ of faith. Martin Marty defines unbelief as "any kind of serious or permanent departure from belief in God (as symbolized by the term 'Trinity') and from belief that God not only is but acts (as symbolized by the historic reference 'Incarnation')."[28] Although Jesus only hints at the three aspects of God in these specific Johannine ὅτι phrases, his relation to the Holy Spirit is also clearly referred to in his lengthy Last Passover discourse. The incarnation aspect is clear from Mary in her confession, John in his purposive statement, and Jesus in the Last Passover discourse.

In an appendix to his *Dogmatics*, Volume 3, Emil Brunner sketches Martin Buber's teaching on the apostles' misunderstanding of faith. Buber sees the difference between the synoptic conversation (Matthew 16:13ff.) and the Johannine conversation (John 6:66ff.) as two kinds of faith, not just the difference between two expression of faith. Buber's thought (via Brunner) is this:

> In the Old Testament, faith is trust and obedience; in gnostic Christianity it is faith in a theology which interprets the fact of Christ. . . . Thus in his opinion the Christian Faith becomes faith in a mythical gnostic doctrine. Through both, through the relation to historical event and through this dogmatic content, the structure of faith is completely altered. The place of personal surrender in trust and obedience is taken by a theoretical "conviction that".[29]

Brunner, however, sees the

distinction not between the faith of trust and "belief that", but between Jewish faith and Christian faith. . . . What we here perceive as faith in Jesus stands wholly within what Buber means by faith, security in God, trust and obedience.[30]

He further criticizes: "Buber's concept of faith does not make it clear that even Old Testament faith is an answer to God's action in *historical events* and in the prophetic Word."[31]

Buber reminds us that we must not ignore the other elements of biblical belief (especially trust and obedience) by shifting to a gnostic faith. Although there *is* biblical emphasis on knowing especially in the Johannine literature, there is no developed gnosticism. Rather the First Letter of John confronts gnosticism with what Robert Law has termed "The Tests of Life": the tests of righteousness, love, and belief.[32] We must stand firm that the element of "belief that" is inherent to the nature of biblical faith.

The Pauline Corpus

In Paul, there is a correspondence between confession and belief: "That if you confess with your mouth, 'Jesus is Lord,' and believe in your heart that God raised him from the dead, you will be saved" (Rom. 10:9).[33] Along with its other elements, faith is simultaneously confession. Rudolf Bultmann expresses it this way:

Faith, therefore, is not "piety" or trust-in-God in general. Rather, it has "dogmatic" character insofar as it is acceptance of a word: "the word of faith" (Rom. 10:8) or "the heard word" (ἀκοή , KJ: "the hearing") of faith (Gal. 3:2, 5). Hence, faith can also be called "faith of the gospel"--i.e. faith in the gospel (Phil 1:27).
"Faith," which arises from "what is heard" (Rom 10:17), consequently contains a *knowing*. That is why Paul can, at times, speak as if knowledge were the basis of faith.[34]

In Thessalonians, what one believes about the historical Jesus predicates what one believes will happen in the historical future, connecting the belief content with hope: "We believe that Jesus died and rose again and so we believe that God will bring with Jesus those who have fallen asleep in him" (1 Thess. 4:14). Faith as belief without an object is not Christian belief at all for Paul; it is futility (1 Cor. 15:17).

The pastorals especially reveal that "a coherent body of tradition had become established to serve as a clearly defined touchstone of orthodoxy."[35] The purpose of the instruction to Titus to rebuke a group of rebellious believers is that the readers should be "sound in *faith*" (ὑγιαίνωσιν ἐν τῇ πίστει Tit. 1:13). The more general statement to Titus is that he should teach what is in accord with "sound doctrine/teaching" (τῇ ὑγιαινούσῃ διδασκαλίᾳ , 2:1). When the writer identifies the older men as a specific group, "sound in faith" (ὑγιαίνοντας τῇ πίστει, 2:2) is a synonym for sound doctrine/teaching. Certainly by the time the Pastorals were written, a certain correctness of doctrine is necessary for the cognitive element of faith.

Content of the Confession

There is diversity among the New Testament writers as to what this specific content is, but nowhere in the New Testament are we given the impression that a totally undefined corpus of belief is characteristic of the Christian faith. James D. G. Dunn finds

> a *fairly clear and consistent unifying strand* which from the first both marked out Christianity as something *distinctive* and different and provided the *integrating centre* for the diverse expressions of Christianity. That unifying element was the unity between the historical Jesus and the exalted Christ, that is to say, the conviction that the wandering charismatic preacher from Nazareth had ministered, died and been raised from the dead to bring God and man finally together, the recognition that the divine power through which they now worshipped and were encountered and accepted by God was one and the same person, Jesus, the man, the Christ, the Son of God, the Lord, the life-giving Spirit.[36]

From another context, Brunner also points out this unifying strand:

> The Word about Christ is at the same time spiritual and historical. This double character refers back to the Incarnation of the Word. Only the Jesus of history can be the Christ. But faith grasps the duality not as a duality but as a unity. The Jesus of history *is* the Christ, the Son of the living God.[37]

Though the body of Christian belief also has content which refers to man (e.g. his salvation, "We believe it is through the grace of our Lord Jesus Christ that we are saved." Acts 15:11), its primary and essential focus is on God and in particular, God as revealed in Jesus Christ. The three main New Testament confessional titles for Jesus are: **Lord** (Rom. 10:9; 1 Cor. 8:6; 12:3; Eph. 4:5; Phil. 2:11, Acts 2:36; John 13:13), **Christ** (Luke 2:11, 9:20 and parallels; John 4:29; 11:27; Acts 2:36; 9:22; 17:3; 18:5, 28; 1 John 5:1; the Hebrew Messiah specifies the historical continuity with the Old Testament believing people), and **Son of God** (Mt. 14:33; 16:16; 26:54; Lk. 22:70; John 1:49; 20:31; Acts 8:37; 9:20; 1 John 4:15; 5:50). Brunner sees that "these three expressions have exactly the same meaning."[38]

The history of the great ecumenical creeds are classic attempts to define the content of the faith. Previous to these creeds the New Testament documents themselves reveal the early Christians' attempts to confess their faith in Jesus in the most relevant and meaningful ways which they could. In this context, James D. G. Dunn comments:

> The confessions lay bare the distinctiveness of the faith confessed in *different particular situations*. We have uncovered no single, final confession appropriate to all circumstances and all times. Any attempt to find a single primitive confession will almost certainly fail. Our investigation has revealed at least three confessions, all of which deserve the epithet "basic and primitive". Three

different confessions--different because the Christians who used them were different, and they used them in different circumstances.   In oversimplified terms, and leaving aside the Son of Man tradition which was an important expression of the eschatological faith of the earliest community, we may say that "Jesus is the Messiah" appears to have been the chief confession of Palestinian Jewish Christians,   "Jesus is the Son of God" of Hellenistic Jewish Christians, "Jesus is Lord" of Gentile Christians.   Or in rather more precise terms,   "Jesus is the Messiah" was the most important confession in Jewish Palestine, "Jesus is the Son of God" in a Hellenistic-Jewish situation, "Jesus is Lord" among Gentiles.[39]

Regarding the distinctiveness of their faith expressed in the confessional formulae, Dunn concludes: "It is, I suggest, *the conviction that the historical figure, Jesus the Jew, is now an exalted being*--that this Jesus is and continues to be the *agent of God*, supreme over all other claimants to the titles, 'Lord' and, 'Son of God.'"   It is worth quoting his specific points in full:

(a)   First, it is *Jesus* who is confessed--not his ideas, ideology, faith or teaching.   It is not the faith *of* Jesus which here comes to expression, but faith *in* Jesus.   The NT knows no confession which is a confession merely of the significance of the historical Jesus.   What Jesus did or said never provides the central or sole element in confessional faith.

(b)   Second, it is the *present* status of Jesus which is confessed--not what he was, but what he *is*. . . .   Only with the confession, "Jesus Christ came in the flesh" does the confession confine itself to a historical retrospect--and even there it is the present, glorious Jesus Christ of whom the confession is made.   But with the three basic confessions it is always the present tense which is used: "Jesus *is* . . .".

(c)   Third, V. Neufeld has reminded us that in each case *Jesus* is the subject of the confession; *it is the historical person who is so confessed*.   In other words, each confession itself maintains the vital link between the historical person and the one who is the present author of life, justification, power.   *Jesus*, the Jesus who was, *is*, now is and continues to be Son of Man, Christ, Son of God, Lord.   Here emerges an important conclusion in our quest for a unifying element within earliest Christianity: viz., the distinctive feature which comes to expression in all the confessions we have examined, the bedrock of the Christian faith confessed in the NT writings, is *the unity between the earthly Jesus and the exalted one who is somehow involved in or part of our encounter with God in the here and now.*[40]

The World Council of Churches Basis of Faith formulated in New Delhi in 1961 is one of the modern attempts at defining those   churches who are eligible to call their members believers:

The World Council of Churches is a fellowship of Churches which *confess the* Lord Jesus Christ as God and Saviour according to the Scriptures and therefore seek to fulfil together their common calling to the glory of the one God, Father, Son and Holy Spirit.[41]

This basis of faith keeps us in touch with the primitive Christian confessions as well as their primitive source and points us toward a trinitarian conception of God without clearly defining it.

Christian belief has often been limited to a set of doctrinal statements to which a believer must give intellectual assent. Intellectual assent to propositional statements alone can never be Christian belief (as the other four elements confirm); neither is it Christian belief which does not have this cognitive element. Martin Marty concurs:

Certainly, few have ever made their faith commitments as Plato did, purely and merely cognitively, propositionally by assent to truths. Again, I'd question whether, then or now, we are capable of making a commitment without some sort of cognition. If you are asked to follow a particular manifestation of the divine, a particular way of the cross to a particular garbage dump called Golgotha, you are indeed involved in a partly cognitive kind of commitment.[42]

The new quest of the historical Jesus questioned whether the gospel intends to convey enough data to convince us of the content of the faith. Although there will be many difficulties in defining the exact content of the Christian faith, this difficulty does not necessitate abandoning the task and thereby defining Christian faith without content. From a sociologist's perspective, Talcott Parsons expressed,

Certainly in the Western tradition, the concept of belief has a cognitive component. That is to say that however difficult this may be in practice, beliefs are capable of being stated in propositional form and then tested by standards of "truth" or cognitive validity.[43]

From the standpoint of biblical theologies, there is no *Christi*an faith without *Christi*an content.

The Origin of the Content

Paul W. Pruyser posits that

belief systems are generated and supplied by the culture. In fact, the production, maintenance, and transmission of belief systems and values are functions which define the word "culture." Durkheim saw beliefs as collective representations which give stability to the social order. Marx saw beliefs largely as ideologies which develop as tools of the social order to maintain its stratification--in other words, to maintain the privileges of the few over the masses . . .
The tenor of most of these studies is that belief, once thought to have been a natural fact of creation or instilled

by divine action, shows a bewildering diversity of origins and correlations with social and cultural processes.[44]

Although one can see--or overlook--instances both inside and outside of Christianity and religion where belief systems have their origin in culture, true Christian belief must resist the *necessity* of the sociology of knowledge.[45]   True Christianity, like its predecessor, true Judaism, is a revealed religion. It is a response to a "given". Sociology, by the very nature of its science, cannot absorb the concept of initiative outside man. As Schillebeeckx writes, "The term 'transcendence' itself does not belong to the sociological vocabulary neither to be condemned nor affirmed".[46]

The Christian faith, however, declares that what has happened in the Christ-event was, in fact, initiated outside human history. The Word which believers believe does not have its origin in the will of man (2 Pt. 1:20-21). Even Christianity's belief content is present because of the action of the Living God. The content of the believer's faith is God as revealed in Jesus Christ and received in the Holy Scriptures.

3.   Trust: Belief In

As the gospel is no mere report about historical incidents, so faith is not just an intellectual belief that historical incidents are true in fact. Bultmann explains that the word of proclamation

> is no teaching about external matters which could simply be regarded as true without any transformation of the hearer's own existence. For the word is kerygma, personal address, demand, and promise; it is the very act of divine grace.[47]

This third element of biblical faith opens the way for the radical encounter of the believer with the person of Jesus. This element becomes the main substance of faith itself--trust, "belief in." Bultmann exalts this element (along with obedience) while diminishing the content element: "In the beginning *faith* is the term which distinguishes the Christian Congregation from the Jews and the heathen, not *orthodoxy* (right doctrine)."[48]

"Belief That" and "Belief In"

Trust is a non-cognitive component, but it is essentially self-consistent with the cognitive aspects of belief. Johannine theology indissoluably links "belief that" (ὅτι) with "belief in/on" (εἰς):   "Who is it that overcomes the world? Only he who believes that Jesus is the Son of God" (1 John 5:5); "I write these things to you who believe in the name of the Son of God so that you may know that you have eternal life (1 John 5:13).

Talcott Parsons looks at the distinction, while at the same time seeing the continuity, between "belief that" and "belief in":

In my view, it would not be appropriate to use the term belief in the latter context if there were *no* cognitive content involved, that is, if the action referred to were completely nonrational expression of emotions. The little word "in," however, suggests a noncognitive component which is not included in "that," which may be called commitment. The "believer in . . ." of course must, explicitly or implicitly, subscribe to cognitively formulable and in some sense testable propositions, but in addition to that, he commits himself to act (including experiencing) in ways which are to put it in the mildest form, congruent with the cognitive components of belief.[49]

In fact, it is "belief that" which gives the possibility for "belief in" to exist at all. It is one thing for me to believe *that* the cross/resurrection event is salvific action. It is quite another thing to believe *in* the saving action of Jesus in the cross/resurrection *for me*. Trust internalizes the objective element by appropriating the subjective element of the Christ event. Trust is the reception of the Christian kerygma into the inner self. Trust takes man out of himself and puts him into Christ and Christ into him.

Trust and Knowledge

Trust also relates to knowledge. John does not abandon the emphasis on γνῶσις in some of the early Christian churches, but instead deepens it to a knowledge characterized by experiential trust. Dunn points out that the Johannine literature uses the verb "know" (56 times) as the near equivalent to "believe".[50] For John, to believe in the Son of God is to know him and vice versa (1 John 5:13, 20).

Trust in the Heart

Even though it is a subjective element, trust is not to be summed up as limited to the emotional sphere of life. Trust is full commitment and ensures that belief resides, in Michael Novak's phrase, at "the core of one's spirit."[51] Trust is a movement of the whole inner man.

This is exemplified in Pauline theology (Rom. 10:9-10) and in a few Lukan manuscripts of Acts 8:37. Πιστεύεις ἐξ ὅλος τῆς καρδίας is much more than to believe with your emotions. Behm shows that "the heart is the centre of the inner life of man and the source or seat of all the forces and functions of soul and spirit" and lists four New Testament attestations (with scripture references):

a. In the heart dwell feelings and emotions, desires and passions. . . .
b. The heart is the seat of understanding, the source of thought and reflection. . . .
c. The heart is the seat of the will, the source of resolves. . . .
d. Thus the heart is supremely the one centre in man to which God turns, in which the religious life is rooted, which

determines moral conduct.[52]

"Believe in your heart" refers to crossing the line between trust and "untrust" with self in the hand. It is commitment of your whole life, extending much further than the mystery religions' "abandonment to the deity by following his instruction and teaching, and putting oneself under his protection."[53] The classical Greek usage rarely rises above intellectual conviction into the region of moral trust. In contrast, the New Testament usage implies a relationship far closer than any Greek would have established between himself and his gods:

> Resting ultimately on a root with the fundamental sense of "binding," and standing in classical Greek as the common term for "trusting," "putting faith in," "relying upon," shading down into "believing," it was rather too strong a term for ordinary use of that ungenial relation to the gods which was characteristic of Greek thought, and which was substantively expressed by πίστις --the proper acknowledgement in thought and act of their existence and rights.[54]

Tillich tackles the existential dimension of faith with his idea of ultimacy:

> For Tillich, "faith is the state of being ultimately concerned." Though the content of faith matters infinitely for the life of the believer, it does not matter for the formal definition of faith. A concern claims ultimacy if it "demands the total surrender of him who accepts this claim, and it promises total fulfillment." The content of the demand and promise accepted in the act of faith can be expressed in symbols, none of which is itself ultimate.
> Faith is an act of the total personality and includes all the elements of personal life: reason, emotion, and the rest. In the past, attempts have been made to reduce faith to one or another of these elements. The effect is always a distortion. For faith tends to transcend all of these even while it includes them all. "It is the unity of every element in the centered self."[55]

Bonhoeffer contrasts faith with the religious act: "The religious act is always something partial, faith is always something whole, an act involving the whole life. Jesus does not call men to a new religion, but to life."[56] Warfield points out that, in the Old Testament, this faith is no mere assent. Rather, "it is a profound and abiding disposition, an ingrained attitude of mind and heart towards God which affects and gives character to all the activities."[57] Trust/commitment is staking one's whole life on the truth of the confession which one has been persuaded (in the best sense of the word) to choose.

The Object of Belief

If the object is important in determining the confession of Christian faith, it is even more so for trust.[58] Although it obviously has psychological aspects, the trust element of belief is not a psychological state as much as a relationship with a living person. The hallmark and motivating power of *Christian* faith is trust in *Christ*. E. C. Blackman specifies this is also true in the Hebrew Scriptures where ־ןׄוׄא in hiphil is to trust. Behind this word is an implied relation, ultimately a personal one, for behind the object, which is the basis of trust, there is a person.[59]

Warfield's thorough analysis breaks down the usages of the noun πιστός and the verb πιστεύω. In the New Testament, the noun and verb are quite evenly distributed and occur with approximately equal frequency (about 240 times each) although there is a concentration of the noun in Paul and of the verb in John.

The usages of the verb with prepositions are most relevant to this discussion. The implication of the construction with ἐν is a firm fixedness of confidence in its object which is the gospel and Christ. The dative, linked with ἐπί and meaning to "believe on", is used only twice besides the Isaiah quotations and is "expressive of steady, resting repose, reliance upon the object." Ἐπί with the accusative is used seven times, five times where its object is Christ himself and twice in Romans 4 where the object of reliance is God, who is described as savingly working through Christ.[60]

Most importantly for our study is the construction of the verb and its object with εἰς which is the special New Testament usage. It is used 49 times, four-fifths of which are Johannine and the rest Pauline.

> The object towards which faith is thus said to be reliantly directed is in one unique instance "the witness which God hath witnessed concerning his Son" (1 John 5:10), where we may well believe that "belief in the truth of the witness is carried on to personal belief in the object of witness, that is, the Incarnate Son Himself." Elsewhere the object believed on, in this construction, is always a person, and that very rarely God . . . , and most commonly Christ. . . . It is probably sufficient to find it in the sense conveyed by the verb itself while the preposition adjoins only the person towards whom the strong feeling expressed by the verb is directed. In any event, what these passages express is "an absolute transference of trust from ourselves to another," a complete self-surrender to Christ.[61]

Warfield's summary continues to emphasize this most characteristic element of biblical faith--reliant trust on Christ for salvation:

> A survey of these passages will show very clearly that in the NT "to believe" is a technical term to express reliance on Christ for salvation. . . . Before the disciples were called "Christians" . . . it would seem, then, that they were called "believers"--those who had turned to Christ in trusting reliance (οἱ πιστεύσαντες), or those who were resting on Christ in trusting reliance (οἱ πιστεύσοντες); and that the undefined "to believe" had come to mean to become or to be a Christian, that is, to turn to or rest on Christ in reliant trust.[62]

The usage of the verb is deepened by the use of the noun πίστις. In its vast usage in the active sense, it is never applied to man's faith in man, rather it always refers to self-abandoning trust with the object as God, Christ, or divine things.

In a number of New Testament instances, there is no specified object for the noun πίστις. This is not because there is no object, but because the object is left to be supplied by the general knowledge of the reader. This implies that πίστις has already become so clearly a technical term in the New Testament that it needed no further definition to clarify that it meant to convey its full sense of saving faith in Jesus Christ. The tendency to use πίστις practically as a synonym for Christianity is sharply pointed out by the phrase οἱ ἐκ πίστεως (Gal. 3:7,9), which comes to mean "believers."[63] Brunner speaks of the absolute usage of the term, "faith":

> The clearest instance of this is Galatians 3:23, "but before the faith came . . . which should afterwards be revealed". Here there could just as well stand "Before Christ came". Indeed, the faith of the New Testament is nothing other than faith in Christ, and therefore it can be spoken of without addition, in an absolute sense.[64]

Faith, in fact, derives its value from its object not its subject. Soteriologically, it is not even faith in Christ which is salvific, but Christ who saves by faith. The object of biblical faith is God himself. The New Testament focuses centrally on Jesus as the Christ, maintaining continuity with Israel's faith in the coming Messiah.

This emphasis on the object of faith is contrasted by Schleiermacher's theology, which emphasizes the trust aspect itself rather than the object of the trust:

> In modern theology Schleiermacher's conception of religion as an original inner experience, distinguished from knowledge and action, has exercised a decisive influence upon the treatment of the conception of faith, by the establishment of the psychological scheme; but owing to his insufficient appreciation of historical revelation, his doctrine of faith bears the traits of a general religion rather than of the Christian faith of salvation.[65]

Trust's psychological value, although significant, is an inadequate foundation for biblical faith.

The Initiative of Trust

The initiator of the relationship of trust between a believer and Jesus Christ is always God himself. From the beginning of man's existence, as described in the Garden of Eden, God has been a God of revelation. He unveils himself and asks man to trust him. There is always enough revealed to establish "belief that" and to build enough facts for a confession. There is plenty of evidence and experience for man to trust God. Yet to trust or not to trust is a choice. Trust or lack of trust (unbelief) is man's reaction to God's primary action.

The Old Testament covenant shows the Israelites to be more children of promise (trust) than children of the law (obedience). Obedience rightly follows, not precedes, trust (Heb. 11):

> The holy walk is characteristic of God's servants (Gn 5:22. 24; 6:9; 17:1; 24:40; 48:15), but it is characteristically described as a walk "with God"; its peculiarity consisted precisely in the ordering of life by entire trust in God, and it expressed itself in conduct growing out of this trust (Gn 3:20; 6:22; 7:5; 8:18; 12:4; 17:23; 21:12.16; 22).[66]

God takes the initiative in trust because he has (and is) the substance of trust, trustworthiness. Man is allowed access into this divine event of trust:

> The main thing to note is that it is man's acceptance of God, and response to God's offer of himself; man's receiving of God's gift rather than his own gift, effort, or achievement. God has spoken his Word. Man can say Yes or No to it. Faith is man's Yes to the Word of God. And when the Word comes into focus in Christ, faith also may be said to center on this focus.[67]

It is not surprising that Christianity came to be seen as a trust event. It was not only unique in its content, but in its way of appropriating the content. What mankind knew of deep trust between human beings became magnified into absolute reliance for Life--past, present, and future. Or more accurately expressed, man derived his inferior, but significant, form of trust between humans from the ultimate example of the relationship between Jesus and the Father and Jesus and His disciples.

Trust is always man's response to God's initiative. To believe in God is simply to let God be God. This is the chief business of faith as trust.

4. Obedience: Belief For

C. Robert Wetzel calls our attention to the fact that for any person,

> simply believing that there is a God is not enough to make him a believer in the Scriptural sense. The more important question may be, "What does the believer do when he believes in God?" Ludwig Wittgenstein reminds us that "what you say won't be taken as the measure for the firmness of a belief. But, for instance, what risks you would take?"[68]

Discipleship, Faith, and Obedience

These are questions that the New Testament writers call us to answer. Belief in the New Testament sense is a full commitment which demands full obedience to the God who calls the believer to discipleship:

> The responsible commitment which is assumed in a small way in all personal knowledge comes into its own in the Christian faith. In Christianity it is not only assumed, it is required. It is not only a premise of epistemology but a developed principle of theology. Faith is "obedience to the truth" (1 Pet. 1:22). Discipleship is an undertaking which grows out of an understanding. What faith has seen, obedience is prepared to sign. This is the obedience of faith to which personal conviction leads.[69]

The equation of faith and obedience is spelled out by Bonhoeffer, *"Only he who believes is obedient, and only he who is obedient believes."*[70] Bonhoeffer further explains the necessity of Christ in discipleship:

> Discipleship means adherence to Christ, and, because Christ is the object of that adherence, it must take the form of discipleship. An abstract Christology, a doctrinal system, a general religious knowledge on the subject of grace or on the forgiveness of sins, render discipleship superfluous, and in fact they positively exclude any idea of discipleship whatever, and are essentially inimical to the whole conception of following Christ. With an abstract idea it is possible to enter into a relation of formal knowledge, to become enthusiastic about it, and perhaps even to put it into practice; but it can never be followed in personal obedience. Christianity without the living Christ is inevitably Christianity without discipleship, and Christianity without discipleship is always Christianity without Christ. . . .
> Discipleship without Jesus Christ is a way of our own choosing.[71]

Obedience is exemplified by Jesus' life, especially in his relationship as obedient Son to the Father. This relationship is stressed in the Johannine expression, "The world must learn that I love the Father and that I do exactly what my Father has commanded me" (John 14:31) and in Mark, "Yet not what I will, but what you will" (14:36 and Matt. 26:39). Paul records that Jesus became obedient unto death (Phil. 2:8). Trusting Jesus then becomes walking the same way that he walked, obedience even in suffering (1 Pet. 2:21).

Looking at the radical nature of Jesus' obedience, Bultmann stresses the inwardness of obedience:

> Radical obedience exists only when a man inwardly assents to what is required of him, when the thing commanded is seen as intrinsically God's command; when the whole man stands behind what he does; or better, when the whole man is *in* what he does, when he is not *doing something obediently*, but *is* essentially obedient.[72]

The Epistles

The fact that "to believe" means "to obey" is especially emphasized in Hebrews 11. In this chapter, *"by faith"* is repeated, continually referring to these actions recorded in the Old Testament: Abel offered God a better sacrifice, Noah built an ark, Abraham journeyed to an unknown place and also offered Isaac as a sacrifice, Isaac blessed Jacob and Esau, Jacob blessed Joseph's sons and worshipped, Joseph spoke, Moses' parents hid him, Moses chose to be mistreated, left Egypt, and kept the Passover, the people passed through the Red Sea, the people marched around the walls of Jericho, and Rahab welcomed the spies. It is obedience by faith which is here emphasized.

Paul. Bultmann shows us

> How naturally πιστεύειν includes obeying may be seen from the use of πείθεσθαι rather than πιστεύειν for receiving the Christian message, . . . Unbelief can be denoted not merely by ἀπιστεῖν but also by ἀπειθεῖν . . . Paul in particular stresses the element of obedience in faith. For him πίστις is indeed ὑπακοή as comparison of R. 1:8; 1 Th. 1:8 with R. 15:18; 16:19, or 2 C. 10:5 f. with 10:15, shows. Faith is for Paul ὑπακούειν τῷ εὐαγγελίῳ , R. 10:16. To refuse to believe is not to obey the righteousness which the Gospel offers for faith, R. 10:3. Paul can call believing confession of the Gospel the ὑποταγὴ τῆς ὁμολογίας εἰς τὸ εὐαγγέλιον τοῦ Χριστοῦ, 2 C. 9:13. He coins the combination ὑπακοη πίστεως, R. 1:5.[73]

The Pauline phrases should also be compared with the negative in 1 Peter 4:17, "those who do not obey the gospel of God" (τῶν ἀπειθούντων τῷ τοῦ θεοῦ εὐαγγελίῳ). The gospel is something to be obeyed in belief/faith.

Bultmann goes so far as to say that

> *Paul understands faith primarily as obedience;* he understands the act of faith as an act of obedience. This is shown by the parallelism of two passages in Romans: "because your faith is proclaimed in all the world" (1:8) and "for your obedience is known to all" (16:19).[74]

And although this is true, God and obedience contain a great deal more substance than Bultmann allows.[75]

James' Action Faith. James takes hold of the task of making sure that faith is active rather than merely passive. For James, faith must have practical, as well as true, expression. Faith must be a persuasion that persists, a belief that moves, a trust that acts, a hope that motivates. He will not tolerate a belief of mind or heart that is not in step with a belief of action:

> As in the paraenetic tradition elsewhere, Jas. is conscious of the need to prove faith (1:3; cf. 1 Pet. 1:7). He demands renunciation of all conduct that conflicts with living faith and confession (1:6ff.). For him, faith and obedient conduct are indissoluably linked. Faith understood merely as trust and confession is not able to save. Only through obedience . . . and conduct which fulfills the commandments of God does faith come to completion (Jas. 2:22).

The opponent that Jas. has in mind does not attack faith but exempts himself from obedience.[76]

The letter of James is bound to give the impression of conflicting with that of the Pauline teaching. Yet, as B. B. Warfield says, this polemic view

is nevertheless a delusion, and arises from an insufficient realization of the place occupied by faith in the discussions of the Jewish schools, reflections of which have naturally found their way into the language of both Paul and James. And so far are we from needing to suppose some reference, direct or indirect, to Pauline teaching to account for James' entrance upon the question which he discusses, that this was a matter upon which an earnest teacher could not fail to touch in the presence of a tendency common among the Jews at the advent of Christianity (cf. Mt 3:9; 7:21; 23:3; Ro 2:17), and certain to pass over into Jewish-Christian circles; and James' treatment of it finds, indeed, its entire presupposition in the state of things underlying the exhortation of 1:22. When read from his own historical standpoint, James' teachings are free from any disaccord with those of Paul, who as strongly as James denies all value to a faith which does not work by love (Gal 5:6; 1 Co 13:2; 1 Th 1:3). In short, James is not depreciating faith: with him, too, it is faith that is reckoned unto righteousness (2:23), though only such a faith as shows itself in works can be so reckoned, because a faith which does not come to fruitage in works is dead, non-existent. He is rather deepening the idea of faith, and insisting that it includes in its very conception something more than an otiose intellectual assent.[77]

Unbelief, as we shall see further below, is akin not to ignorance, but to disobedience (ἀπείθεια, the root of the English word apathy). One Johannine verse (John 3:36) suffices as an example, at this point, of the contrast of "he who believes in the Son" (ὁ πιστεύων εἰς τὸν υἱὸν) with "he who does not obey the Son" (ὁ δὲ ἀπειθῶν τῷ υἱῷ).

5. Hope: Belief Until

As subjective elements, trust and hope are at least very closely related; for many theologians, they are one and the same. From our perspective, we see hope as one of the elements of Christian belief/faith.

For the Reformers, "Faith is called to life by promise and is therefore essentially hope, confidence, trust in the God who will not lie but will remain faithful to his promise."[78] For Arthur Rich,

Hope, the eschatological hope that is grounded in Jesus Christ is not deduced from faith, it IS the faith; . . . "Without God faith and hope are groundless", says Rich, "just as without faith and hope God is without sense". "Hope belongs to faith like warmth belongs to fire" he adds.[79]

For John Calvin, "Wherever this living faith exists, it must have the hope of eternal life as its inseparable companion, or rather must of itself beget and manifest it."[80] More specifically, Calvin sees

> that in one word hope is nothing more than the expectation of those things which faith previously believes to have been truly promised by God. Thus, faith believes that God is true; hope expects that in due season he will manifest his truth. Faith believes that he is our Father; hope expects that he will always act the part of a Father toward us. Faith believes that eternal life has been given to us; hope expects that it will one day be revealed. Faith is the foundation on which hope rests; hope nourishes and sustains faith. For as no man can expect anything from God without previously believing his promises, so, on the other hand, the weakness of our faith, which might grow weary and fall away, must be supported and cherished by patient hope and expectation. For this reason Paul justly says, *"We are saved by hope"* (Rom 8:24). For while hope silently waits for the Lord, it restrains faith from hastening on with too much precipitation, confirms it when it might waver in regard to the promises of God or begin to doubt of their truth, refreshes it when it might be fatigued, extends its view to the final goal, so as not to allow it to give up in the middle of the course, or at the very outset. In short, by constantly renovating and reviving, it is ever and anon furnishing more vigour for perseverance.[81]

"Thus," as Moltmann puts it, "in the Christian life faith has the priority, but hope the primacy."[82] He sees all of Christianity through the eschatological perspective:

> From first to last, and not merely in the epilogue, Christianity is eschatology, is hope, forward looking and forward moving, and therefore also revolutionizing and transforming the present. The eschatological is not one element *of* Christianity, but it is the medium of Christian faith as such, the key in which everything in it is set, the glow that suffuses everything here in the dawn of an expected new day. For Christian faith lives from the raising of the crucified Christ, and strains after the promises of the universal future of Christ.[83]

Brunner also sees faith as almost identical with hope:

> Faith knows no other theodicy than the Eschatological Hope. For it breaks through the veil we spoke of, and shows that it is not the true reality. But faith as hope is the knowledge of that manifestation of glory which alone removes the cause of declension from faith, the cause of doubt, and makes manifest the love of God as the true reality in the face of all doubt. The faith which contains in itself this hope, which indeed is almost identical with it, is the faith which has passed through death until life and the certainty of the eternal goal which is promised to faith.[84]

The General Epistles

In the "Faith Hall of Fame" in Hebrews 11, the Old Testament characters are given as examples of faith largely because their faith consists of trusting hope, which issued in the obedience we have already discussed. They lived in faithful hope until their death even though "they did not receive the things promised; they only saw them and welcomed them from a distance" (vs. 13). Their commendation was for their faith, that is, trusting God for the future even though there was no fulfilment of the promise (vs. 39).

More generally, the Letter to the Hebrews encourages the readers so that they would not fall away from faith into hopelessness:

That in the Epistle to the Hebrews it is the general idea of faith, or, to be more exact, the subjective nature of faith, that is dwelt upon, rather than its specific object, is not due to a peculiar conception of what faith lays hold upon, but to the particular task which fell to its writer in the work of planting Christianity in the world. With him, too, the person and work of Christ are the specific object of faith (13:7.8; 3:14; 10:22). But the danger against which, in the providence of God, he was called upon to guard the infant flock, was not that it should fall away from faith to works, but that it should fall away from faith into despair. His readers were threatened not with legalism but with "shrinking back" (10:39), and he needed, therefore, to emphasize not so much the object of faith as the duty of faith. Accordingly, it is not so much on the righteousness of faith as on its perfecting that he insists; it is not so much its contrast with works as its contrast with impatience that he impresses on his readers' consciences; it is not so much to faith specifically in Christ and in Him alone that he exhorts them as to an attitude of faith--an attitude which could rise above the seen to the unseen, the present to the future, the temporal to the eternal, and which in the midst of the sufferings could retain patience, in the midst of disappointments could preserve hope. This is the key to the whole treatment of faith in the Epistle to the Hebrews--its definition as the assurance of things hoped for, the conviction of things not seen (11:1); its illustration and enforcement by the example of the heroes of faith in the past, a list chosen and treated with the utmost skill for the end in view (11); its constant attachment to the promises (4:1.2; 6:12; 10:36.38; 11:9; 13:39); its connexion with the faithfulness (11:11, cf. 10:23), almightiness (11:19), and the rewards of God (11:6.26); and its association with such virtues as boldness (3:6; 4:16; 10:19.35), confidence (3:14; 11:1), patience (10:36: 12:1), hope (3:6; 6:11.18; 10:23).[85]

The First Letter of Peter calls the readers to a living hope in the midst of their trials of various kinds. The writer sees the trials as refiners of the faith of the readers. Mostly Gentiles, they are not in imminent danger of falling back into Judaism as were the readers of the Letter to the Hebrews, but this aspect of hoping faith is extremely relevant to their present sufferings. The object of their faith and hope is God Himself (1:21; 3:5), who raised Jesus from the dead and glorified him. The full eschatological dimension of hope is referred to when the readers are exhorted to "set your hope fully on the grace to be given you when Jesus Christ is revealed" (1:13).

Warfield sees the tone of the hoping faith in this letter rooted in the character of Peter as revealed in his recorded speeches in Acts.[86] The letter stresses the relation of faith to the coming salvation: "The reference of faith in Peter is therefore characteristically to the completion rather than to the inception of salvation (1:5.9; 2:6, cf. Ac 15:11)."[87]

This is consistent with the fact that in the Johannine literature one of the consequences of faith is hope. "Whoever puts his faith in the Son has eternal life" (John 3:36), "Whoever hears my word and believes him who sent me has eternal life and will not be condemned; he has crossed over from death to life" (John 5:24, cf. also 6:47, 54). "God has given us eternal life, and this life is in his Son. He who has the Son has life; he who does not have the Son of God does not have life" (1 John 5:11-12). The future eternal life is a present possession for the believer, accenting the present and future dimensions of hopeful faith.

Os Guinness looks at the creative tension inherent in Christian faith as seen in Hebrews 11:

> The Hebrew word for faith has the same stem as the word for hope and the root meaning of both is tautness or tension. Faith which lacks this is less than it should be. The Christian view of things is pitted ultimately against the vision of other faiths and world views. It stands over against every perception of reality which is finite from end to end. Faith sees the infinite as well as the finite or it sees nothing. The tension of faith results from its being stretched between God's promise and God's fulfillment, and if one or other of these is thought to fail, the line of faith will sag or snap.
> Faith's calling is to live in between times. Faith is in transit. It lives in an interim period. Behind faith is the great "no longer." Ahead of it lies the great "not yet." God has spoken and God will act. Christ has come once and Christ will come again. We have heard the promises and we will witness the event. However long the waiting takes, it is only the gap between the thunder and the lightning.
> Faith's task is to join hands with the past and the future to hold down God's will in the present. The present moment is the disputed territory for faith, a no man's land between past and future, ground either to be seized by obedience or lost to disobedience. Visionary faith stakes out its possession of the land and does so with energy and enthusiasm that come from its knowledge of what the reclaimed land will one day be.[88]

In the synoptics, what Warfield calls "miracle faith"[89] stresses moments in which people put trust in Jesus for a specific event. This shows that faith has a temporal future hope as well as the longer-term eschatological dimension. The beginning temporal hope gives sight (in a different context, "Because you have seen me, you have believed," John 20:29) to build the eschatological dimension while the overarching eschatological hope then has new power in temporal moments ("Blessed are those who have not seen and yet have believed," John 20:29).

Faith as Hope in Paul

Bultmann sees that for Paul

> "*faith*" is also "*hope*." "Faith" is no self-contained condi-
> tion of man's soul, but points toward the future: "he who by
> faith is righteous shall live" (Gal. 3:11; Rom. 1:17). "For
> if we have died with Christ, we believe that we shall also
> live with him" (Rom. 6:8; *cf*. I Thess. 4:14). "for with the
> heart man believeth unto righteousness and with the mouth
> confession is made unto salvation" (Rom. 10:10 KJ).
>   The "righteousness" which is the goal of "faith" is no
> quality which adheres to man, but is his relation to God. If
> it has become a present possibility, this "present-ness" is
> not a temporal and therefore a temporary state. Rather, its
> "present-ness" is that of the eschatological Now. That is,
> it is always both here and ahead of the already rightwised
> believer as future to him.[90]

A key passage in Paul for this hoping belief is Romans 4:18. In the context of Abraham being justified by his faith, Paul writes, "Against all hope, Abraham in hope believed . . . ." As Moltmann says, "Where the bounds that mark the end of all human hopes are broken through in the raising of the crucified one, there faith can and must expand into hope."[91] Paul's prayer at the end of the Roman letter emphasizes the relation of hope to belief, "May the God of hope fill you with great joy and peace as you trust in him, so that you may overflow with hope by the power of the Holy Spirit" (15:13). Hope does not stand on its own for Paul; it is believing which causes hope. Hope without belief is baseless.

Romans 8:24f. identifies the unseen dimension of hope for which faith gives a solid substance. This alleviates the need for anxiety on man's part "because he has turned over his anxiety about himself and his future to God in obedience."[92] O. Michel points out that faith merges into hope here since it contains the element of being sustained.[93] The first letter of Peter adds the possibility of relieving oneself of anxieties of the temporal future: "Cast all your anxiety on him because he cares for you" (5:7).

In the context of the author's suffering, the Second Letter to Timothy emphasizes hope which comes through belief (πεπίστευκα), "I know whom I have believed, and am convinced that he is able to guard what I have entrusted to him for that day" (1:12). This suffering motif is also prominent in Peter. Moltmann says of hope in suffering,

> Hope finds in Christ not only a consolation *in* suffering, but
> also the protest of the divine promise *against* suffering. If
> Paul calls death the "last enemy" (I Cor. 15:26), then the
> opposite is also true: that the risen Christ, and with him

the resurrection hope, must be declared to be the enemy of death and of a world that puts up with death. Faith takes up this contradiction and thus becomes itself a contradiction to the world of death. That is why faith, wherever it develops into hope, causes not rest but unrest, not patience but impatience. It does not calm the unquiet heart, but is itself this unquiet heart in man.[94]

It is both the restfulness and restlessness of hope which is an element of Christian belief.

Other Elements Considered

Fear

Bultmann makes us consider what we might not have considered otherwise, that is, that, "Such 'hope,' nevertheless, has a peculiar correlative in 'fear' (φόβος), which is an indispensable constitutive element in 'faith,' inasmuch as it guarantees the centering of the believer's attention upon God's 'grace.'"[95]

Bultmann quotes Rom. 11:20-22, warning the readers that the unbelieving Jews "were broken off because of unbelief, and you stand by faith. Do not be arrogant, but be afraid." He brings home his point:

Faith would be cheated of its purpose if the believer were to consider himself insured by it. God's "kindness," in which faith takes comfort, is only valid "provided you continue in his kindness." The man of faith, who in view of God's "grace" is freed from fear, must not forget that the grace that emancipates him is the "grace" of a Judge. When the man of faith looks to himself, his faith must ever contain "fear" as the knowledge of his own insignificance and his constant dependence upon God's "grace."[96]

Slightly diverting from Paul, Blackman reminds us that the two basic attitudes of trust in God and fear of God were not incompatible to the Hebrews. The fear of the Lord is closely connected to wisdom (Isa. 11:2; Ps. 111:10; Prov. 1:7). "The only reasoning that mattered for them was that which started from the presuppositions of faith--a faith, moreover, which trembled in reverence before God."[97]

Having expressed his view that hope and fear equally belong to the structure of faith as correlatives, Bultmann then refers to Phil. 3:12-14 upon which he comments:

Existence in faith, then, is a movement between "no longer" and "not yet." "No longer": The decision of faith has done away with the past; nevertheless, as true decision, the decision must be maintained--that is, made again and again anew. As that which is overcome, the past is always with us, and faith must remember the past as that which constantly threatens. Paul's "forgetting" does not mean putting the past out of mind, but does mean constantly holding it down, not letting one's self be caught by it again. "Not yet": giving up that which is past, i.e. surrendering a possession which had given a supposed security, precludes taking a new possession in exchange for it. Viewed from man's side no one can say, "I have made it my own"; and yet in view of the fact that "Jesus Christ has made me his own," it can be said, "Nevertheless the hoped-for has already occurred."[98]

Even though this discussion appears rather convincing, it seems more in touch with Pauline thought that fear moves one to faith, rather than being an element of it. It may also keep a believer from falling away from faith when he is in doubt, but it does not constitute a part in the substance of faith itself. Faith, as reliant trust and confident hope, is the antithesis to fear (Rom 8:15, cf. also 1 John 4:18).

It is true that Paul sees fear as having some part in the Christian life, but fear is largely a check to see if faith is genuine. When faith looks to God's grace and not man's own self, fear is needed only to remind one to beware of falling back into man's own achievement. When the believer looks to himself, he has ceased to have reliant trust in Jesus alone and has forgotten the hope to which he was called. He then needs fear to make him return to faith. The two strands of faith in God and fear of God exist side by side in the Christian life, but it is rather misleading to see fear as a constituent of faith.

Love

Love also has a very close connection to faith. The Pauline triad, "faith, hope, and love" (1 Cor. 13:13), is almost inseparable, with love emerging as the greatest. The Johannine litmus test for outsiders to ascertain who are disciples is love not belief (John 13:35). Brunner points out that for Paul, "the connection between faith and love was a much more intimate one, one that was indeed [sic] implied by the very nature of faith. For Paul, faith is indeed nothing other than the reception of the love of God."[99] Although love is the greatest for Paul, with regard to freedom in Christ, "the only thing that counts is faith expressing itself through love" (Gal. 5:6).

The intimate connection of faith and love must be maintained. But even though they are married to one another, love also has its own life "separate" from faith. It would tie love down too much to make it an element of belief. Although both faith and love (along with hope) are eternal, love is the greatest of the triad. Although love issues from faith as do obedience and hope, love is not *inherent* in the word, conception, and action of faith in the way that obedience and hope are.

Others

There are other terms that are used as near synonyms for believe. Bauer and Zimmerman point out that John uses "to believe" meaning "to hear", while "to believe in him" means "to come to him", "to receive him", or "love him".[100] However important these are, they cannot be considered elements of biblical belief.

Conclusion

In conclusion, we could do no better than to quote the old biblical scholar, B. B. Warfield:

> It is only a question whether "The Christian religion" is designated in it [πίστις] from the side of doctrine or life; though it be from the point of view of life, still "the faith" has become a synonym for "Christianity," "believers" for "Christians," "to believe" for "to become a Christian," and we may trace a development by means of which πίστις has come to mean the religion which is marked by and consists essentially in "believing." That this development so rapidly took place is significant of much, and supplies a ready explanation of such passages as Gal 3:23.25, in which the phrases "before the faith came" and "now that faith is come" probably mean little more than before and after the advent of "Christianity" into the world. On the ground of such a usage, we may at least re-affirm with increased confidence that the idea of "faith" is conceived of in the NT as the characteristic idea of Christianity, and that it does not import mere "belief" in an intellectual sense, but all that enters into an entire self-commitment of the soul to Jesus as the Son of God, the Saviour of the world.[101]

DIMENSIONS OF RELIGIOUS COMMITMENT

An interesting excursus from the biblical material is to note Charles Y. Glock's proposition that "all of the many and diverse manifestations of religiosity prescribed by the different religions of the world" can be classified under five dimensions of religious commitment: 1) experiential (feeling, emotion), 2) ritualistic (religious behavior and practice), 3) ideological (beliefs), 4) intellectual (information and knowledge), 5) consequential (the effects in the secular world of religious belief, practice, experience, and knowledge).[102]

Our biblical elements are closely interrelated and cannot be strictly organized under Glock's dimensions, but they may be seen to touch upon and agree with his categories in the sense that they seem to fit the empirical reality revealed in Christian belief. Although they are not equal to these dimensions, our elements at times converge with them. A suggested comparison:

Biblical Elements	Glock's Dimensions
1. CHOICE	Intellectual, Ideological, Experiential, Ritualistic
2. CONFESSION	Intellectual, Ideological
3. TRUST	Experiential
4. OBEDIENCE	Consequential, Ritualistic
5. HOPE	Ideological, Experiential

There are other sociological models which emphasize various aspects of religion which could be considered,[103] but Glock's model is the most relevant for this discussion.

THE NATURE OF UNBELIEF

Put simply, unbelief is the absence,[104] rejection, or opposite of belief as we have described it. It spans the five elements by its void, denial, or choice of an alternative.[105]

The element of obedience is especially important here in the πείθω stem. Disobedience and unbelief are virtually equivalent terms as seen most vividly in John 3:36. The double word groupings in both noun and verb with their alpha privitives become almost synonymous in certain passages even though ἀπιστία is more a state of mind while ἀπείθεια is an expression of that state of mind. Ἀπείθεια is not always a complete refusal, but simply disobedience, lack of belief, doing nothing with God's revelation.

On this issue, Bultmann stresses the unbelief which results from lack of hope:

> The unbeliever insists upon living out of his own resources and so is anxious about his own future in the illusion of being able to dispose over it. Though the man without faith naturally has his hopes, too--just as those "who have hope" (1 Thess. 4:13), of course, also live with certain hopes-- still they are no real hopes. This man who is concerned for himself factually lives in fear, shutting himself up against the future, which is not at his disposal. The man of faith is relieved of this fear because in faith he has let anxiety about himself go.[106]

Moltmann stresses similarly when he writes of the sin of despair:

> If faith thus depends on hope for its life, then the sin of unbelief is manifestly grounded in hopelessness. To be sure, it is usually said that sin in its original form is man's wanting to be as God. But that is only the one side of sin. The other side of such pride is hopelessness, resignation, inertia and melancholy. From this arise the *tristesse* and frustration which fill all living things with the seeds of a sweet decay. Among the sinners whose future is eternal death in Rev. 21.8, the "fearful" are mentioned before unbelievers, idolaters, murderers and the rest. For the Epistle to the Hebrews, falling away from the living hope, in the sense of being disobedient to the promise in time of oppression, or of being carried away from God's pilgrim people as by a flood, is the great sin which threatens the hopeful on their way. Temptation then consists not so much in the titanic desire to be as God, but in weakness, timidity, weariness, not wanting to be what God requires of us.[107]

Besides obedience and hope already mentioned, the remain-

ing three elements are also inherently absent in unbelief, but
the usages of unbelief, unbeliever, and derivatives usually
encompass all rather than stressing one element above the other.
Trust is perhaps especially considered to be negated in Matthew
13:58; 17:20; Mark 6:6; John 16:9; 20:27; and Romans 3:3. Confession is probably most strongly referred to when the council of
the elders met together and asked Jesus if he was the Christ.
Jesus replies, "If I tell you, you will not believe me" (Luke
22:67). Other passages stressing confession are the alternative
ending of Mark (16:11-14), John 20:25, and 1 Tim. 1:13. The
element of choice comes into its own mainly with the term, "unbeliever" (ὁ ἄπιστος) used in Paul (1 Cor. 6:6; 7:12,13; 10:27;
14:22,24; 2 Cor. 4:4).

Reasons for Unbelief

The biblical material rarely sees a need to ascertain the
causes of or reasons for unbelief. Mainly, it simply states the
fact, "They do not believe." Occasionally, almost as an exception to the normal assumed reasons, another explanation is given.
Four stand out in relief: The gospel of John records that a
group of Jews still would not believe even after Jesus' miraculous signs and explains through quoting Isaiah 6:10 that they
cannot believe (12:37-41; cf. also Mark 6:52). Luke's gospel
records a different side of unbelief when after Jesus' appearance
to the disciples, it records that "they still did not believe it
because of joy and amazement" (24:41). The Second Thessalonian
Epistle records a very strong statement, "For this reason God
sends them a powerful delusion so that they will believe the lie
and so that all will be condemned who have not believed the truth
but have delighted in wickedness" (2:11-12). In several passages,
it is clear that men refused to believe (Acts 14:1; 19:9) or
rejected the truth (Rom. 2:8).

Besides these occasional usages, there seems to be two
confluent streams of thought in the biblical view of those who
"do not believe": that is, that people are chosen to belief
(predestination) and that the unbelievers are responsible for not
coming to faith. These thoughts are most clearly seen in the
Gospel of John. The former is most clearly stated in the words
of Jesus when many disciples were offended by Jesus' "hard teaching" and deserted him, "This is why I told you that no one can
come to me unless the Father has enabled him" (6:65). Responsibility is spelled out strongly in the previous chapter where
Jesus discusses the various testimonies to his credibility, which
are evident, "yet you refuse to come to me to have life" (5:40
cf. also 3:18; 8:24,46; 12:44-50; Mark 8:17-18). A passage about
the unbelief of the Jews (10:22-42) includes both of these
aspects, i.e. "You do not believe because you do not belong to my
flock" (vs. 26) implying predestination and, "I did tell you, but
you do not believe" (vs. 25), implying that they have had enough
evidence so that they are held responsible for their unbelief.

Hebrews is very strong on the responsibility of unbelief,
showing that it is possible not to be unbelieving. "*See to it*,
brothers, that none of you has a sinful, unbelieving heart that
turns away from the living God" (3:12) and, "*Make every effort* to
enter that rest, so that no one will fall by following their

example of disobedience" (4:11). Compare also Ephesians 5:6, the alternative reading of Colossians 3:6, and Titus 1:16; 3:3. On the other hand, the Pauline corpus is clear that the faithfulness of God does not rely even on man's faith (Rom. 3:3; 11:32; 2 Tim. 2:13).

Brunner tackles the question of the reasons for unbelief, bringing in unbelievers' own perspectives:

But what is unbelief? Why does man not hear and acknowledge the claim and assurance of the Lord? What else could unbelief be than the will to assert one's autonomy? Unbelief does not indeed see it thus. It is quite unable to see itself as unbelief, but understands itself as an *inability* to believe and a *duty* not to believe. . . .
But what unbelief does not recognize is the occurrence and the motive of this displacement of the question from the dimension of historical encounter into that of objective truth. This motive is nothing other than the will to maintain autonomy. "Were there gods, who could endure not to be a god?" The claim to autonomy, resentment, the arrogance that cannot bear not to be God oneself, are the reason for unbelief. The flight of man from historical reality into the dimension of objective truth is caused by his refusal to face God's claim, for if he did so it would be an end of his autonomy.[108]

This is born out especially in the Genesis account of the first people's distrust of God's word (3:1-7).

In the context of the biblical theology of names for God, Carl F. H. Henry approaches unbelief from a unique perspective:

The whole history of unbelief may be summarized as a "calling God names"--sometimes blasphemous, sometimes ridiculous, always somewhat derogatory--indeed, as a refusal to identify him by his true name. The subject of theology (in its narrower reference to the nature of God) might even be approached through a dictionary of divine "names" since every age has added to "sacred nomenclature" by the coining of new God-names. Over against the human misnaming of God--both by the coarse caricatures of atheism, the earthy epithets of secularism, and the polite profanity of speculative philosophy--biblical theology insists on a self-named God.[109]

Pseudo-Unfaith, A Contemporary Phenomenon

While looking at the perspective from which others view unbelief, it is worth briefly noting Arthur Rich's notions of faith and pseudo-faith, unfaith and pseudo-unfaith as interpreted by Harold Tonks:

"Pseudo-faith is a religious phenomenon passing itself off as faith". Real faith is only ever faith in the presence of unfaith--"Lord, I believe, help my unbelief". Faith is unsafe--in principle and always. Furthermore, it has an eschatological placing: it can have no sense or knowledge of finality. But pseudo-faith clothes itself in this finality:

it turns the category of the ultimate into things that are at
our disposal, possible. . . .
"Just as *pseudo-faith* goes too far in the face of faith's
temptation to unfaith by taking the path of a world-view
founded on religious dogma, so *pseudo-unfaith* goes too far in
the face of unfaith's temptation to faith by taking the path
of ideology founded on an irreligious or atheistic dogma."

What Rich has in mind is that true faith and true unfaith
are existentially very draughty and exposed corners to stand
on. Both are glad of the shelter of their pseudo-ver-
sions.[110]

What Rich calls pseudo-faith, the New Testament often calls
unbelief. But in our day when open unfaith is much more prevalent, we will do well to consider the pseudo-version of unbelief
"when you have become just one more ideologist".[111]

DOUBT: UNBELIEF IN BELIEVERS

Of course, unbelief may also exist side by side with
belief. When this occurs, it becomes doubt, the state of being
in two minds or perhaps two hearts. This is partly because of
the nature of both faith itself and of human beings since the
fall.

Francis M. Tyrrell points out from a Thomistic perspective that in the intellectual aspects of belief,

Assent and deliberation coexist, and because the intellect
has not been satisfied by its own proper motives, its faith
assent can even be accompanied by doubts arising from the
absence of such evidence. Thus by its very internal dynamic,
belief is open to unbelief. In fact, it would appear that
the inclination to unbelief is built into its very structure.[112]

Jean Lacroix gives his comments on the unbelief of believers in *The Meaning of Modern Atheism*:

More generally we must rediscover the tradition of
negative theology, and learn at least this much from
Kierkegaard, that there is a struggle between doubt and
certitude at the heart of belief, because the dialectic
between belief and unbelief cannot take place at any other
level. It is rooted within, at the kernel of faith; it is an
inner need of faith; it enables faith to become more aware of
itself in the teeth of outside criticism. In recent times a
too facile apologetic has tried to insist on the implicit
belief of the unbeliever and to make him admit the existence
of God in spite of himself. Perhaps the time has come to
change the emphasis, and to stress rather the unbelief of the
believer.[113]

The classic biblical portrayal of belief and unbelief
existing alongside one another is Mark 9:24, "I do believe; help
me overcome my unbelief!" Because so many believers identify

with the unbelief in this man who came to Jesus, his statement
has become for some an example of true belief, which is seen to
be inseparable from unbelief. Brunner, however, correctly points
out that this saying "is not the expression of faith. No Apostle
speaks thus of faith. These words are rather an expression of
the beginning of faith, of faith extricating itself from unbelief." Brunner continues by explaining the continual struggle to
retain faith:

> We shall not understand this rightly until we have learnt the
> cause of unbelief, and the relapse from faith into unbelief.
> But the believer knows well that he must continually struggle
> in order to retain his faith. Faith is not a condition
> (*habitus*), not a virtue, but an act. We are continually
> returning from unbelief, from godlessness, to faith and can
> obtain the certainty of faith only through the act of abid-
> ing, through "dwelling in Him". Faith is "the actuality of
> response", the actuality of hearing and answering. . . .
> For this reason faith must continually be won afresh in the
> struggle with unbelief. It exists only as the fight of
> faith, as a continual transition from unbelief, from the
> desire to rest in oneself, to life in the presence of God.[114]

PART TWO

APPLICATION:
BELIEVERS AND UNBELIEVERS
IN BIRMINGHAM

CHAPTER FOUR

THE METHODOLOGY:

RANDOM SAMPLE, IN-DEPTH INTERVIEW

We must clearly declare the interests of the study at hand. This study takes the perspective of a theological, not a sociological, eye. There is no attempt in the method to gain sociological analyses and answers. The initial methods borrow from sociology's time-proven lessons, but both the questions and the answers proposed are thoroughly and unashamedly theological.

The approach of this research has been to give adequate attention to make sure that the sample was taken and the interview given by the best of techniques currently available, using sociological tools only to eliminate major bias, but claiming no value-free objectivity.

There is a perpetual disagreement among sociologists as to the best method of research, depending on the subject and object of research. Bryan Wilson is an advocate for studying the structures of unbelief. He suggests "that belief systems do not in fact inhere only in individuals but that cultures carry belief systems and unbelief systems."[1] He feels, then,

that the principal thrust of research into unbelief ought not to be a head count of individual dispositions but an analysis of social institutions, of organization and of communities, and of patterns of social relationships within them in order to discover to what extent these communities, organizations and structures are informed by supernatural conceptions of the world and are characterized by the behavioral correlates of such beliefs.[2]

Wilson sees that,

We ought not to suppose that changes in individual choices about belief have themselves produced a culture of unbelief; for individuals to have developed the consciousness of choice there must have been significant changes in social and cultural institutions.[3]

He thinks that the culture of unbelief will not be explained solely by survey research, but survey research does have appropriateness in modern conditions because of the prominence given to individual choice: "in politics (democracy); in economic consumption (the competitive market); in moral attitudes (the permissive society); and in religious belief (denominationalism and tolerance)."[4]

Charles Y. Glock, however, takes a view that fits more in line with our purposes here. He sees the first task is

> to refine our conceptualization so as to establish, insofar as possible without empirical work, the referents for supernatural and natural objectivists beliefs which exist in that setting. . . .
> The next step involves empirical tests of the conceptualization as elaborated for each setting. These tests would be constituted by interviews in dept [*sic*] with a sample of the population in the different settings, the sample could be relatively small, since no quantitative purpose is to be served by these tests. The depth interviews would be virtually open-ended at the beginning and would become more directed as the interview proceeds. The open-ended phase would be concerned with establishing the perspective from which respondents themselves view belief and unbelief. Do they consider themselves as believers or unbelievers, and by what criteria do they arrive at their judgments? . . . Through the interview attempts will be made to establish the saliency of the issues under discussion.[5]

Although not denying the validity nor the importance of Wilson's statements on the structural culture of unbelief, the model which Glock gives works better with the qualitative, theological questions which we wanted to answer and is roughly the one which we followed in our random sample, in-depth interview approach.[6]

The Population

The population was a small area of the Erdington section of northeastern Birmingham. This area would in popular language be termed a working class area, more specifically in the middle to higher part of that designation. Only one or two had incomes, education, or occupations that, were it possible to shift classes, might have put them in the middle class, yet their backgrounds were thoroughly working class. Its housing is part owner-occupier, part council and a few privately rented houses.[7]

This area was chosen because the study is to focus on people who were raised in a nominally Christian, British culture. The study did not intend to include those who were raised under the strong influence of other religions.[8]

The population was further limited to men. There is standard agreement that there is less belief and church activity in males than in females.[9] This study's purpose was to get at unbelief, nonbelief, and irreligion at their strongest and so weighted the population in terms of the most known adherents. From the wives of men who listened to the interviews, it was my impression that, with only a few exceptions, they followed the general trend of being more believing than their husbands. The area was also chosen because of its close proximity to the home of the researcher.

The Sampling Frame

The sampling frame was specific polling districts of the Register of Electors of the Birmingham, Erdington Constituency. There were 4,146 names of men and women on the entire frame, which would make a population of about 2,000 men's names on the sampling frame.

The Sample

The sample was a simple random sample of fifty men chosen from Kendal and Babinton Smith's *Table of Random Sampling Numbers*.[10] In Williamson's view, it was a rare sample since it incorporated as many as fifty informants.[11] Names which were obviously women's names were omitted, but names of questionable sexual origin were pursued and omitted only when it was verified that it was not a man.

Age Range. Since the sampling frame was the Register of Electors, the sample was limited to men eighteen years and older. There was no pre-set upper limit and the oldest men interviewed were eighty-four. The mean average age was 50.86 years and the median ages 53/54. The average between the extremes is fifty-one. Broken down into age groupings, they were:

Age Range	Actual Ages	Number/Percentage	
18-29	18,19,20,20,21,21,24,24,25,28	10	20%
30-39	30,30,30,36,37,39	6	12%
40-49	40,42,42,43,44,44,45,48	8	16%
50-59	53,54,55,58	4	8%
60-69	60,60,62,63,63,63,67,67,68,69,69,69	12	24%
70-79	70,71,74,74,74,78	6	12%
80-84	82,82,84,84	4	8%

This appears to be a reasonable age range, although with a higher percentage of pensioners than the civil population and a lower percentage in the 45-64 age range.[12] It may be that this reflects the population area age range, but this has not been examined.

Housing Type. The area included a council owned estate as well as privately owned homes. The houses were mainly terraced and semi-detached, but there were also some privately rented and co-ownership flats in a block about four stories high. Also included were some council bungalows for pensioners and a nursing home. No one from the sample was actually a resident at the nursing home, although two were from the pensioner's council bungalows.

Twenty-eight (56%) of the men lived in houses that were owned by themselves or their parents, while twenty-two (44%) lived in rented accommodation. Of the latter, two (4%) were privately rented and the rest were rented from the Birmingham Council.

The Approach

The approach was made personally at each man's door. It usually included an introduction something like the following:

Hello, I'm Roger Edrington, a student at the University of Birmingham. Your name has been selected at random from the electoral register to be one of the fifty men in this part of Erdington to participate in a research project.
The project has to do with finding out about the important moments in your life, your opinions, concerns and values. I hope that we can find out what is important to people so that we can really provide for people in a way that will help. So we may be able to find out some things from you that would help others.
The interview usually lasts between forty-five minutes and an hour, depending on how much you have to say. If this is a convenient time, I'd be happy to come in and talk with you about it now. If it is not a good time, I'd like to make an appointment with you for another time."

The words "belief", "unbelief", etc. were carefully avoided in order to keep from establishing a religious framework for the questionnaire. A few times, men did ask whether the interview had to do with church or religion. I did not want them to expect those questions, but in a very few cases I felt obliged to tell them that there were some questions relating to the church or religion among the other questions. Honesty was maintained at all times, sometimes clearly saying that I did not want to bias their answers but would be happy to explain things later.

The Response

I was persistent in showing the men their importance to the project and although cordial did not accept refusals willingly. Even so, nineteen of the men who were approached did not participate in the interview for a variety of reasons. This was a 27.5% non-response rate. Moser and Kalton guess that a typical non-response rate is around 20% for a survey of a few questions and explain that if there is anything more than those few questions, the non-response rate is always higher.[13] In view of the time required of the informants as well as the serious nature of the interview, the response rate seems to be very high indeed.[14]

There was a strong tendency in some women to refuse for their husbands or, in one case, for her son. Some of these men I still managed to get to and interview, but three of the refusals were of this type--two after agreement had been received from the men and appointments made. One of the latter women threatened to call the police because of my hardly hard-sell approach! Two men objected that they were too old, one adding that he couldn't hear and the other that, "Our opinions don't count for much. We don't have any opinions any more, we just live from day to day."

One man arranged an appointment and seemed to studiously avoid me from there on. I gave up after calling six times. After the same amount of tries I gave up on a young man who was

never home. I left the latter two notes, the first of which he
responded to by ringing me at one o'clock in the morning to
arrange a time to see me at my house. He did not arrive there
either.

Some of the refusers might have made for interesting
interviews. One man took ten minutes to tell me why he didn't
have time to participate, and, also revealed extreme bitterness
toward the rest of society, "I take care of myself and they take
care of themselves. They could drop the bomb on the lot of them
tomorrow. The British have no respect for themselves." Several
of the other refusers also *appeared* to have a rather bitter view
toward life. Others seemed to react to the seriousness of the
questions regarding their "concerns and values" and refused
quickly. "No, no, I'm alright," said one, while another gave the
classic reply, "I don't want to get involved." One potential
informant's wife had died eight months ago and said he might be
willing to be interviewed in a few years. In addition to these
nineteen, I rejected one young man in the potential sample since
I knew him and he knew me. There was no one else in the sample
that I knew or even recognised, even though the population area
was very close to my home. No one gave any indications whatsoever of knowing me.

The sample was well spread throughout the population with
only one road giving cause for wonder. Five out of five potential informants refused to participate from that road which made
up 3.95% of the total population. The refusals, however, were
for a variety of reasons and didn't appear to have any special
significance.

One can only wonder what the results might have been if
those men who did not seem willing to give their views had participated. However, we can be contented with the fact that the
great majority were willing to let their courses be charted.

The Interviews

The interviews were carried out over a four week period
in February and March of 1984. The interview was designed as a
semistructered, in-depth one using a normal, sociable conversation.[15] It put a high priority on the individual telling his own
story of present values and beliefs as well as past experience.
The entire interview schedule is included in appendix 1.

The interview had two major parts. Part one (the first
sixteen sections of questions) was designed to find out what was
important to the men: their values, concerns, and changes of
direction in life. It was also to check the saliency of their
belief, i.e., whether Christian belief or other beliefs so motivated their lives that the beliefs would appear without specifically religious questions being asked. After the first few interviews I tended to ask question number thirteen about death as a
bridge question between the first and second part (that is between questions sixteen and seventeen), since the question about
death was often seen as a "believe in God question", as one young
man put it [32]. Part two contained questions regarding specific
religious beliefs, practices, and background followed by a few

personal data questions.

The order, however, was not strictly adhered to, sometimes following the man's natural bent toward a related area which might be the answer to a question further down the list. Secondary probe questions were used where necessary and, although most questions were worded similarly, no necessity was seen to word the questions in exactly the same form every time. Except in cases where a religious belief or practice came out early in the interview, the first part of the schedule was not intermingled with the more specifically religious content questions of the second part.

A number of sociologists looked at the projected interview schedule and their help appreciably reduced the bias, but it was also found that some of the "biased questions" actually provoked the opposite response to the expected one when the pilot interviews and later the actual interviews were put in practice.

Every interview was tape recorded with a small tape recorder run on the men's own mains electricity supply. Rather than objecting to this process, they seemed to expect it. No one hesitated or appeared self-conscious in any noticeable way and appeared very much at ease. The men seemed to be as accustomed to tape recording as they would be to any of the other technological equipment in their home and my tape recorder was quickly disregarded. The men often didn't even break their sentence when the tape recorder shut off automatically and I changed the tape. This did, of course, mean that sometimes a sentence or two was lost, but the immense gain in having all of the data on tape and then transcribed on paper outweighed it. This gave final access to all the material and eliminated selection bias at the time of the interview.

At least as early as 1956 some sociologists were confirming that tapes do not increase resistance or decrease or destroy rapport, rather they enhance rapport because the interviewer is free to concentrate on the interviewee more.[16] This study showed that, even on the mainly unspoken subject of religion, tape recorders were a great aid rather than a hindrance. The men would have been far more put off by someone writing down everything they said.

All of the interviews were carried out in the men's own house, although I would have been willing to do the interview elsewhere if this was thought better by the men. I wanted the men to be comfortable in their own environment where they felt free to be honest. In my introduction to the interviews, I stressed as standard my need for them to be honest and my promise of confidentiality. I didn't know just how important that statement was until a number of men quoted my honesty statement back to me before they shared one of their most carefully protected secrets.

I always attempted to get the men on their own if possible. Only in a few cases was this entirely impossible and we sat in the presence of the ear (and sometimes eye) of a wife or one time a father. On the whole I did not feel that this influenced the quality of the responses, but there were one or two cases where the men may have told me more on their own. The fact that some men who spoke to me alone told me that their wives did not know some of what they told me or, in some cases, that they had never told anyone some of those things makes me wonder what stories might have come from the men where there was another listening ear.

Overall there is the mark of extreme honesty about the interview data. The one exception is the man who later told me that he was hungry which perhaps explained his abrupt answers. Even he, however, told me that he had confided in me an experience that he had never before revealed to anyone else.

J. Russell Hale's words with respect to his interviews with the unchurched in the USA are worth recounting here:

Whether the words are those of a ventriloquist or not, I heard them from the mouths of live human beings, not dummies. And it is no more possible to detach the words from the storytellers than to detach art from the artist, music from the composers or memoirs from the autobiographer. To dismiss the stories is to question the integrity of the authors.[17]

I cannot help but accept as genuine the great majority of material.

The interviews appeared to be successful in not giving away the interviewer's own religious stance since a number of informants asked quite unknowing at the end of the interview whether I was a believer or not. I resisted the temptation to answer any of the informants' questions during the interview or to tell them too much about the nature of the questions before they were asked, but I was always willing to tell them whatever they wanted to know after the interview was finished.

CHAPTER FIVE

THEIR SELF-DESIGNATIONS:

WHAT THEY CALL THEMSELVES AND WHY

One of the interesting aspects of any people is what they term themselves. When asked how they would describe themselves in terms of beliefs or lack of beliefs in the Christian faith, the answers were not as predictable as one might have expected.

"Believers"

Only twenty-eight (56 percent) of the men called themselves believers of some type, although there was a great deal of diversity about what it meant to be a believer as well as regarding the intensity of belief.

One regular church-goer was keen to say, "I believe the lot I do" [30]. Another man said the same but was quick to add, "Although I don't go to church" [36]. Still another was keen to justify the latter, "People say if you believe in him but don't go to church, you're an hypocrite, but I don't look at it like that. I've got just my beliefs just the same as they have who go to church all the time" [24].

Others with this self-designation of "believer" were not so sure but still wanted to be called believers. One informant said, "I wouldn't class myself a very high believer, very high in that way. . . . 70 percent believer" [10]. Another described himself as 60 percent believer and 40 percent "the other way" [43]. Going up the percentage scale was the man who described himself as, "Almost a believer. I would think about between 80 and 85 percent a believer" [44].

Others attempted to reveal this mixture in words rather than percentages, "I like to think I believe. Sometimes I have my doubts" [17]. Another regarded himself as the middle standard, "I would say I was average. I'm a Christian, I believe in Christ, but I would say that I was not a great believer, just middling I suppose" [14]. A regular church-goer was perhaps saying the same thing, "I'm about half way up the ladder as regards the--I'm not a great believer but I'm a Christian and that" [50].

One spelled out the assumption that others only intimated, "I believe in a lot of things and there are certain things that you disbelieve in. I mean that's got to be automatic I think" [19]. Another seemed to speak plainly for "everyday believers": "Well, I just believe just a certain amount, you know, not a lot. Just everyday way. . . . I do believe in him to an extent" [41].

"Agnostics"

A step beyond those people who had described themselves with some mixture were those who were much more in the middle of belief and unbelief. When asked to describe themselves these twelve men (24 percent) could not come off the fence. Some of their words: "I don't believe. I don't disbelieve" [46]; "Half and half" [47]; "Right in the middle" [31]; "Open" [38]; "Agnostic" [29,18]. The three most often used words among this group were, "I don't know": "I wouldn't describe meself. I should say, 'I don't know' I suppose. I wouldn't say I'm an atheist because I don't know" [26]. One man's attempt to label himself was, "A don't know believer" [22].

One was extremely cynical when asked for his description of himself, "Believe nothing you read, nothing you hear, and only half of what you see." His, "I don't know", was the sample's most strongly stated example of his earlier stated, "I'm not interested. . . . I'm not bothered. I don't care" [9]. In contrast was the humility of the young man who said, "I'm ignorant to it. I don't know enough to say whether I believe in it or I don't believe in it. That's why I'm just half and half" [13].

"Atheists" and "Unbelievers"

At the other end of the scale were the people who when asked for a tag were happiest with being called unbelievers of some kind. There were nine (18 percent) of these men. All these men were categorical that there was no God. One exception was the man who quantified his beliefs as a "considerable lack. The only time that I have any beliefs is when I am in trouble. I'd call myself an unbeliever" [6]. Another left a 1 percent openness in his unbelief. He said, "I'm probably 99 percent against it, but the other 1% [is] probably stood in the corner of me somewhere saying that I suppose anything is a possibility" [25]. One of these self-termed unbelievers added that he would also call himself a socialist [33].

Also in this category must be placed the man who didn't want to use the terms believer/unbeliever, but described himself as a, "Freethinker who doesn't believe in one religion being superior to another" [5]. This makes up the total to ten (20 percent) of the sample who were placed in the "unbeliever" category.

"Christians" or "Non-Christians"

When specifying themselves as a Christian or a non-Christian, all who called themselves believers also termed themselves Christians as did two who clearly termed themselves unbelievers. One gave no explanation but the other realising the problem admitted, "I don't know how to work that out" [25]. Another man who didn't believe in God at all seemed to change in mid-stream as he re-thought,

> Non-christian. Oh, no, now, now, then, that's a different question. I believe in the good things. I believe in helping anybody if I can. I wouldn't stamp on anybody or anything. If that is the way a Christian is, that is the way I will be [16].

It is interesting that half of those who were some type of agnostic called themselves Christians or nearly so. Said one semi-retired businessman, "I would say that I was a Christian but agnostic all the same." Earlier in the interview he had explained, "I do try to carry out the teachings of Christ. Not because so much that they are the teachings of Christ, but because I know they are the right things to do" [18]. Another expressed a similar sentiment, "I would say I was a Christian because me attitudes are Christian. My attitudes are to help people and things, a Christian attitude. I don't hold animosity about certain people" [26]. Many of those who termed themselves believers also described Christianity in similar terms, as will be shown in a later section.

Some of the agnostics wanted to qualify their Christianity by defining themselves as, "A non-practicing Christian" [13] or, "A not sure religious Christian", as another said with "a touch of the Mark Twain's like here" [22].

This study gives general credence to the hypothesis that men are more likely to identify with the term, "Christian" (72 percent) than with the term, "Believer" (56 percent). Not only were more men willing to identify with the term "Christian", but the qualifications on "Christian" were much less than with "believer". "Christian" was a term most could happily identify themselves as while "believer" had a good many problems associated with its identification. It seems that for many, their beliefs are not necessarily connected to their actions as "good Christians".

Reasons for Particular Stance

The three traditional viewpoints toward Christianity--believer, atheist, and agnostic--can further be used as divisions for revealing their reasons for believing, not believing, and being uncertain or uncommitted. Specific questions were not asked as to why the informants believed or disbelieved but, even so, many seemed to want to give their reasons.

Reasons for Believing

In those who called themselves believers in God, five reasons were present. Some of the men had complex reasons and so brought more than one reason to our listing.

1. Childhood upbringing. Several wanted to explain their belief in God mainly by their upbringing. The older men especially found this significant in a day of changing values. An 84 year old explained, "It is something that I've been brought up to, right through life, to appreciate the things in life which are provided from above, in my opinion" [7].

A regular church-goer spells it out:

It's in your upbringing, isn't it? Well, I mean I was brought up to that in early years, you see. And if you were brought up in Ireland more so, it's a very Catholic country Ireland is, and it's part of the day's work really. You started from young and it's something that you do. It's the matter of the thing to do really [50].

He also said that God or belief in God hadn't influenced his life as did another older man, "Well, I say it doesn't influence your life, not in my way of thinking. It's just the way you are isn't it? The way yourself, your mother, your parents bring you up" [35].

Another man was a great defender of God when people doubted because of suffering. One of his main reasons seemed to be that he "wouldn't like to think after being taught at school and at church that there isn't a God or Jesus Christ" [8]. A twenty-four year-old echoed his reasons with regard to the story of Jesus, "I think it is true--only because I was taught it since I can remember. Nobody's ever told me it's not true so I believe it is true, I suppose. I think it is true" [14].

2. Prayer Answered. One of the strongest examples of a person trusting God because of an answered prayer is from a young man who

turned around and prayed and prayed that that girl wouldn't be pregnant. And I trusted him for the fact that he would help me and he did! I am convinced that somebody up there must have liked me and it's nice to grab onto something and believe it. I certainly do trust him.

That's why I believe in God because I did pray to him and obviously he produced the goods. Although I'm not religious, I've said that, but when you are in trouble, you tend to cling onto something [3].

A pensioner described his experience of coming through a serious illness: "Life's made up of experiences, what you are experiencing at the time. It's what comes out of that. . . . Well, really speaking, it has perhaps brought me a bit nearer to religion" [4]. Experiences of prayers answered when his son was ill and getting together with his wife were also important to his belief.

3. A Sort of Deductive Reasoning. Another man has had several experiences of praying. He cries out when he wants help. He explained, "I [am] probably hypocritical. I only pray when I want help, when the wife's bad, the children's bad or something like that." It is not so much the answers that are important in his belief, but the *fact* that he prays that spurs his otherwise rather confused belief. "I kept bringing God into it, so there must be something there, mustn't there?" [12]. This reason is almost a sort of unconscious deductive reasoning: I pray, therefore God is.

4. Fate. Several of the men indicated that their fate was to believe in God:

> I don't believe in forcing people to go to church. I believe that religion in people should come. They've either got it or they haven't. They should voice their own opinion and they should judge themselves. I don't think that you can make anybody religious, but you could send a child to Sunday School and Church every week, but I don't think that you could make that child religious unless it has got religion in it. . . . You have either got religion, you either believe or you don't [12].

For another man faith is "something that just might be with me" [4]. The correlative is the man (an "I don't know") who explained, "I'm afraid fate has decreed that I shouldn't take much interest in it [religion]" [22]. For these men, the fact that they believe is something in which they have no choice. Belief for them is caught like the flu.[1]

5. Classical Arguments. One cited his version of the argument from creation: "I believe in a Creator. Scientists have proved that atoms--and when we die we go to dust in the ground. Well, somewhere along the line, something had to be started. It couldn't start on its own" [17]. Another believed because of Christianity being proved by time:

> I believe mainly because I don't think anything could have existed that long that wasn't based on a truth to start off with. I think there had to be some, how much truth it's hard to say, but I think there had to be something in the truth of it to start off with for it to live so long. Because as you know yourself, religions have come and gone and quite a lot of them. . . . It's got to be more than people assuming or something, then inventing their own gods. There's got to be more truth in it for it to have lasted [32].

Reasons for Being Uncertain

Of those who were unsure about the question of God and Christianity, these were the reasons given for their uncertainty:

1. The Need for Proof. These reasons were stated mainly in the standard sort of phrases one hears: "I have to see it before I believe it" [38]; "Nobody's ever come back to tell you" [22]; "I'm the sort of a person, a practical sort of person. If it can be proved by writing it down or showing me, I'll believe in it. I can't believe anything I can't see" [26]. One man's already quoted philosophy of life is more positivistic than the positivists, "Believe nothing you read, nothing you hear, and only half of what you see." Later, he realised his contradiction when he said, "Seeing is believing [laughter]--to a degree" [9]. For him and perhaps other agnostics there seems to be a kind of proof needed of the quality of which not even science could meet the qualifications. It should also be noted that one man who couldn't believe anything which he couldn't see was open to certain psychic and religious experiences although they had not had a major effect on his beliefs.

By proof, most of the men mean a miracle or some spectacular event: "I'd have to see a miracle, I suppose. Or an angel. I've already seen a few when I've been drunk" [38]. It is interesting that one of the other quoted men did have an experience of having a fluffy angel land on his hand and talk to him, but this was not adequate for him to put his trust in God, "Because I haven't really had enough experience" [26].

2. **Scientific Conflicts.** A related area was that several of the agnostics found uncertainty over the issue of science and Christianity. One explained it, "Nobody's actually proved it, have they? Yet science can prove but the Bible can't" [26]. An eighteen year-old described the conflict of the teaching at school which he had not resolved:

You had it drummed into you at school. One person might be saying, "God created this and God created that." And the next person said that Charles Darwin said that you got evolution coming through it from this angle and that. Darwin is saying that we evolved from this, a little tiny germ and you think, "Well, who put that there?" There's got to be some, somebody's got to have put it there. Either way I suppose both of them are right, but you've got to wonder whether God just put us straight on the earth as we are or whether we evolved from the monkeys and further on like that [13].

Another began his questioning with what he saw as a scientific problem, "I don't see how a child can be born to a virgin," and then moved on to hypotheses that many would call pseudo-science:

I read a piece in the paper about spacemen. We are always on about UFO's and God knows what. And this man was talking about spacemen coming down. The halo we see around Christ is actually a bubble from a spaceman. I suppose that one sticks in my mind because, I don't know, it is a nice theory.

Yet he stressed, "I suppose that really I want to [believe]" [20].

Another man was much more involved with thoughts of what a third man called "ufology" [39]:

I wouldn't say that I believe or disbelieve in a God. I take it that there's someone or something as regard to importance and a much higher intelligence than ours. On that line, my thoughts are that there is a superior race.

He had many questions to which the superior race gave a possible explanation:

Are we just a spin-off of another planet? Were we put here for a reason? My mind's involved [with] a lot of things that can't be explained. I mean if you go back thousands of years to the Aztec Indians, I mean how did they get their dwellings up in the mountains? There was no cranes in those days, no wheel, but then they've got building up in the mountains, and yet there was no rocks in the immediate area for them to build with.

When asked his conclusions, he replied,

That they were led by a superior race that at the time were here on earth then doing it. When, again in the Bible, Moses went up to Mount Sinai--was it for the Ten commandments?--he came down with white hair. I mean they could have been radiation burns. I don't know. . . . And was there a super- ior race at the time here on the planet then, setting us in one way, in one direction, watch how we go on, then leave us alone? But keep an eye on us so that we don't get too near what we're looking for, what we're trying [to] find out. I mean we always delve into the mysteries, aren't we? [46].

Unlike the atheist grouping, who are convinced by scien- tific and pseudo-scientific arguments, this group has to keep other views in tow at the same time. It appears the existential questions of life restrain the scientific answers of fact. The men remain in two minds and cannot decide.

3. **Suffering and Evil.** It is no surprise that perhaps the greatest existential questions of God and of suffering and evil are always linked together. It is man's great dilemma from which the agnostic grouping sees no escape. It is an obstacle for which they can neither defend God like some of the believer grouping nor turn away from God like the unbeliever grouping.

One man was still in the midst of his grief over the loss of his wife--"the biggest shock of me life"--at the time of the interview. He expressed it in tears, "I've lost complete confi- dence in Jesus since he took me wife and son." He still prays a little prayer every night "just before I drop off. But is it worth it?" The evil further away from home is also a problem,

That's what turns me against it, all the bad what's going on in the world. Look at that bloody bloke coming out in Ireland and all with his wife and daughter and whallop! If there was a Lord, he'd stop all that, wouldn't he? Or would he? Would he? [47].

Another informant sees his break with the Catholic church, because of suffering and evil in the world, as one of the important turning points in his life:

I was baptised and educated a Roman Catholic. At school I

always lived up to the religion. After I left school, I
didn't live up to it. I didn't practice Roman Catholicism
and I haven't since. For the simple reason that I'm not sure
whether there is a God or not. I'm very doubtful. I think
that if there was a God, he wouldn't let so much suffering go
on in the world as there is. He wouldn't let nunneries catch
fire in America and a good many nuns lost their lives. It's
things like that make me doubt; the suffering in India;
Africa makes me doubt [18].

Some of them saw another possible side to the issue,
although not usually through a very sound theological argument:

But I've seen so many tragedies when I was younger and had so
many personal involvements with people and illnesses and
children and I just think to meself, "If there's anybody up
there, why the hell is he letting all this go on like?" And
another person would say, "Well, he's taking them to a better
place," and all this, that, and the other. And I wouldn't
argue, I wouldn't answer it because they may be right [46].

Reluctant to make the classical objection, another
stated,

Alright I'm going to say it, I mean everybody says it. If
there is a God how can he let this happen? But it's going
through life, it's sort of a sorting out process I suppose,
he's sorting the weak out from the, like the weak countries
and strong countries. You know, in a way they're sorting a
chap out [26].

Another wasn't exactly enamoured with the stereotyped
other side of the argument he might hear:

The only times that I've wondered if there is a God is when
you see all the trouble that is in the world, especially with
children suffering. . . . That's when I think, "Well, if
there is a God to see little tots that's suffering." But
then you come up, if you was to ask that of a priest or
whatever you call them, what's he turn around and say? "God
moves in mysterious ways." A load of bull! [22].

4. Ignorance. An eighteen year old, whose Roman
Catholic mother and auntie and non-religious father were all
respected by him, gave his reason as, "I just say that I'm ignorant to it. I don't know enough to say whether I believe in it or
don't believe in it. That's why I'm just half and half." He
thought that he would think about it one day, but for now, "I
don't think that I am old enough to try and understand it. I'd
rather wait" [13]. No one else was quite in the same self-
proclaimed position of ignorance--or perhaps honesty.

5. God is not plausible. A polytechnic student describes his shift in beliefs and his present conclusion,

I've changed a lot because two or three years ago I was very
much I suppose what you would say atheist. But now I con-

sider myself more sort of an agnostic. You know, I don't know if I shall ever move toward actually believing in God one day. But at the moment, I just think, well when you die that's the end. . . . if it was possible I would like to have a belief in God, but I just can't find it plausible at the moment [29].

This sort of general view of implausibility is perhaps representative of what happens in others who did not give precise reasons.

6. **Apathy and God is not relevant.** Although these were not given as reasons for their uncertainty, two showed disinterest in God to the extent that it may help describe their lack of certainty. One was strongly stated, "I'm not interested [in whether God exists]" [9], while the disinterest of the other, a nineteen year-old, was expressed as a casual drift, "When I was at school, I believed in God more. But once I left--isn't it?-- it like gradually wore off." The latter said three times, "It gradually wore off", and added, "As I got older, I ain't really bothered to think. I haven't really thought about it." At the same time he expressed some belief in God, "I kind of believe in him, but I can't say I don't think he'll be up there. I don't know about God. I believe in him, but I don't at the same time" [23].

7. **Fate.** Since one man felt that "fate is what sees you through life," it was bound to shape his view of his own religious state:

I'm afraid fate has decreed that I shouldn't take much interest in it [religion]. If it had been the other way about, I might have turned out to be a priest or a vicar or whatever you call them, you never know. One never knows do they? [22].

Reasons for Not Believing

There were ten men (20 percent) who considered themselves clearly unbelievers in God's existence--or left room for only a drop of doubt or openness to the other viewpoint. It is interesting that we do not find these men believing in fate as the reason for their position with regard to God. On the whole, these men feel that they have a choice with regard to belief in God and they have decided that there is not one.

As would be expected, all of them take a secular view toward life and give general sort of reasons for their unbelief, which they came to as youths or have never believed in God.

I always felt that I was open for anything, you know. I'll take anything with an open mind I hope. I hope that's true anyway. To me it didn't seem logical. Perhaps I'm too cynical or what I don't know. But it just doesn't seem logical to me. I like things to, you know be there, to be explained perhaps. That's a better way of putting it. It just doesn't seem to be that logical,

said one in explaining how he came to the conclusion that there was no God [33].

"I'm afraid it just doesn't ring true," said another when speaking of "all these angels, harps, and Jesus Christ crap." This informant, who was raised in a strongly Roman Catholic family and was an altar boy for a while, found his change from belief to unbelief happening almost imperceptibly:

It just happened. I didn't realise it. When I did go to Mass, I thought to myself, "That's a lot of crap he's speaking there. I can't take that in." There was things I couldn't explain why I didn't believe. I just didn't. I mean to say, I sat and talked to priest and what have you, it still didn't ring true [39].[2]

A third expressed similarly, "It don't seem to be true. It seems to be a fairy story to me," when speaking of his impression of the Bible. "Nothing but good, good, good. Everything that went on in the Bible was always good, everything always had a happy ending" [25].

Two others depicted their general unbelief in different terms: "Religion don't mean nothing to me" [16]. ". . . Nothing around me has really affected me with anything to do with religion" [5].

Of the more specific reasons they gave for not believing in God, three were about the same as for the agnostic's uncertainty and there were two others which pertained to their response to the Church, Christians, or religion.

1. **No empirical proof.** After specifying himself as "nothing" with regard to beliefs in the Christian faith, a pensioner revealed his empiricism, "I've always said that I'm a person who's got to see something happen to convince me that it has actually happened" [1]. In speaking about the afterlife, an eighty-four year-old gave his reasoning, "You see so many funerals about and you never hear speak of anybody coming back--no form at all" [15].

An engineering student indicated that scientific explanations are the only valid ones:

I am skeptical about the basis on which God is founded whereas quite a lot of things can be explained today. A lot of things can't, but I mean, who can prove the feeding of the five thousand? I mean it was just written down by somebody. I mean, they could have fed fifty people with a few loaves. It's too questionable a subject.

The same man also showed that there may have been a higher being which was "perhaps some extra-terrestrial lifeform. Perhaps they've advanced to some fantastic technology to where they could break down distances in time." His grounding: "You've got to base it on what people say, what experts say, religious experts, astro-experts say" [6].

With the one exception, the men in this grouping do not appear to be so enamoured with empiricism and science as the agnostic grouping. This stronger form of unbelief appears in many cases to be more ideologically based, although this is hard to chronicle from the data.

2. **Apathy and God is not relevant.** All of these men had some view that God, religion, Christianity, certainly the church was irrelevant. Two very different personalities illustrated the extent of the irrelevance. They also shared a common lack of thinking about "important issues" even though their natural intelligence level was widely divergent.

One explained about the most important things in life, "I think you could worry yourself sick if you thought about a lot of these sort of things, so I don't bother, you know." And regarding life after death, "I don't believe in it at all. If we have religious people come to door, I turn them down. I'm not bothered about religion" [21].

The other had no ideas as to what is the most important thing in life, saying, "I don't think above day to day." When speaking about his answer regarding "absolutely nothing" happening after death, he elaborated,

> I'm not certain about it, but I'm not prepared to let myself believe in religion. . . . I think it's a weakness. If you can't turn to yourself, you have to turn to somebody else or a fictitious somebody else. You've got to believe in a fantasy world. It's a weakness in your character. That's probably just a bland way to look at it.
>
> I mean there's religious people, like we get the Jehovah's Witness on the door and we argue blue on the doorstep, he tells me the end is nigh, etc. If it is, I'm not worried about it [49].

3. **Suffering and Evil.** Most of the men, no matter what their grouping, mentioned somewhere the problem of suffering and/or evil in the world. However, this grouping of men were troubled enough to use it as a reason to keep them from believing in God. They would have had great expectations from a God if there were one: "Starving and atomic bombs and war and that's what puts me off actually believing it" [25]. Another explained:

> Ever since I could make my mind up and that, I remember not believing in a God. To believe in God with all the different things that happen, that they shouldn't happen. Like the murders and [one thing and] another. If there was a God above, he wouldn't let all of these things happen. . . . If God would change these crimes, then I would believe [15].

One felt that if there were a God, he was "sleeping on the job a bit":

Because with the amount of suffering in the third world countries, only simple things like the droughts, I'm sure that he could send a little bit of rain their way. That's the way I look on it. I suppose the vicars and that would argue against that, but surely he could do simple things like this. Even if we can help them ourselves, he could do things like that.

I mean, we can go and help them ourselves, but it costs money and governments don't want to spend money. So it ends up with you having to do it all [6].

Another felt that it was during the army that he made the decision not to believe in God, "All these wars and things like this. If they were bothered, they could stop all the killing. I did start to think that there can't be one" [16].

4.   The Incredibility of the Church. The previously mentioned man recalled an incident in the army which combined the problem of suffering with the failure of the church to do anything about it:

There was one incident when we used to have half-hour sessions talking about the news. This lad was a politician like. He wanted to know why the church had so much money, so many millions in the bank and they have got government advisers how to spend it and speculate it. He spoke his mind. The padre—that was it—he wouldn't let him go any further, you know what I mean. He wouldn't let the lad say what he wanted to say. It made sense what he said. So many people suffering and they've [the church] got millions and millions. Why don't they spend it on those who need it? [16].

Another man echoed this complaint, "The churches are far too rich for my liking for a start. No man, no church, nobody should have the vast amounts of money when anybody is starving at night" [39].

A different man reported his interpretation:

I think religion is a farce in some ways. Take Northern Ireland. The Catholics are supposed to be one of the strongest breeds of church-goers a going, I should imagine. Yet they are doing all this to it. To me, they shouldn't even let them in the churches. If a church is a place of good to repel evil, then what the hell are they letting them type of people into the churches over there for, I don't know. They should ban them all. I couldn't care anyway meself, but when you think of other people that are real thoughtful about it, they are letting their side down sort of thing. If I spoke to one of them, they would tell me all about their beliefs of God and everything.

His view of the church also gave him the impression, "I think that it would ruin my life, the way I live, if I was to become a church-goer" [25].

5. **Problems with religions.** Not only are there religious wars which caused some of the men to be put off religion, but the less violent fact that religions don't get along also put their hackles up:

> The Jesuits can have absolutely [*sic*] belief in something and everything else doesn't exist. The Church of England doesn't exist, the Buddhists don't exist. They do, but they are wrong. And that is absolutely crazy because there are millions and millions of people who think as absolute Buddhists or absolute Taoists that they are right and everyone else is wrong. So I'm much more a freethinker [5].

Seeing the religious experiences of others as, "Some sort of inner experience as opposed to a religious one" is an explanation for one man "why I don't believe in God": "I think that there are that many weird and wonderful religions around now that it's hard for me anyway to see them as being true or to be what" [33].

Another sees faith as oppressing certain people:

> And faith is alright, but just pure unadulterated faith to me is no good. That's just what it was like. There's millions dying in the world through that. . . I mean to say, you take for instance the Mexicans. You know yourself the Yanks are robbing that country blind. They lent them money and they're getting back so much extra, you know. This country as well, they're all doing it, all the big capitalist countries are doing it. And them people, a lot of them people are fed on religion. "Oh, don't do nothing about it. It's wrong to do this and that." They'll never get anywhere without a struggle. And I don't necessarily mean guns and stuff like this. But you know, come out of the mud huts at least and forget the priest. It won't happen, you know. If he's told he can have a new school, he'll just shut up. He's doing a job. He believes in what he's doing, I'm not saying he doesn't, but I think he's hurting most of them. Like meself, they've been led to believe wrong things in the beginning, you know.

His graphic style shows up another religious contradiction which he cannot tolerate:

> You take the Falkland Islands. Our lot blessing our boys going out there and their priest blessing their men, instead of as the Bible says [unintelligible on tape]. It's stupid! you're going out to kill each other and you don't even own an ounce of the land and you don't own nothing here. Most of the people at home, they've got nothing. They haven't even got control over their rent. They've got nothing and they're going out to massacre each other. And there's priests on the dock blessing them, you know. Fellows carrying the picture of the Virgin Mary on his gun. Poor old Argentinian, he's dead now, you know. OK, he might have had a belief, but is that belief going to keep your family? It's not. So as far as beliefs are concerned, I'm afraid it's a no-no with me. Never convince me [39].[3]

CHAPTER SIX

THEIR PRACTICE:

HOW THEY VIEW AND LIVE THEIR BELIEF AND UNBELIEF

Their Values

What someone values is always a slippery substance to hold. It is not so much what people say they value, but how they live which proves their values. This research could not touch the values revealed by their lives and had to suffice with what the men said was important to them. Even if it is not always accurate in the sense of what their lives prove, it still reveals something of their beliefs about what is important in life.

The major question from which the information is gleaned is "When you are alone and thinking beyond the day to day problems, what do you consider to be the most important concern or concerns of (or thing or things in) life (or your life)." The answers to this researcher did not disclose any lost secrets of working class values, but only confirmed what might be expected. There was little difference in stated values between any of the self-designation groupings.

Most often mentioned was the individual's health, listed by 36 percent of the men (30 percent of atheists, 42 percent of agnostics, and 36 percent of believers): "I think the important things in life really mostly is your health. If a man or a woman's got good health, they've got nothing to worry about or grumble about" [48]; "The most important thing in life undoubtedly is good health" [18]. Another, whose mother had had some mental problems, added mental health; he replied, "Health and sanity, I would think. That's all I could say really. A good sound mind really. Health. They're the most important things" [46].

Family and the concerns around it were mentioned by 30 percent of the men, making it second on the list of important things and concerns: "It is more or less, as I say, family concerns" [19]; "The most important thing about life is keeping the family together and healthy" [28]; "All I want to do now is watch my children grow up and just lead a quiet life. That's all I want to do now" [12]; "The knowledge that you've got your wife and your family and you can't wish for nothing more" [36]. An atheist gives a biological justification for the same:

My family. I don't normally think above that to be honest
with you. . . . There's nothing else I find more important.
. . . You know, you are biologically here to survive the
best you can. And it's in you to defend and look after your
family. It's as simple as that. Unless you're a lunatic,
there's nothing else. That's life, isn't it? You've got to
get by and survive the best you can. Your family, you've got
to look after them. That's life [39].

Some were very clear that they didn't ever think beyond
the day to day problems. "I think you could worry yourself sick
if you thought about a lot of these sorts of things, so I don't
bother, you know" [21], said one atheist. An agnostic agrees, "I
never bother about things like that. No way. In latter years,
you change as you get older. You don't worry so much" [9]. The
more positive side was taking each day as it comes. One believer's most important thing in life is "to waken up in the
morning and see life around you" [50] while another expressed it,
"Just living, just being alive. As long as I can get up every
morning, go out and do me job, I'm quite happy" [27]. Others
were concerned to emphasize that they had "no yearns on big
things" [31].

Other important things mentioned several times were work
(14 percent), money (10 percent), and personal happiness (8
percent). These three were mentioned much less often by those in
the believer grouping than those of the atheist and agnostic
classifications, money not being stated at all by the believer
grouping. One, however, should be wary of giving that any
significance. An agnostic cautions that "The people who don't
say, 'Money' are two faced. It ain't true because without it, we
can't do nothing. So the first one has got to be money" [20].

Other important items mentioned only once were: "Humanity"; "A home of me own"; "Good relationships with other people";
"Self-respect"; "Being able to care for somebody else"; "Understanding"; "Concern for yourself; looking after yourself"; "Doing
something in life, it's not personally what you feel yourself";
"You must think and you must meet with other people, this is what
life is about."

Although the question was usually phrased in both an
individual and general way, only three people volunteered values
beyond themselves and their family. Their concerns had to do
with world peace, hunger, and crime. Another question asking
their worries about the future of the world brought out the grave
threat which most felt about nuclear war. Often even that threat
was not considered worth worrying about.

The fact that these men reflected so few values beyond
their own personal contacts may reflect the personalistic bias of
the interview schedule, but it may also point to the probability
that the sphere of their values is the microcosm of their own
family. Looking beyond the day to day concerns was impossible
for some and unnecessary for others while those who did gaze up
slightly never looked toward the horizon. The eternal values of
poets, philosophers, theologians, or even song writers were out
of the range of their vision which was focused on the concrete
affairs of life.

Their Morals

Morals have often had their basis in religious values and cultural patterns. The test for this interview was to see if the men were conscious of making their decisions about moral issues on the basis of any religious or "outside" standard.

Views on Abortion

They were first asked about one of the controversial issues in personal morality: abortion. The question was really to see on what basis they made their decisions rather than what their views on abortion were. However, their views on abortion are given here as it shows some interesting trends. The following chart is a summary of their views delineated by the belief groupings:

27 consider abortion as wrong or mainly wrong.
      3 Atheists   5 Agnostics   19 Believers

    15 of these see abortion as totally wrong, giving no qualifications.
      1 Atheist   1 Agnostic   13 Believers

    12 qualify their belief in some way
      2 Atheists   4 Agnostics   6 Believers

19 view the issue of abortion as totally up to the individual or always acceptable.
      7 Atheists   6 Agnostics   6 Believers

3 gave no information on this issue.
1 replied, "I never give it a thought really. You see, I've got no children of me own" [45].[1]

This leads us to ask a number of questions about the tendency of those in the believer grouping to see abortion as wrong or mainly wrong. Does declaring yourself a believer and moral conservatism regarding abortion have a social or ideological connection? Or does belief in Christianity in some way inform morals in this direction? Lest Christian believers be too hopeful that belief actually informs in any way, we must note that these men do not read the Bible, go to church, or even discuss religion at all with anyone, so are not in an advantageous position to be informed by anything except common religion.

Determining Morals

How they determine their moral beliefs is an unknown area for many of the men. They often found it difficult to reflect on how they made their moral decisions. Just over half of those who gave answers to these questions agreed that they made their moral decisions through independent thinking": "Me own thinking, like. I don't talk it over with others" [1]; "Listen to both sides and then decide in your mind what you're going to do" [6]; "Well just me own beliefs really, I think. I just decide meself. I don't usually turn to anybody if I think it's right" [25];   "According to what your mind says" [30].   Some mentioned that they listened to all other views from TV, radio, papers, and friends in the pub, "You put all those into one basket and then form your own opinion of it" [3].

Seven of the eight atheists revealed that their own independent thinking was the basis for their moral views while 50 percent of the agnostics and 37 percent of the believers gave similar answers.   Another three men (9 percent of those who gave answers) used their own thinking but were unwilling to make at least some of their moral decisions alone and so seriously included the views of some other person or persons.

Six of the men (18 percent) saw some inherent or external unquestionable standard of right and wrong, which did not need a rationale.   Very unsure in so many other areas, this agnostic leaves no room for doubt in morals: "There's only two: there's a right and a wrong, a right way and a wrong way" [22].   Another was equally strong, "If something is right, to me it is right. If it's wrong, it's wrong" [28].   This subgrouping thought that, "People should know right from wrong" [34].   One called it, "Common sense" [4] while another dubbed it, "Instinct" [38].   The other with this opinion had an outside view of right and wrong which is "instilled in everybody I think.   Well in myself, we know what's right and wrong due to the law.   We know the law can have it's own little silly idiocycracies, but that's neither here nor there."   As an atheist with a more than average church connection in his youth, he quoted "the old thing from the Bible I suppose, 'Do unto others as you would like to have them do unto you' sort of thing."   He wasn't always so sure, however, adding, "Although it never usually works out that way.   You know, you never know whether you're doing right or wrong whatever step you take, and you don't know how it's going to affect somebody else sometimes" [33].

This uncertainty about morals is a byproduct of uncertainty about truth in general (discussed in the next section). Although they were willing to make moral decisions, they had no certainty whatever that they were right.   One example of this was a man from the believer grouping who felt that abortion was always wrong, yet he was very unsure of how he determined his morals:

> I don't think anybody can answer that one because you never know what's right and wrong.   You might do a thing that you think is right and it turns out the opposite way.   Or you might say, "It's wrong to do that," and on the other hand you might have been right [36].

An agnostic made a similar statement,

> Well somebody over there will say black is white and I might say white is black.   So where do you go?   You can think you are right.   I can think that what I say I'm right, but it doesn't mean to say I'm right and it doesn't mean to say I'm wrong [9].

Or as another agnostic states more pessimistically after recalling his own decisions, "Most of the time it's wrong" [23].[2]

Four (12 percent) of those in the believer grouping thought that their morals were determined by their "upbringing" [50]: "I think it is the life that we were led ourselves, how we were brought up, and how we were led to understand the rights and wrongs of things" [14]; "I mean, you used to be at the school and all this and you learn, don't you, from school the right and wrong. Not the church, the school" [37].

Another believer gave a practical helping motive as his basis for morals while still another gave the most "outside" basis in the sample, "I look toward the Lord's side of it," and quickly qualified, "I'm not religious in the sense of I go to church every time" [48].

Their Truth Claims

At the heart of every religion is a truth claim. The important point is to discover in what way it claims to be true. It is very clear from looking at the data from these men that every man values his own ideas. His own ideas are considered as important--if not more important--as those of any scholar, politician, or most especially for this study, vicar. The authoritarian age has been shattered and every man is free not only "to do what is right in his own eyes" but also to believe whatever he wants. Yet for many of them, with the new-found freedom--often denied them by their forefathers--comes uncertainty at best and deep confusion at the worst. They are free to choose their own beliefs, but also feel ill equipped to do so.

For most of the men, their beliefs--whether about the existence and nature of God, the afterlife, the efficacy of prayer, or the ability of God to help, whether well-thought out, imbibed from others, or caught from fate--have no conviction of certainty. Said one young agnostic, "I think you must accept you've got your view, but that may not be the right view. . . . I don't believe in certainty" [29]. As the interviews shifted from describing the important moments in their lives and their concerns and values to the specifically religious questions, many also shifted their intonation to the uncharted uncertainty that is a part of the world view which they share--whether believer or unbeliever. For many of these men some things are postulated as true without question, while at the same time uncertainty bubbles at the heart of their own existence--never mind God's existence.[3]

One would have expected the agnostics to be uncertain about the questions of God's existence. Their uncertainty looms even larger about the more unknown afterlife: "I think. I don't say I believe" [9]; "I can't say and nobody else can say because they haven't come back from the grave to say" [22]; "I mean a person living can't tell me and the person dead can't tell me. It's only assumption--in my opinion" [31]. About his view of abortion, the latter pictures what was true for many others about the whole of their beliefs, "I mean I might be wrong in saying it was right. I might be right in saying it was wrong" [31].

Yet this deep uncertainty was revealed completely across the spectrum. At this level at least, the entire world is viewed through the spectacles of uncertainty. The only possible exceptions were a few of the atheists and a few of the believers who were more sure of their positions. One regular church attender was not at all sure about the nature of the afterlife, but he was quite certain that there would be life after death,

Well, I suppose you can't be a hundred percent sure that you're right, can you, but I suppose it's just faith really. As I say, when you have moments to yourself, when you pray or you just think about it, you feel there is somebody there, there is somebody listening and I'm just sure that there is [11].

Another in the believer grouping was "as certain as I'm sitting here" that "when I'm dead I'm dead" [36].

Religious Pluralism

Along with uncertainty about God and all things religious is the accompanying religious pluralism. Representative of the agnostics was the sample's only businessman who stated, "I don't believe that there is anything wrong with any belief or section of religion. They are all good if practiced correctly" [18]. Another agnostic, who confessed that he really wanted to believe in God, confirmed the value of "belief in something": "I think that we have to believe in something the same as I have to believe in my ability to earn a decent living for me family" [20].

An atheist made his pluralistic tolerance plain,

Everybody to their own beliefs. As I am, I don't ask anybody to be like me. If they want to believe--out in India they have thirty-two different religions, they worship the cow, they worship the sun--if that's what they want to believe in, it's up to them [16].

The man who called himself a freethinker gives his version of the kernel of religion and why he doesn't believe in religion. When he speaks of religions, he is adamant that they must be on a total equality basis:

Some religions ought to be wrong. Because if one is right, the others have got to be wrong. Except in one belief that good is over evil, that's the only one that counts. Everything else is--because half of the wars that happen are over religion. So how can people be so blind to seeing what is right and what is wrong? If their religion is right, why can't they see that other people's religions are right? That's why I don't have any belief in religion because to me there is only one thing: good over evil. The rest is only created by myths throughout the ages. The Jesuits can have absolutely [sic] belief in something and everything else doesn't exist. The Church of England doesn't exist. The Buddhists don't exist. They do, but they are wrong. And that is absolutely crazy because there are millions and

millions of people who think as absolute Buddhists or absolute Taoists that they are right and everyone else is wrong
[5].

One of the men who had strong personal convictions about
Christ and particularly in prayer expressed similar thoughts:

To me, if people believe in something, I think they are a
better person for it, regardless of what it is. As I've
said, you can take a Red Indian who used to have the totem
pole. But he believed in something and that was stronger
than him [4].

A man who describes himself as, "Almost a believer" extends the
equal value of religious positions to atheism. He says regarding
his son, "He is an atheist. But I don't think he's any the
worse for it. . . . He has already proved to me what he's done
in his short life. I think he's done very, very well" [44].

One of the strongly devoted Roman Catholics added his
pluralistic tolerance when answering about the difference between
true believers and those who are not,

There's very good people that's not Christians. They've got
their philosophy, they've got their way of living the same as
I've got mine. And I believe in letting them do what they
want to do. If a person believes in Buddha or believes in
what you call him, Simma [?] or their gods or different
religion, they are doing good, just as good as me. I don't
frown on anybody's religion. Let them believe what they want
to believe [34].

Another in the believer grouping responded to the same
question, "Just their own choice, what they believe in; same as
the different religions really, isn't it? People believe in the
religions. If they are happy with that, I'm happy the way I am"
[40]. An Irish Catholic who attends mass regularly shows his
latent pluralism using a picture of the great British drink,
"It's not everybody's cup of tea. It's your faith and that's
what it is; that's what it amounts to, isn't it?" [50].[4]

Autonomous Nature of Their Beliefs

Correlating with the pluralism is the men's insistence
upon their beliefs as autonomous. Not only is there no agreed
upon corpus of truth, there is little agreed upon basis for
truth. Perhaps a scientific rationale presumes for a basis, but
its interpretation is so varied and its facts so muddled that few
scientists would recognize their product.

What is agreed is an absolute adherence to one's own
right to make up his own mind.[5] Not only do they defend this
for themselves, the atheists especially and the agnostics to a
certain extent also defend it for their children, especially in
the area of religion. The interview's intention was to discover
the intensity of their beliefs by asking whether they would like
their children (or grandchildren) to grow up to believe the same
things as they do (question number 25.1). The unexpected re-

sponse, however, was to unleash many of the men's convictions that their children should have the right to believe whatever they like.

The atheists who gave responses were unanimous in their wish for their children to think freely about religion without any parental interference: "I'd like for them to think for themselves" [39]; "If they want to become a religious freak, that's OK" [5]; "They have to do what they think is right" [15]; "I'll leave them to do their own thing when they get older" [25]; "I don't really think it's up to me to make that decision. I should never force any kids of mine to go to church or anything. And I'd be very angry if anyone tried to force it onto them" [33]; "I wouldn't influence them if I could help it. My parents didn't influence me. It's just a decision I made for myself" [49]; "While they was infants and that, I would like for them to believe in the good things, perhaps even to believe in God until they are old enough to question it themselves" [6].

The agnostic grouping were half and half as might be expected. Half of them had the same desire for the autonomous thinking of their children: "No, they make up their own mind about what they believe" [9]; "I would leave it up to them" [13]; "I'd give them--it's their freedom of choice, isn't it? Like if they didn't want to go to church, I'd leave it up to them" [23]; "No, because their mind's their own now. They decide" [26]; "I would like for them to believe in whatever they want to believe in. . . . it's entirely up to them" [38]. The other half would be happy if their children were either like themselves in beliefs or were any religion similar to the one in which they were raised. A single man qualified, "I hope to help them find their own way" [29].

Most surprising to the interviewer were those responses in the believer grouping who often seemed so uncertain about the value of their own beliefs. Twenty-six said that they would like for their children or grandchildren to believe the same as themselves, two qualifying it by saying they hoped that they would do better than they had done, while three moved toward the more autonomous approach with statements like, "I would like them to. I wouldn't force them to" [27]. Only two of them volunteered that they wanted their children or grandchildren to have complete freedom to believe what they like.

The Private Character of their Religions

What is absolutely clear is that whatever their religion is or is not, it is private. It may well only be unfolded for observation when an unknown interviewer comes along to ask them about it. 79 percent of the men about whom we had the information never talked with anyone about their religious beliefs. Most had no information about the religious beliefs of their workmates, friends, or even families. An agnostic spelled it out in the classic phrase, "Religion is a private thing" [26]. An atheist also recited his doctrine, "If there is such a thing as God, it is a personal thing" [39]. The extent of privacy was

explained by a man in the believer grouping, "I think that the
only person who knows if he is a true believer is the person
himself" [10].[6]

Discussing Their Religion

To a question about whether they talk about the subject
to friends, workmates or family, many simply answered, "No," or
"No, never" or "No, not really". Typical of the longer comments
were: "A question like that never arises" [1]; "We don't discuss religion" [9]; "It never comes into a conversation, so
there is never an argument over it" [13]; "They never mention it
and I never say anything to them" [27]; "Well, you see, it's a
thing that you don't talk about--religion--at any time really.
Religion and politics, it's something taboo" [50].

One elaborated on the irrelevance and embarrassment of
the taboo question and the resulting social pressure of his not-
so-long-past teenage years,

At eighteen, you don't really consider religious beliefs.
You are only chasing the girls and things. You don't consider such questions like, "Is there a supreme being?" If
you talked about that in the pub, everybody would look at you
nonsensically and laugh at you. It's not a question that
would come up [6].

Another pointed out that the word, "God" is used but only in
swearing or joking. "It's not something that you ever talk about
unless somebody says, 'Oh, God!' and you say, 'You called' [3].[7]

The few (18.6%) who sometimes talked about religion only
did so occasionally or if something came up, or if they argued
with someone about it. An agnostic student said, "It comes up
occasionally, every so often but not much. It's not really the
main topic of conversation. It just comes up more accidentally
than anything" [29]. One used to talk about it with "one particular boy" at work [44] while another was prompted by working
"with a certain amount of coloureds. As you probably know yourself, [they] are religious freaks and they do talk about the
church and things like that and giving, and things like that, to
the church" [28].

One man who called himself a believer gave an interesting
twist to the fruitlessness of discussing God:

It's not a good topic of conversation to get onto that you
believe in God. Because, you know, it is a long drawn-out
one and, of course, you can always get involved in some sort
of argument. I don't really talk so much on the subject
except when as I say, when you've got a friend who's an
atheist, you are sometimes drawn into conversation expelling
the theories of being an atheist and that when you're gone
you're gone, you know. I feel there's got to be something
more, so I would be drawn out against an atheist but not
against someone who believes. I feel that just discussing
God with someone who believes in any case is achieving nothing really. There is nothing you can prove. You can only

just work over each other's knowledge, which seems a point-
less exercise really. So I would only be drawn out by someone who is an absolute nonbeliever [32].

One ardent Roman Catholic, who had only missed mass nine
times in twenty-five years, didn't talk with people about his
beliefs much, but he didn't deny his beliefs any more, which he
used to do. He still expected that his workmates would get the
impression that he's not religious and thought that a lot of the
other workers covered it up, "trying to go about like they are
men of the world like, you know" [34]. A man who had regularly
attended the Methodist Church all his life said about his workmates, "But you see, you don't know half of them what they do
believe and you haven't got the opportunities of probing their
background" [2].

The only one who indicated that he talked a lot about his
beliefs was an eighty-four year old Roman Catholic who attended
mass regularly. His workmates had often made fun of him, "'Ah,
go and kiss the pope's feet'"[30], but it didn't bother him. He
was, however, a protruding exception from the men--and society--
who rarely discuss religion, God, or beliefs.

At least three older men revealed the hiddenness of their
religion from their wives. One man said the Lord's prayer every
night, but embarrassedly added, "The wife doesn't know that I do"
[24]. Another confided, "All that I am telling you now, I never
tell my wife nothing. I leave them to their own. If they pray,
they might do for all I know. I never ask her." When asked his
reasons for not talking about it, he found it difficult to express the extremely private nature of his prayer, "I don't know
actually. I don't want to ask her. I leave it to her own
feelings, like. I suppose she does say a few prayers, like if
there is any trouble" [8]. Another expressed at the end of the
interview that I knew more about him than his wife does [4].
There are, of course, other intimate things that men keep from
those most intimate (theoretically at least) of all partners, but
it seems that religion/God/belief is one of those items that gets
discussed with no one. Even sex seems to be more openly discussed (and practiced!) than religion.

One in the believer grouping thought that the atheists
made themselves known, but in this sample, they even seemed to
follow the pattern of privatistic belief. One spoke for others
when he said, "I don't go round trying to prove my point to other
people" [49] and another expected a reciprocal agreement from
believers, "I don't mind, they can go to church if they want to.
I don't go and tell them that it's wrong to go to church. And I
don't expect them to come to me and tell me that I'm wrong not
going to church" [21].

Outside Help In General

This privatistic nature of religion converges with the
general impression that the men were often isolated from any
substantial outside help for the direction of their lives. Many
could name no one who had given them any help over the whole of
their lives. Some of the ones who did say that they had received

help mentioned things like help with the garden, moving house, getting a job, or being loaned or given money. Some had received meaningful help from parents, wives, or relatives while others seemed to mention, "The Missus" or, "The wife", teachers, and relatives, yet without any real conviction. Most were in the pattern of the man who had "helped myself more or less" [45] and expected that this is the way life is.

The men most likely would not have anyone that they could count on for advice in a difficult situation or would not consider going to anyone for advice. Rather they would work it out themselves. This self-help was sometimes considered a virtue along with minding one's own business and keeping "ourselves to ourselves more or less" [41]. At other times the questioning seemed to make the men aware--or face--their alienation from other men. "We just muddled through some way or the other" [41] was perhaps a much more universal motto than most would have felt comfortable quoting. They not only revealed specific alienation from people in relation to (talking about) God (or perhaps alienation from God in relation to people), but alienation from people in general. Privitised religion and general privitisation of life work hand in hand.

Their Secularity and Religiosity

Over and over--whether agnostic, atheist, or believer grouping--these men proclaimed what became almost like a confession of faith: "I'm not religious." Whatever their beliefs were, they didn't want to be known as religious.

For many in the believer grouping, religion was related to going to church, hence, "I'm not religious in the sense of I go to church every time" [48]. For others, not being religious protected the privacy of their religion: "I'm not a deeply religious per[son]. I don't show that I'm religious. I just, it's sort of something with me" [4].

For one atheist, his "I'm not religious" was a slogan to keep away the threat of the "weakness" of the religion that "I'm not prepared to let myself believe in" [49]. For the atheists, the statement usually came out when talking about death. For them, death was a purely secular matter and although they were willing to "go through the usual procedure" [16], presumably a religious service for the sake of the family, it was surely the sphere in which they did not want religion involved.

As discussed elsewhere, many have unashamedly explained that even for those who believe in him, God or belief in God has had little influence on their lives. Their desire was to be independent of God, only calling upon him as "the last alternative" [32], which one hopes never comes.

The Secular Becomes Sacred?

It is chronicled *ad nauseum* that the Western World is

becoming increasing secular. One of the men from the believer category in the sample gives his own analysis:

> I think faith is going to be shaken in years to come. I think more people are going to become disbelievers mainly through science. . . . I mean I disbelieve more now than when I was younger, mainly through the advancements of science really. Things you always took as basic, you know, they can explain away why things happen here and there. Things that people always had blind faith in, I feel now they can always explain [32].

Bonhoeffer writing from prison agreed:

> Man has learned to cope with all questions of importance without recourse to God as a working hypothesis. In questions concerning science, art, and even ethics, this has become an understood thing which one scarcely dares to tilt at any more. But for the last hundred years or so it has become increasingly true of religious questions also: it is becoming evident that everything gets along without "God," and just as well as before. As in the scientific field, so in human affairs generally, what we call "God" is being more and more edged out of life, losing more and more ground.[8]

Feuerbach also chronicles this shift, "Faith has been replaced by unbelief, the Bible by reason, religion and Church by politics, heaven by earth, prayer by work, hell by material wretchedness, the Christian by man."[9]

However, a number of thinkers point out that even though our day is nominally secular--we no longer say, "Holy, Holy"--but we fool ourselves if we think that we do not worship. In fact, we have desacralized the sacred and have resacralized the unholy. We have become like the primitive, seeing society and movements as holy.[10]

Jacque Ellul sees that "man cannot live without participation in the sacred":

> The forms and meanings of the sacred today can no longer be those of an enduring sacred. Man is forced to create something to serve as a sacred. Is it substitute or reality? I can't say. In any event, it cannot be said that man is no longer religious just because Christianity is no longer the religion of the masses. To the contrary, he is just as religious as medieval man. It cannot be said that there is nothing sacred now just because we claim to have emptied out the sacred from nature, sex, and death. To the contrary, the sacred is proliferating all around us.[11]

Ellul sets forth the proposition, "That the modern sacred is ordered entirely around two axes, each involving two poles, one pole being respect and order and the other transgression. The first axis is that of 'technique/sex,' the second is the 'nation-state/revolution' axis."[12] He sees technology as particularly relevant to our working class men:

> Technology is the instrument of liberation for the proletar-

iat. It need only progress for the proletariat to free itself a little more from its chains. Stalin names industrialization as the sole condition for the realization of communism. Every advance in technology is an advance for the proletariat.

This is indeed a belief in the sacred. Technology is the god who saves. It is good in its essence. Capitalism is abominable, sometimes demoniacal, in its opposition. Technology is the hope of the proletariat. The proletarian can put his faith in it because its miracles are at least visible and progressive. Much mystery still attaches to it, for if Karl Marx could explain just how it was that technology would liberate the proletariat, that is certainly not at the level of the proletarians themselves, who know absolutely nothing of the how. For them it remains mysterious. They have simply the formula of faith, and their faith is placed enthusiastically in the instrument, so mysteriously active, of their liberation.[13]

Although this appears to be true at the societal level, there was very little evidence of awareness of this factor in the men interviewed. Of course, this becomes even more dangerous when one is unaware of one's gods and myths. Yet one must also take seriously the fact that most of these men see themselves as thoroughly secularized. They would tend to agree more with T.S. Eliot's, "Choruses from *The Rock*":

> But it seems that something has happened that has never happened before: though we know not just when, or why, or how, or where.
> Men have left GOD not for other gods, they say, but for no god; and this has never happened before.[14]

Peter Berger summarizes: "If commentators on the contemporary situation of religion agree about anything, it is that the supernatural has departed from the modern world."[15]

Bonhoeffer's view of thoroughly secularized man is well known. He relates on this subject:

> The usual interpretation of idolatry as "riches, debauchery and desire" seems unbiblical. That is a bit of moralising. Idols are objects of worship, and idolatry implies that people still worship something. The truth is, we've given up worshipping everything, even idols. In fact, we are absolute nihilists.[16]

What is probably true for most of these men is that they find nothing very important at all in life. Perhaps they valued the relationship with their family, "the wife", a few personal friends, but they gave no hint of sacredness even in these relationships. These were often strained or broken or simply all that they had. These men appear to be described accurately by Paul as "separate from Christ, . . . foreigners of the covenants of promise, without hope and without God in the world" (Ephesians 2:12).

There are perhaps bigger gods worshipped by bigger people. For example, "Premier Khrushchev, addressing himself to

Abdel Nasser, said, 'I am warning you in all seriousness. I tell
you that communism is sacred.'"[17] However, these men are not big
men with big gods, they are merely men with tiny or non-existent
gods.

Their Views of God in Their Religions

The secondary question, "What do you think God is like?"
is almost too metaphysical for the theologians who write tomes
about the subject, much less these men who have often shown their
microcosm of values to be the nuclear family. The "beyond physical", i.e., transcendent nature of God is for many completely
unknown and too much to grasp, "I think that there is something
out there but that we don't know about, that we can believe in,
that we don't know much about. There must be something" [14].
Their feeble attempts to explain the nature of God fail to say
much of significance--often not unlike those of the skilled
student of God, "It's alright for these blokes who write books,
but they don't tell you, they don't put it plain enough for you
to understand because I don't think they know theirselves" [43].

They often do reveal, however, their view that the metaphysical God, as they conceive him, is irrelevant to their lives.
It is so "beyond physical" that they can have no contact with
him. An atheist describes a view of the supreme being which
could possibly be acceptable:

But I always looked on God as say a computer, you know. You
imagine this computer there on it's own. Now they say God
knows everything, but just say this computer had everything
except awareness. And it needed awareness, so it bursted
itself say into thousands of pieces, right? And each piece
had a bit of awareness of its own, each piece maybe bumped
into another piece. It done something, but each piece had
something happen to it and then eventually all these pieces
got back together in one machine. I look on a supreme being
possibly something like that. Along those lines is acceptable to me. But all these angels, harps and Jesus Christ
crap I'm afraid it just doesn't ring true, you know [39].

That they have views of God--whether they believe in Him
or not--is indisputable. However, it is difficult to get them to
reflect on God and even more difficult--if not impossible--to
untangle their views from a mass of statements about their values, concerns, important moments, convictions and beliefs. After
the general question regarding the nature of God, they were also
often given directed areas to consider, i.e. "What kind of power
does it/He have? Are there things that it/He cannot do? Does
it/He have feelings? What sort of feelings?"

Power

Of those who believed in God and spoke about his nature,
more than anything else they picked up on the power conception of
God. He has, "Tremendous power" [4], "Great power" [37], "All

power" [43], "Power to help people through prayer" [44], "The powers over everybody" [45], and "The power of the world in his hands" [48]. Another saw him as the power to give, "I think God gives you everything like, the children and. . . . Think about it in that light like and it makes you feel happy that he has given you something" [27].

A Roman Catholic, vitally involved in church life, elaborated on a classic theological problem,

> I know we're all supposed to believe that he is all powerful and almighty. IS HE? I think he could be if he wanted to be. But if he was supposedly all powerful and almighty, he knows everything. As I mentioned before, if he knew everything, we would all be living a sort of predestined life, but the greatest gift he gave us supposedly was freedom of choice to do as we wanted to. I always like to think he is powerful and almighty, could do everything if he wanted, but perhaps doesn't. He gives us choice, freedom to do what we wanted [11].

Some saw God's power as limited in some way:

> It's like that negro spiritualist, "He's got the world in his hands." But he can't do everything. Because if he could do everything, there wouldn't be these third world countries starving and drought and banish wars if it come to that. YOU DON'T THINK HE CAN DO ANYTHING ABOUT THAT? Well, if he could have done, he'd have done it a long, long time ago [36].

Another thought God's power was in the past although largely because of people's response, "I've never gone into it a lot, but I think that he had a lot of power but I don't think that he has it with people today. I don't think that people turn to it today" [10]. Another limited his communication with God, "It's not someone you can speak to" [32].

The only information one pensioner gave about God was his thought that, "When bad things have all happened, when we get these extra gales and storms and I always think that he is provoked" [19]. Another man early in the interview spoke about an accident with one of his children and was attempting to explain why it happened:

> It is hard to say why these [things] happen. It could be the sins of the father, as they used to say. . . . Now I'm only going by the biblical term, "The sins of the fathers shall fall upon the children," and I was trying to think if I had done anything which had caused it, but I couldn't. I've lived quite a normal--I mean I drink a little and have a smoke or two and perhaps have a few swear words sometimes. But that's as far as I ever went.

Later he spoke about his view of Jesus:

> I don't think that he was a man for revenge. He don't put the spell on the parents of children. No, I don't believe in it. I don't blame Jesus Christ at all. Therefore, I don't believe in the Bible as it says, where it quotes that about

parents of the children.   No [8].

One man who saw God as having "tremendous power" explained a
little of his view of God as he was speaking about how one
relates to God in fear,   "If you believe in God, you fear God.
You fear because it is like the parent and the child.   If you
love God, you will fear God" [4].

Some could not speak of the power of God without mention-
ing it's antithesis, suffering and evil. Of course, atheists and
agnostics had already used this as a reason to prove God's non-
existence or to show how it was impossible to decide.   Here those
who believed in God brought it up to mention their number one
doubt or to make a theodicy.

Anthropomorphisms

Some of the men were keen to describe what God was like
by anthropomorphisms.   One saw him as, "Possibly a larger version
of Jesus with grey hair, perhaps with a halo over his head" [3].
An agnostic describes God as, "Human like" [13].   One asked the
interviewer a question about God,

Do you think he's still alive up there, do you?
WHAT DO YOU THINK?
Blimey, he must be old? God.
DO YOU MEAN JESUS GOD?
The first one. He must be very old [37].

Some clearly identified God with Jesus, "My image of him
would be the image of Christ.   That's the person that died for us
on the cross" [28].   Another said that "the only thing that I
could picture him as is that he was a priest.   He was a man who
brought in the days of the market squares and the religious
places and that.   He used to go about preaching" [10].   A third
gave his hope:

I hope that he is all nice like we see in the books.   We see
a nice little white man that comes from the Middle East with
fair hair and blue eyes.   If Jesus was Jesus, he would be
black as a nigger, more or less.   You would be coming from
that part of the world. . . . I hope he is like what I've
been brought up to believe--if I do go to meeting him [17].

Another saw that it was impossible for God to materi-
alize, "I believe in God, but when you actually come down to
actually being a person, I don't believe this . . . not material-
wise, if you know what I mean" [40].

Impersonal God

One was clear that God was not a person you could speak
to (although he does pray) but, "It's almost like a force that
steers your life really" [32].   Another saw God as, "Your mind
more or less" [35].   In this same vein, although not clear
whether it was impersonal or not, was one who thought "that he
puts thoughts into your head" [12] while an agnostic considered,

"I always think God is in your thoughts as such.   If there is a
God, he will take judgement on you as a person through your
thoughts,   not on whether you are willing to go to church every
week" [38].

The Unknown Name of God

        Perhaps the most beautiful portrait of God was painted by
a man who did not know at all that he had described a view of
God.   It was rather his reason for believing in God because he
prayed in that situation:

        There was a captain in the Gurkha rifles and he carried me
        across the paddy fields and the Japs were shelling over him
        and he was ill himself.   He was rotten with dysentery. I've
        never seen him since and I don't know his name, but I think
        of him [12].

This was a picture of many of these men who seemed to think of
God and what he had done, yet had not seen him and did not know
his name.

Their Views of Jesus

        The central question of the New Testament is Jesus' own,
"Who do you say that I am?" Preceding this question, the men
were asked to tell the story of Jesus in a few words and what
they made of this story. Most gave the bare skeleton of Jesus'
life,   starting with his birth and ending in the crucifixion and
sometimes resurrection.   One confessed what others revealed more
subtly, "I only know Christmas and Good Friday and that's me lot"
[21] while another expressed it, "Apart from him being born and
crucified, in between I ain't got a clue apart from some of the
miracles he did" [26].

        The Christological question did appear to be one that put
them in their respective groupings, but even so, there was much
variety and inconsistency.

The Believers

        More than half of the believer grouping (57 percent) gave
some kind of answer that related to Jesus' godly or messianic
character.   The most common designation was, "Son of God" which
ten (36 percent) of the believers gave in mainly that form.   It
was not always clear what they meant and it appeared sometimes to
be more a quoted title than a believed confession. Some of those
who designated Jesus as Son of God were clearly unsure.   One
concluded that he believed it, "But of course, you don't know
whether this is the fact or not.   I mean he could be a terrible
charlatan who's got away with it" [32].

        Other   appellations in this 57 percent of the believers
were: "Messiah in so much as he came to earth to serve a purpose"

[3], "The Lord who died on the cross" [7], "God" [24], "King of the Jews" [30], and the non-biblical but very strong "God of all Gods" [28]. Another added, "Jesus is Jesus. He was born as Jesus, the man to rule. Well, he made the world in seven days, didn't he?" [42].

Others in the believer grouping gave answers which may be considered less than a Godly or messianic description, but their often unexplained terms could have many meanings. Three described Jesus as a good man or example to follow. One portrayal was less than clear that it should be in this category, "Well, he must have been a man like, well, he was probably in good health and that. He must have had powers, you know, good powers" [45]. Another saw him as a man who "healed the sick like, brought the goodness out of people." He didn't believe God could be a person and so explained Jesus as:

A person like the first kind of a doctor like because he was a curer, wasn't he? He did heal the sick. So I mean whoever started it off made him a God-like figure then, you know, because he cured somebody that they knew and they carried on from there. So a God-like figure become--I mean like when you think about it, I'd say he was more religious than a priest, when you think about it, because he was doing God's work--isn't he--or doing Jesus' work. He's curing the sick. A priest is only preaching to you about what he did [40].

Others called him: "A saint" [10] and "Son of Mary" [8,43], while another simply spoke of the mythical conception of Jesus [44].

One might have expected the regular church-goers with other obvious signs of the elements of biblical belief to confess also with the biblical heritage, but it was not quite so simple. One gave the standard Petrine confession [11] while another said, "He was the King of the Jews" after previously stating, "He was an ordinary man and aged thirty-three" [30]. The third man made his confession, "According to the scriptures, he was the Son of God" but added that he wasn't sure whether he was or not, "I don't really think it matters. . . . I mean he lived the right life, the good life and his example is what matters" [2]. A Roman Catholic gave what seemed to the researcher an extremely out of character answer, "I believe that he was some being from outer space. It was something that was higher [unclear on tape]. It took something to create that universe out there and whoever invented it, whoever made it or whatever became, it goes over us [unclear on tape]" [34].

The Agnostics

This was one of the points where they were most unsure. Six of them (55 percent of those who gave answers) said that they didn't know. "I don't have a clue, have I?" [47] said one while another wondered "whether he was somewhere from another planet, I don't know." [26]. One who said he didn't know re-thought as he answered, "To be quite honest, I do believe there was Jesus. There's something in the back of my mind that tells me there was." He went on to ask a question of the atonement prompted by going to Roman Catholic mass with his girlfriend, "If God is such

a great man, if he is a man, why should Jesus Christ have to beg
forgiveness for us? Surely he would be understanding to that
sort of level" [38].

The other five agnostics divided on their descriptions of
Jesus. One informant asked questions which showed the way he was
predisposed to think,

I don't know without sounding ridiculous really. It could be
just an alien, couldn't it? I mean what was his halo? What
was the halo that's always on pictures? What is the halo?
Was it a ring of radiation, heat? [46].

Another described Jesus as a "kind of hero": "He was a helper,
weren't he, sent down [by who is up there] to try to sort out the
problems" [23].

One man thought he was, "A man like you or I" [31] while
still another thought of him as, "Just an image, a sort of ideal
type of how to live your life" [29]. A pure, "ignorant" agnostic
mused on the confession that he must have heard from Roman Catholic family members and it's implication for the nature of man,

His son. Then again, if you say he was his son, then that
means we must be moulded on God. We must all be the same,
look the same type of thing, unless he could change us into
what he wants us to be, which means that he has got more
power than what anybody can imagine. He has got power over
everything [13].

The Atheists

The atheists were not so sure that Jesus, the man, even
existed. They spoke hypothetically, "If he existed . . ." [6]
or, "If there was such a man" [16] or, "A good fairy tale. . . .
But I can't actually believe the story itself" [49].

If he did exist, they thought of him as fairly ordinary,
as, "Somebody who just got wound up in the events around him and
got persecuted" [49] or,

Just an ordinary man. He was a bit of a prophet in his time
is what I think he was. . . . He was a communist, a long
haired hippie if you want to put it that way, you know. And
he was a bit out of his time [39].

Alternatively, they described him as some sort of good
man: "He done good and tried to do good" [16] or,

I suppose that it was an extraordinary being coming to life
and putting the world to right as it was. Everything was bad
to start with and Jesus come along to put the world turning
in the right direction as it were. But to me that never
happened [25].

To a socialist who thought that there, more than likely, could
have been a Jesus, Jesus was,

Probably a very intelligent bloke, probably somebody who was
probably morally right who wanted to do something for the
area because it must have been pretty bad to live in those
times anyway. No medicines and things of that nature. He
might have even have been a herbalist for all we know. . . .
And who threatened the social structure of the day [33].

The other three thought Jesus was: "Some other being from
another world" [6], "A very religious person" [1], and the extremely bold, "Nobody in particular" [21].

Summary

Looked at over all, 35 percent described Jesus as "the
Son of God" (23 percent) or some messianic or godly title, 15
percent depicted him as some sort of good person, 8 percent saw
him as an ordinary person, 6 percent as some kind of alien, 21
percent just didn't know, and the remaining 15 percent gave
miscellaneous answers.

Their Prayer

One of the most interesting aspects of their religions--
as with any religion--was to find out about the prayer in the
lives of these working class men. Thirty-six (72 percent) of the
men admitted to praying of some kind or the other while the other
fourteen (28 percent) of the men never pray now at all, although
they may have in the past.

Reasons For and Circumstances of Their Prayer

Of those who do pray, 30.5 percent pray at least once a
day and the same percentage pray occasionally, which can mean
anything from *nearly* every night to "not often".

The remaining 39 percent pray only in some sort of stress
or troubled situation or if they want something. From the believer grouping comes a response quite typical, "If I'm in trouble or anything like that, I do pray to God because I want to
believe in him. But when I don't want to believe in him, I don't
believe in him" [17]. An agnostic recognises his lack of consistency:

You know sometimes we contradict ourselves. I mean, you've
just asked me whether I believe in Christ and I've just said,
"I don't know." And yet me one thought in life is that I
don't want to bury me own kids. And I'll say, "Oh, Jesus
Christ, I don't want to bury me own kids." I think that is
terrible. But who am I talking to if I don't believe. Who
am I talking to? I don't know. I can't answer that [9].

The prayers in stress or trouble range from when "the
kiddies have been very ill" [19] or "if I have been particularly
worried about an interview or an exam" [6] to an atheist who

prays before he is about to get hit on his motorbike [49].

Some of those who pray are content to be as blatant as one of those in the believer grouping who appeared to treat prayer almost like going to the corner shop, "I just do the standard praying if I want something" [40]. Others are more subtle, but also seem to join him in the queue at the corner shop even though the transaction seems to have little or no effect on the life of the pray-er.

Changing the analogy to health and wholeness, the men only go to God for the same reasons that they go to the doctor's surgery, when they are ill. Some of the men see themselves as hypocritical or selfish, "It's probably hypocritical. I only pray when I want help, when the wife's bad, the children's bad or something like that" [12]. It is not just one man who confessed something similar to praying "when Villa have played in the League Cup Final as daft as it may sound" [17].

Looked at from another angle, 54 percent of the men either never pray or pray only in stress, trouble, or when they want something. 26 percent pray some sort of prayer at least once a day while another 20 percent pray sometimes.

Dividing up into the self designations, we find that even though they don't believe in God, four of the ten atheists pray. Of the twelve men in the agnostic grouping, four never pray at all, six pray sometimes (two of those only in stress), and two pray every night before they go to bed.

Believers. One might expect those who call themselves believers to talk to the God in whom they believe. There was certainly a much higher proportion in the believer grouping who did and all of the five who regularly attended church prayed. Nine (32 percent) of these twenty-eight men prayed every day. Fifteen (54 percent) of them prayed sometimes (including over half of them who only pray in stress, trouble, or for help) while four (14 percent) of the believers do not consider themselves to pray now at all.[18] Included in the latter group is the young man who has prayed only once in his life. The prayer was answered for him in a dramatic way which influenced his "110 percent" trust in God, but he has not prayed since.

Among those who pray sometimes are those who fervently believe in "just an ordinary prayer like that, nothing long, it just lasts about two or three minutes to say what you've got to say" [8] as well as those who "turn to God almost as the last alternative, when there is nothing else to turn to really" [32]. Typical of many in all groupings is the man from the believer grouping who says, "The only reason that I shut my eyes and think is when I want help. I'm probably selfish really. I only pray when I want something" [12].

Privacy of Prayer. Overall for those who did pray, prayer exemplified the private nature of these men's religions. Prayer was deliberately not defined by the interview for the men and they overwhelmingly considered it to be private prayer. A few mentioned that they prayed in church. For one man this was when he got "dragged along" by the wife [6] and for another when he regularly attended mass, which was the only time this man prayed. The latter, however, even saw his prayer in mass as being "more or less on me own like" [50].

For these men prayer was the ultimate in privacy of religion. Their wives often did not know that their husbands prayed and they, in turn, would not ask if their wives prayed. If you were praying, "You'd probably feel embarrassed if somebody caught you like. I would myself" [12].

The place of prayer, therefore, became not the church but the private "prayer closet," for one, at least theoretically, the water closet. "I think religion, if there is such a thing as a God, is a personal thing. And if you do any praying, you don't go to a church, you know. You can pray in your home, you can pray in the toilet if you want to" [39]. A believer explained why he stopped attending church, "I felt, 'Well you can make anywhere your altar' if I want to pray to God. I got to go to church and I don't want to." His method of prayer was explained by his theology, "You needn't say it outloud, almost in a whisper because God is everywhere" [8].

Another elaborates on the place of prayer,

I don't believe in all the performances like. You can pray and think in the Lord and think about the Lord just sitting. There may be a nice piece of soft music on the radio and you can relax and think then. In the eyes of some people, they think that to go to the Almighty, you have to go to the correct place at the correct time. I don't believe in that. I think a person can still be dedicated and all that in a nice way without all the rigmarole [10].

Secular Prayer

One atheist answered first that he didn't pray and then mused on the nature of his wishes.

I don't know if you could say it's praying, perhaps it is the same sort of thing that people go through. You say, "I wish that this will happen," or whatever or something else. To yourself. If you could class that as praying, perhaps it's the same sort of thing [33].

The Results of Prayer

The men seemed to remain in their groupings with regard to what happens when they pray. Of the eight agnostics who prayed, five of them felt that nothing happened either to them or to the situation about which they have prayed. The exception was the one who thought, "You seem to get enlightened and you've got something off your chest which you probably can't tell anybody else" [31]. He also believed that it seems to help him and has changed the situation. Another didn't believe that anything happened yet later confirmed his agnostic position, "I can never

really tell, can I?" while he concedes to the fact that he "would
feel uncomfortable if he didn't [pray], that's all" [18]. The
other man did not give any information.

The two of the four in the atheist grouping who reported
information on the results of their prayer were at the ends of
the spectrum. One felt that nothing happened when he prayed [49]
while the other had been 90 percent successful in the situations
about which he had prayed. The latter added, "It usually makes
me feel better. I usually feel a lot come off my shoulders. I
don't worry so much either" [6].

The twenty-four men in the believer grouping who pray
found that more happened when they prayed. (Is it because of
their faith or is their faith produced by this?) Nevertheless,
three of them still felt that nothing happened. One spoke of
when he prayed at mass every Sunday, "No, it doesn't change
anything. It's just something that I do and I want to do and I
do it and that's it" [50].

The Effect of Prayer on the Pray-er. More of the believer
grouping felt that something happened to them than happened to
the situation about which they were praying. Eighteen of them
(64 percent) confided that something happened in them when they
prayed. Two of those who regularly attended church depicted the
strongest feelings: "I just think you feel a sense of companion-
ship with the Maker" [2] and, "I always get a feeling that I'm
not just saying it to myself and I'm not the only person who's
just hearing it. I believe that God does hear me. I feel quite
good about it afterwards" [11]. Others seemed to express the
habit or duty of prayer, "I feel that I've done what I should do,
if you put it like that" [43] and, "It hasn't changed me, no, but
I feel that I'm doing right" [7]. Others had the benefits of
relaxing, feeling better, contentment, or a little bit of confidence.

The Effect of Prayer on the Situation. Ten of those who
felt better for praying also felt that the situation changed at
least sometimes or they thought it might. Another two also
reported the situation changing in some way or the other. One of
the latter depicted it this way, "Well, I think he can be a bit
lenient like, you know what I mean. He can make it more lenient
for them, soften the blow and what you like, you know" [34].

Typical of the vagueness of the answers to prayers were,
"I haven't done so bad up to now so I imagine that he has really"
[12] and, "Any situation like when the kids [are ill] and when
they are better, to me in my mind, God has done that for me.
That's only in my opinion and in my mind like" [27]. Another
spoke of his hopes and prayers:

> Somebody what's ill, you think, "I hope he will make them
> feel better." And couple of days later, somebody comes and
> tells you that that person is feeling better like. I'm not
> one of those who always believes that your prayers are always
> answered. I don't think they are. . . . Because I think it
> is a lot to ask for myself. For all the millions of people

who do pray to the Lord or the Almighty to expect for all
those prayers to be answered, I think it is asking rather a
lot [10].

Another explains his persistent prayer in a similar vein,

Has he heard me? . . . Well, if he's got a bit of spare
time. He's a pretty busy man, isn't he, sort of thing. He
can't listen to millions, can he? As I say, in a spare
minute sort of thing like, I hope he listens to me prayer
like sort of thing. I say the prayer over and over again in
case he doesn't hear. He's a very busy man. I suppose he
can listen to everybody really [42].

There was no very strong certainty about the answers to
prayer, with the exception of one man, but even he didn't seem
absolutely certain that his time for answered prayers might not
be up:

For me, anything I've always prayed has always come out
successfully. So I can't fault it myself. You don't know.
I suppose if you lost somebody, you'd be the opposite. But
for my mind, anything I've always prayed for has always come
out on the right side, so I can't fault it myself [32].

Their Views of Death and Afterlife

Paul Tillich, in his classic work, *The Courage To Be*,
distinguishes three types of anxiety in men. One of them is
relevant here: "Nonbeing threatens man's ontic self-affirmation,
relatively in terms of fate, absolutely in terms of death." He
states further. "The anxiety of fate and death is most basic,
most universal, and inescapable."[19]

If this is true, the men in this sample are either unrep-
resentative or dishonest or, because this research was not designed to test for psychological anxiety, it did not touch the
heart of their concerns. It did, however, ask how they felt
about the fact that they would die one day.

They overwhelmingly answered in nearly the same words:
"It don't bother me at all", "I'm not worried one little bit", "I
don't worry about it", or "I never really thought about it."
Their reasons for not worrying do not have to do with great hope
of afterlife but with death's persistent universality: "It is
inevitable"; "It's got to happen. Nothing you can do"; "All the
worrying in the world won't change it"; "Here today and gone
tomorrow"; "That's a foregone conclusion, isn't it? Nobody lasts
forever"; "It's a cert on that. I don't know when it is, but
it'll come".

Since the data had a loud ring of authenticity about it,
one would suspect that Tillich's statement refers more to middle-
class than working class people--or at least it does not appear
to refer to the British working class in the mid-1980's.[20]

Fear of Death

Only five men mentioned fearing death at all including one who spoke of past fear. The atheists had no one admitting to fear. Perhaps their majority faith in no afterlife protected them from at least anxiety about hell. However, only a few in the sample mentioned hell and they placed it mainly on earth.

Leaving this World. One of the men agreed with Tillich's universality assuming he would be among the majority, "It scares me, obviously." However, his fear was not of the hell of the past but of missing "all the things I'm looking forward to, i.e. getting married and owning a house and having kids" [38]. Another spoke similarly, "It frightens me. . . . Silly really, I suppose it's to think that you'd be leaving your kids . . . never seeing your wife and family again" [27]. A third spoke of "more or less what you leave behind. . . . Well, I'm frightened of death anyway, you know 'cause I worry about my fear and what happens afterwards" [40].

A few others who did not mention fear said that they were only concerned about leaving their family or one hoped "that I have a little bit of warning. I don't want to drop down here. I want a little bit of warning--to let somebody know you're off" [47]. One seemed to think he would receive this warning since he hoped that reincarnation was "something that I would like to keep there and reflect on when the time is near" [3].

For one agnostic, death

> used to frighten the hell out of me. . . . I think I was frightened because I didn't know what it was. I knew, you knew what death was naturally, but you only know death outside when a person's dead. You don't know what's happening beyond that. I think that's what worried me more than anything, not knowing after that. But I have had one or two experiences with people that's gone.

These nearly inside experiences have made him "not worried anymore" [46].

Fear of Nothing. Only one was articulate about the present anxiety of non-being that "frightens the living daylights out of me." He explained to the interviewer,

> I don't suppose it is dying. It's the same as flying. When you get down to it, flying doesn't frighten anybody. Crashing does. Dying don't frighten anybody, it is what's after, it's nothing.
> SO IT IS THE NOTHING THAT FRIGHTENS YOU?
> Yes.
> YOU DON'T WANT TO BE NOTHING?
> No, I don't [20].

The Process of Dying. A few others didn't agree about dying not being the major problem. They concurred more with

Bonhoeffer's rhetorical question, "Do we not attach more importance nowadays to the act of dying than to death itself? We are
much more concerned with getting over the act of dying than with
being victorious over death."[21] "Everybody has got to die," said
an agnostic who said that he had already experienced clinical
death,

> But I want it to come quick. It's terrible how people can--
> in a way I do believe in euthanasia of a sort. I mean when a
> person is really in dead pain and nobody can--I mean they
> wouldn't let a blooming horse suffer or a dog suffer [26].

Afterlife

Belief in some kind of life after death followed roughly
the belief groupings with the exception of the extreme variety in
the believer grouping.

Believers. 39 percent of the believers thought there was
some kind of afterlife, whether it be reincarnation, heaven and
hell, or just heaven. The regular church goers appeared to be
the strongest in the certainty that there was an afterlife, but
about its nature one didn't have "the foggiest notion really" [2]
while another hadn't "got a clue" [11]. Two others spoke in
terms of heaven and one of them also of hell. The former knew
his "soul will be judged" but didn't know what the judgement
would be, "It's according to what the Lord says" [34].

The church attender with the least evidence of elements
of belief described the afterlife in terms of "another world" and
"what we're led to believe", adding that he believed it "to a
certain extent". He didn't know about his own future after
death, "It's something that's really a mystery, I suppose. I
don't know. It's not everybody's cup of tea. It's your faith
and that's what it is. That's what it amounts to, isn't it?"
[50].

18 percent of the believers came down on the side that
there was no life after death at all. "Death. That's it. I don't
believe in life after death. I can't see it" [40].

The most popular position for the believers was uncertainty whether there was anything after death or not (43 percent). Three contemplated reincarnation while two mentioned
heaven and hell "according to the preaching" [7], but "I just
can't make up my mind. I'm just hoping that there is a heaven
and it is a nice place to go" [28].

One man didn't know the results of this study or even his
own final conclusion when he began,

> I think everyone has the basic belief in afterlife. I don't
> think the human race as such can accept that when you die
> you're gone. I think it's what keeps half the race going is
> the belief in the afterlife. There's going to be something
> afterwards and you're not just going to die like an animal.
> But I don't know [32].

Another also made a universal statement,

> I don't think anybody knows that really. I don't think
> anything happens to you. I don't know whether your soul goes
> to heaven or whether it doesn't, I don't know. I would like
> to come back and tell people this, but I don't suppose I
> shall.

His final statement on the subject gives reason for his believer
grouping, "Only the Lord knows that" [48].

      Agnostics. The agnostics, of course, found themselves
mainly in the "I don't know" classification which is their general hallmark. Two-thirds of them could not commit themselves as
to whether there was an afterlife or not. Like no other belief
grouping among the men who didn't know about the afterlife, three
of these two-thirds of the agnostics called for a need for proof
of the existence of the afterlife.

> Nobody has ever come back to tell me that there is a life
> everafter. So as far as I am concerned, there ain't. The
> vicars and everybody else tell us, but nobody's come and told
> me. I don't know. We're only on this earth for about eighty
> years, aren't we, and you're a long time dead [20].

Two of those who didn't know considered the possibility of reincarnation.

      Four other agnostics (the other one-third) were convinced
or nearly so that there was no afterlife, "Well, unfortunately
at the moment, I just think that, well, that's the end. It will
just be it" [29].

      Atheists. Eight out of ten of the atheists stood firmly
on, "Once you are gone, you are gone and that's it" [5]. The
other two weren't so sure. One of them had "no idea" because he
had "never give it a thought to tell the truth" [25]; while the
other had an interesting theory, "I think like a piece of paper
burning, you become something else. But not necessarily an
afterlife. You might just become a type of energy, you know.
Possibly. I'm not really sure on that point" [39]

Their Personal Wrongdoing

      Most religions have something to say about personal right
and wrong, its practice, causes, consequences, and how to deal
with it. Christian belief in particular has quite a lot to say
about this and various theological traditions have laid different
emphases on this. What do these men believe about their own
lives? Is it obvious, as is so often assumed, that consciousness
of doing something wrong is universal? The questions (section
number 15) did not define wrong, so the men interpreted it in
various ways. When necessary, I defined it as, "Something morally wrong, against your own values or beliefs."

The men were radically divided over their own wrongdoing. Twenty-three (47 percent) of the forty-nine who gave information were clear that they had done something wrong. They resounded: "Plenty of times" [1], "Millions of times" [9], or, "Oh, all the time" [11]. They often brought all their fellow human beings into their plight, "Nobody's perfect" [42], or, "Everybody does" [17,32].

However, not everyone agreed to being placed into that universal state of wrongdoing. Seventeen of the men (35 percent) asserted that they had never done anything wrong or perhaps only when very young, "I used to pinch a few chocolate biscuits" [29] or had acted "a bit of a darling when I was a kid, you know, playing it up, playing rounders in the street and cricket in the street and the coppers used to chase us. But nothing really" [47]. Another nine men (18 percent) qualified their wrongdoing with statements like, "I haven't done a lot [wrong] really" [14] or "I might have done [something wrong]" [8] that they need to be classified as mainly having done nothing wrong. Seen from this perspective, this places 53 percent of the men having done nothing wrong, or nearly nothing, while 47 percent see that they have done wrong in their lives. Reinterpreting the "mainly no" group as "sometimes yes," there are 65 percent who say they have done wrong and 35 percent who say they have not done wrong.[22]

It should be pointed out at this stage that the interpretation of doing wrong ranges from stabbing someone to taking chances motoring, from abusing certain privileges to drinking and driving, from being arrested for being drunk and disorderly to disciplining the children improperly, from pinching time from work to stealing birds eggs as a child.

What is most interesting is how the different belief groupings see themselves in relation to doing wrong. The more these men believe the less likely they are to believe that they have done wrong. 78 percent of the atheists, 67 percent of the agnostics and only 29 percent of the believers were clear about their own personal wrongdoing. On the other hand, 22 percent of the atheists, 17 percent of the agnostics, and 46 percent of the believers saw themselves as having not ever done wrong. (The latter group of believers included three of those who regularly attended church while the other two were in the opposite extreme, clearly aware of their wrongdoing.) If we look at the grouping of those who see themselves as not doing wrong including those who felt that they almost never did wrong, we find 22 percent of the atheists, 34 percent of the agnostics, and 71 percent of the believers in this category.

One has to contemplate the meaning of these findings. Does being a believer actually make one better morally and without sin, thereby rejecting a number of sound theological traditions which would claim the opposite? Or does being a believer go together with self-righteousness, using the belief as a way of justifying or camouflaging the wrongdoing? Does it depend on what kind of a believer one is since they are divided on this issue?

Forgiveness

Whether these men had a felt need for forgiveness is also an important issue for Christian theology and for the communication of such. Forgiveness is at the heart of the Christ event and the Christian proclamation.

Forgiveness was not usually defined in the interview and people mainly interpreted it as a need for forgiveness from a person whom they had wronged. In the main they did not see it as a religious word.

The men who admitted wrongdoing and spoke about this issue of forgiveness were again divided. Five out of six of the atheists (83 percent) and three out of five of the agnostics (60 percent) admitted needing forgiveness while the others did not. Half of the believer grouping felt a need for forgiveness while the other half did not. This followed the same pattern as the wrongdoing.

Although "having feelings of that nature [i.e. feeling a need for forgiveness]", an atheist spoke about forgiveness in a way reminiscent of the Lord's prayer, "I think that you had better reverse that, 'Am I a person who gives forgiveness?' The answer would have to be, 'No' because I'm a person who doesn't give forgiveness and I don't look for forgiveness" [1]. Others showed the desire for forgiveness, but it was not always realised, "It's nice if you can mention what you've done and get forgiveness for it. But if you'd rather not mention it, then you've got to do without it" [49] or, "It is nice to have forgiveness but it is not always possible. Yes, I do need forgiveness. I need someone to agree that I've done wrong, but it is not absolutely essential" [5]. An atheist showed a point of inconsistency in his need for supernatural forgiveness, "If there is a Lord above, I've asked him to forgive me" [15].

Only one in the believer category mentioned that he would "ask God to forgive you if you have done anything untoward" [8]. Another believer positively states that he does not need forgiveness "from anybody else" including God, "I think that I can forgive myself" [17]. A practicing Roman Catholic explains it more in terms of human failure than a need for God,

> I don't run off to the confession box or anything like that and ask for forgiveness. I just think it's human failure. Everybody does it and I suppose we should ultimately try not to do it next time, but invariably we do it. I suppose we should always be trying to make ourselves better in that respect, but I wouldn't say I feel very guilty about it [11].

Besides personal forgiveness which was not always wanted and was often illusive to those who wanted it, the remedy for these men's wrongdoing was not very satisfying to most of them. Typical of what they do when they do something wrong were these replies: "Try to do better next time" [9], "Justify it" [18], "I just have to shrug me shoulders or make sure it don't happen again" [26], "Try to make amends" [34], and "Sit down and try to forget it" [36]. Some were willing to apologise or talk it over with the person that they felt they had wronged while others must stoically take the consequences.

The European Value Systems Study Group uncovered facts which merge with the findings of this study indicating that even those men who admitted wrongdoing did not understand it as sin, "Younger people tend--as Stoetzel's European analysis suggests-- to regret doing wrong more frequently than those aged over 30 years but to be less convinced about the existence of sin."[23]

Their Religious Experience

Eleven of the fifty men gave me specific religious or spiritual experiences either when I specifically asked for it or earlier in the interview.[24] One young Roman Catholic church-goer's experience of seeing a vision of Jesus in the cloud came out as the major turning point in his life. Others were not so sure that their experiences were religious or spiritual after they described them. One recounted experiences of hearing things on the very old wooden stairs at his work place, "I wouldn't call it a religious experience, more of the paranormal I would say" [32].

As might be expected, there was also the mark of privacy about these experiences. One man trusted me with an experience which he has "never told anybody" [45]. Another wasn't going to tell me his experience then later changed his mind saying, "I haven't told my wife about this . . ." [26], and the church-goer, mentioned above, said, "I've only told a couple of people this. I'm not that sure actually that I still believe it myself" [11].

Of the experiences that they narrated, four of them happened as children, four of them to men while they were in their twenties, and three to men who were more than thirty.

Most of them were unsure about how to interpret their experiences, especially those whose experiences involved some sort of ghosts, dreams, or visions of dead people. Four of them found themselves in these situations. One saw a ghost with two other teenagers while another had an experience of seeing a man, who had perhaps lived in the house before, at the bottom of the bed. He put this down to the war yet thought it was real. He also had a dream he relished of flying like a bird, which was a "marvelous sensation" [12].

Another had a vivid dream with his deceased mother in it, which he credits as a pivotal point in his not worrying anymore about her. He also had an appearance from his dead granddad, "He came to me in the room because they had known I was upset, I wasn't bad, I was just upset in any case. And I was fine after again." Another strange incident he thought might also be ex-plained by his granddad,

I don't know whether you would call it religious or spiritual really. I was driving a car and I came to a hump-back bridge and someone put their hand on me shoulder and told me to stop

and I did. And when I stopped a lorry came over the other
side, which I wouldn't have got through. But there was no
one there [46].

One recounted an experience when he was six years old,

My mother had hit me for doing something. I came out crying
and I distinctly remember someone saying, "Don't cry little
boy. Go in and say you are sorry." I remember going back in
telling my father that I had heard somebody say to say that I
am sorry. My father believed me and went out and no one was
there. And yet I really did think that I heard somebody
say.

The man was in two minds as to how to interpret the experience.
He considered that perhaps he had imagined it as his "head was
all full up of things", yet he concluded, "I am convinced that
somebody spoke to me, whether it was God or whoever" [3].

Three of the men had had a vision of Jesus or what they
thought might be Jesus. The least sure of identifying the manifestation was the man who first said it was a ghost then unfolded
this story,

I had this vision of seeing this person in white--and the
light was on and it wasn't dark; it was night but the landing
light was on--walking to my sister's bedroom and back into
the bathroom. And it wasn't once I saw it. I was just wide
awake, watching it never looking at me--dressed like a Jesus
figure in white, long hair, long robe. And I wasn't scared.
I was scared the next night. . . . It was real [17].

Another reported an experience when he had his top teeth
extracted at the dentist when they gave him gas:

That's a funny sensation, I never told anybody, but as I was
coming around, I seen a picture of God, you know. And he
said something to me. I don't know what it was. And I come
round. The next thing I could see the chappie, the dentist
[45].

The most convincing picture was given by the young man who was
sleeping downstairs one Saturday morning and had just awakened,

I just looked out the window and I always think I saw, you
always picture a face like Jesus, going past in the sky in
the form of a cloud. I always remember seeing this vividly
actually 'cause the clouds were rolling by and this one
seemed to stop there for about ten minutes--just the face
[11].

Still in the vein of the heavenlies was the man who was
very distressed and depressed over being made redundant:

And I sat in the toilet crying. Now, I was praying for
somebody to help me. And through the window of the toilet
came a fluffy angel. "Remember the angels," she said. And
this was five o'clock in the morning. And he came and landed
on me hand like that and it was a tremendous feeling went

through me and the next thing I do was, I don't know what it was, but I phoned the Samaritans up and spoke to somebody at the Samaritans who talked to me and then I was alright when I came out of work.

He had also had the experience of "something horrible" blowing out a match in the garage where there was no draft and also an experience of someone watching him in a certain room at work, "I always say that when I went through that bad patch that some bugger had put a curse on me. I still reckon he has now. Oh, I believe it now. I'm a very superstitious person" [26].

Two fairly traditionally evangelical, religious experiences were recounted. The first one felt that his experience hadn't influenced him and was only for the moment:

In the Salvation Army, only as a child, you go underneath the flag and they kinda baptise you. If you go to the Salvation Army, they give it out, "Come up to the bench for repentance." . . . Oh, you always have a good cry when you go there. They make you cry . . . by asking different questions [36].

The other had an experience which might be termed "the call":

When I was about twenty-one, I used to go to a Bible class, like, on a Sunday and it seemed as if God wanted me to help spread the gospel. I thought of it, "Well, I'm working and all that and if you start trucking like that to your workmates, they would ridicule you and call you a Bible puncher." I just went from there and just did nothing about it.

He further described the experience as "just a kind of quiet solitude. I didn't actually see God, but it was just a kind of feeling that he was trying to tell me something like, not to do this, that, and the other" [8].

Interpreting Experience By What Framework?

For these men, there was no blanket rule about how they interpreted their experience. The experiences all seemed to depend, at least to a certain extent, on the framework in which they already lived.[25]

Personal Changes. It should be noted that spiritual or religious experiences alter some of the men quite radically while others are hardly touched, some of them adding that the experience does not give enough evidence in order to fully believe. There is no example in this sample of anyone totally changing his whole framework of thinking and acting on the basis of a religious experience.[26]

The first example includes the framework of a devoted Roman Catholic family. Before his experience of seeing a vision of Jesus in the clouds, he "had stopped going to church." After that he stated,

I always go to church now and I get a lot more out of it now.
. . . I think it made me more sure that there was more
belief in God and as I say now, I get a lot more out of, for
instance, going to church than when I used to go to church.
I think it was mainly just to please my mother and father
really. I just used to go and stand at the back and just be
bored for forty-five minutes or an hour or whatever it was.
But now, I get much more out of going.

He explained how his renewed faith helped in specific circumstances,

I felt really I was getting comfort from somewhere and I
thought I got over it quite quickly actually. Just on occasions when you feel a bit down or whatever, you know, I just
think to myself you always feel that there's somebody there
and you feel happier [11].

The man who had a fluffy angel land on his hand links
that experience to the time that he was giving up tranquilizers
and later gave up cigarettes. But it did not push him over the
brink of his skepticism to actually trust God "because I haven't
really had enough experience." His transformation seemed rather
less than radical. "Probably in a way some of my views on religion have changed since then. Let's put it another way, I think
twice before I put it down." Elsewhere, he limited his changes
to "just my private thoughts" [26].

The effect on the man who saw a picture of God after
coming out of gas in the dentist's chair remembered that, "It
affected me more or less as if I was God meself. . . . anybody
arguing or like that, you know, you tell them to stop it and all
that kind" [45].

The man who explained his experiences of someone on the
stairs was aware of his different framework of interpretation and
elaborated:

So really, the more you learn on the subject the more, I mean
if you've never gone into, for instance, the subject of
parapsychology, then you're never going to question. You
know, well, people would say, "I've heard a ghost on the
stairs." If you've never heard the other side of the argument, you just sort of say, "Well, this is a ghost. I've
heard a ghost. That's what it is, a ghost." But you know, I
don't personally think that if you are taken from this life
for another existence, it is not going to be left to just
roaming around scaring people witless. I feel that probably
most of these experiences are caused by the mind of the
people, you know, in the situation [32].

Even having appearances from dead people which gave one
agnostic comfort and saved him from disaster were not enough to
make him give up his joint framework (of belief and unbelief) for
one or the other or a third framework:

I mean I have never had an experience enough for me to turn
around to anybody and say, you know, "That's the answer." I
just couldn't do that. . . . I think me mind's mixed up,

really, on that. . . . I don't believe, I don't disbelieve.
The old saying is, "Seeing's believing," but I've had experiences which I suppose you could say I've seen, but it's not
enough to convince me as to whether it's religion or it is
some superior. . . . I would say in my mind, "It's one of
the two." That there is a religious side to it or there is a
superior side to it [46].

Experiencing the War. None of the men spoke about the
war when speaking directly about religious experience, but being
in the war was an important experience for some of the older men,
which moved some of them to consider their beliefs. It may have
had other religious ramifications as well. Several men spoke of
the war as, "Six wasted years", even though there was great
comradeship unequalled since they have been in civilian life.
Such emotional experiences brought some men to belief in God and
some to unbelief.

An ardent atheist found the war to be the moment when he
decided that he didn't believe in God. Besides the bad experience with the padre mentioned in chapter two, the suffering of
the war was too much to reconcile with God. "All these wars and
things like this. If they were bothered, they could stop all the
killing. I did start to think [in the army] that there can't be
one" [16].

By contrast, some of the men were moved toward belief by
their equally frightening and tragic experiences in the war:

Let me put it like this, during me war service, I mean I come
under some pretty heavy shellfire and gunfire and I'm not
kidding you, I wasn't interested in God at that time, but
during the war, I don't mind admitting that I actually
prayed, especially under shellfire [24].

He has prayed the Lord's Prayer every night since that time.

Another man saw that it was a "damn miracle" that they
won with the ancient weapons recovered from the Oxford museum.
The even more important reason, already cited, for believing in
God more in the army was because people prayed,

Well, I do believe in God. I say I don't, but I do. While
I'm in church I sing my head off, but you won't get me in
church. . . . I do it because I remember when I was ill and
I remember when this captain of the Gurkha Rifles carried me
across this paddy field and the Japs were shelling over him.
I always remember, "Oh God! Oh God!" That's what comes out
of your mouth. He's got to be there for you to do that,
that's my opinion [12].

This experience, a graphic portrayal of what Christians believe
the love of God to be like, was also given as his non-eschatolog-
ical experience of the sense of being saved by Jesus Christ.

Another veteran also saw people praying as a convincing
reason to move toward faith:

When you saw these chaps that were getting knocked about, I
don't know whether it is just a way of saying it, but a lot
of them people just said, "Oh, God!" and "Oh, Jesus!" . . .
You have the faith that you are going to be kept safe, if
it's possible [19].

    Prayer. People also interpret the answers or lack of
answers to their prayers in different ways. The way one sees
God's response or lack of response to prayer seems to have the
effect of sometimes prompting trust while at other times it seems
to change nothing.

    One man

turned around and prayed and prayed that that girl wouldn't
be pregnant. And I trusted him for the fact that he would
help me and he did! I am convinced that somebody up there
must have liked me and it's nice to grab onto something and
believe in it. I certainly do trust him.

For his answered prayer he trusts God "as much as I trust my
mother, brother, and grandparents and I trust them 110%." But
that was "the only one time" he has prayed in his life [3].

    Another informant found that, "Life's made up of exper-
iences, what you are experiencing at the time. It's what comes
out of that." What came out of an experience when he was eighteen of having suspected tuberculosis, which at that time was "a
death sentence", was that "it has perhaps brought me a bit nearer
to religion." Within that context, his prayers for his son when
he had meningitis and even that he "would somehow get together"
with his present wife convinced him that "the important things in
life" get answered [4].

    On the other hand, another man claims that, in the big
things, "He never answered me prayers." His son, daughter and
wife had all died despite his prayers for them. He still prays a
simple memorised prayer but, "Does it do any good?" On the
question of the existence of God, "Well, I ain't sure. Half and
half. I wouldn't mind if he'd give me any proof that he's around
[47].

    An atheist speaks in a different--"hypocritical"--vein
when he speaks of his prayers answered 90% of the time in stress.
He tries to explain, "It is hard to say that you believe because
you don't know whether it is some extra force plying to you or
the fact that now you have confessed this, you relax more and
hence your mind become more susceptible to changing problems."
Even though his prayer is so successfully answered, it doesn't
change his beliefs. He still doesn't believe in God and wouldn't
consider changing his mind about it [6].

Specific Religious Experience Questions

    Besides the open-ended questions about religious experi-
ence and other questions which unintentionally prompted the recounting of religious experiences, the interviewees were also

asked whether they had experienced eight specific categories of religious experience which were termed in fairly traditional Christian language.   Four of these were "positive" experiences: a.   a feeling that you were somehow in the presence of God or in contact with something holy or sacred; c. a sense of being saved by Jesus Christ; e. a sense that God truly loved you; and g. a sense that you were healed or someone was healed of an illness in an unexpected way.   Four of these were more "negative" experiences: b.   a feeling of being afraid of God; d. a feeling of being punished by God for something you had done; f. a feeling of being tempted by the devil or something demonic; h. a sense of the presence of supernatural evil or something demonic.

Of those thirty-seven men who replied, "No" to whether they had ever had an experience which they would call religious or spiritual, nineteen said that they were either sure they had or probably had one or more of these specifically mentioned religious experiences. This makes a total of thirty (60 percent) who either had experienced something they termed religious or spiritual or had an experience included in the limited list of specifics.[27]   It is important to note, however, that some of the specifics were clearly re-interpreted as secular experiences by some of the men, particularly temptation and healing.

The full listing of the answers to these specifics is appended in appendix 2.   Suffice it to mention at this stage that the men reported a great deal more "positive" religious experiences than "negative" ones by quite a margin.   Each of the "positive" experiences were reported by about one-third of those who were asked and responded positively or negatively, which was about the same as the highest response to the "negative" experiences, which was the experience of temptation. The lowest number of men reported experiences of being afraid of God (12 percent) and experiencing supernatural evil (14 percent) with only a few more recounting that they had been punished by God (20 percent).

It is perhaps interesting in what many of the men inferred was an evil age that few men saw any religious connection to evil.   All of the general groupings, including the "believers", are perhaps so thoroughly secularised that they do not see evil as having religious significance unlike both the Old and New Testaments which emphasize "principalities and powers" in society as well as the more familiar demonic in the individual. However, the vivid exception to this pattern in the men was the man who had none of the specific religious experiences except that which had to do with supernatural evil [25].

The fact that these men have not experienced God's punishment and have not been afraid of him may mean that perhaps the God in which they either believe or disbelieve is not a God to be feared.   Is this perhaps the negative reaction to the caricature hell-fire preaching of the past and/or the positive teaching of the love of God in the present?   Or is it a belief that God is somehow impotent and all the shouts, blasphemies, and rejection by man cause no reaction in God?[28]   An exception to the rule was one pensioner who linked belief in, fear of, and love of God: "If you believe in God, you fear God.   You fear because it is like the parent and child. If you love God, you will fear God"

[4].

Of extreme interest for communication of the doctrines
and experiences of Christianity was the way people responded to
the question regarding a sense of being saved by Jesus Christ.
This was expected to be a question of, "You mean my soul saved?"
[17]. However, only two of the fifteen who were sure that they
had or thought that they had had this experience interpreted the
question in this way. One was a regular Methodist church-goer
[2], the other an agnostic with an evangelical background [31].
A strong Roman Catholic interpreted it in a moral sense, "I could
have been a blaggard up in London, but my mother was praying for
me. . . . I think these people's prayers are the things [that]
kept me on the straight and narrow. I could have been the worst
blaggard that ever was born." When a further probe asked specifically about his soul being saved, he elaborated,

To be quite honest with you, the reason I'm saying the rosary
is that God will save my soul. Because I believe there is a
hereafter and you either go up or you go down and I want to
try and make it. Put it this way, I'm a betting man. I back
myself each way. To be quite honest, I have a sense of
humour as well [34].

The great majority interpreted the question with respect
to physical salvation. Most of these were with regard to their
lives being saved: a fellow was buried in the coal pits and
saved, another stuck on a cliff, several would have died had they
not had medical help which they attributed to God saving them
while another already mentioned was saved by an officer carrying
him across the paddy fields in Burma. Also previously mentioned
was the man who explained his ex-girlfriend not being pregnant as
God's salvation. A seventy-four year old man, who used to smoke
sixty cigarettes a day, thought,

It was Jesus Christ who more or less getting me to pack up
smoking. Yes, I think so really. It was the fear of these
illness, you know. And the way I just packed it up, you
know. I think he really helped me there and I've never
craved for one since [48].

The Place of the Church in Their Lives

The interview probed both the present church relationship
and the past church background of these working class men, who
have been traditionally considered beyond the ambit of active
church life. The sample confirmed and perhaps went beyond the
traditional expectations.

Regular Attenders

Five of the men in the sample went to church at least
once a week.[29] Four of these were Roman Catholics and one was a
Methodist. Their ages were 24, 53, 55, 82, and 84. All of these
men were raised in the church and had attended regularly since

childhood. One recounts, "I attended mass every Sunday from the time I was a toddler; my mother carried me up." He had only missed mass nine times in twenty-five years and missed Ash Wednesday mass only because of this interview. He explained,

> I believe the one thing, you go to mass. I believe in the mass. I believe the sacrifice of the mass. . . . It's laid down by St. Peter the first time. I believe in the Catholic church as regards to what has been laid down. Some of the rules are only [made by] human beings. They've made mistakes. They've made a hell of a lot of mistakes. You can put that down to being human. Everybody. There's no one's that's infallible. The pope is supposed to be infallible, but we know he's not [34].

Two had short breaks from their regular attendance. One explains, "I suppose it must have been fourteen till about sixteen or seventeen when I stopped or just went and stood at the back. I started going again when I was about seventeen" [11]. Another fell out of the habit when he was about 26 for "it could be six, seven months, probably more than that." The latter felt that, "Religion can be carried too far as well", by which he meant, "These people that goes to church every day or twice a day, I don't think there's any reason for that." He goes every week himself, "I always find if I don't go to church, I feel uneasy as if something was going to happen. When I do go, I don't feel that at all. It's just probably one of those things" [50]. The youngest specifies, "I go because I enjoy going. I like going" [11]. As only 10 percent of the sample, their joy of going to church is shared by a very small minority.

Occasional Attenders

Nine (18 percent) of the men reported that they attended church occasionally now. For all but one this meant three or less times last year. The exception was a clear unbeliever (agnostic grouping) who said he was "open to belief". He had attended mass about ten times last year with his girlfriend even though he objects to much of the Roman Catholic practice. His theology, however, did not give a very high priority to going to church, "I tend to think, as I said before, I've always believed that if there is a God, he'll understand you through your thoughts. I don't think it's got anything to do with going to church" [38]. Of note is the fact that four of the nine who attend church occasionally were in the agnostic grouping while the other five were in the believer grouping. All of the occasional attendances do not add up to one regular attendance.

All three of the occasional attenders who would fill in, "Roman Catholic" if they were filling out a form reported that they were members of a church (although one qualified it by saying that he was not an active member) and the rest (four Church of England and one Methodist who sometimes attended a Baptist Church) were not members of a church. All except two of these men had quite a lot of religious teaching in childhood (Sunday School, church services, mass, and/or catholic school), but haven't attended church regularly since they were teenagers (or for one, age twenty).

No Church Attendance

The overwhelming majority (72 percent) have never (or a few once or twice) attended any church service on a Sunday since childhood (with the exception of one who attended a Bible class until he was twenty-three). The only times these men have been to church since childhood are the proverbial "funerals and marriages and christenings" [8]. Of these, two (4 percent of total) had *never* attended any church or Sunday School at all in their lives.

Twenty-eight had attended Sunday School for some portion of time, quite a few every Sunday for a good part of their childhood, but a number had only been to Sunday School occasionally and/or for only a year or two. A few (six) had been to church as well as Sunday school in their childhood and four men had been to church only as a child (two of them also to Roman Catholic schools). Two of the men went only to a youth club or boy scouts and the occasional obligatory Sunday morning or evening at church while two others mentioned clubs or Boys Brigade along with Sunday School.

Overall there was some Sunday School attendance as a child with little church connection. Although (with a few exceptions) Sunday School was regarded as nice, it did not appear to influence beliefs much and certainly did not help these men to come into *any*, much less a strong, relationship to the church.

A surprising factor was that the age of these men seems to have little bearing on the church connection, with perhaps the older men staying in Sunday School a little longer and/or with a little more consistency. As an example, an eighty-two year old [15], a forty-five year old [26], and a thirty year old [25] all had similar backgrounds of attending Sunday School occasionally when they were nine or under and have never been to a church service except for the three significant ceremonies of life. A seventy-four year old expressed it for many others in his own grammar, "I haven't been to church once since I've been growed up, you know" [47].

Those in the atheist grouping had not been involved at all with the church since childhood. Even compared to those in the whole sample who had also not been to any church since they were children, the atheists' Sunday School and church involvement was even lower than might be expected. Only two of them had had a regular association with any church for most of their childhood. Six of the men indicated that they had never been to church in their lives except for weddings, funerals, and christenings. Most of them had Sunday School experience for only a very short time, if at all.

The conclusions about the atheists' lack of church involvement are not clear. Most of their decisions about belief in God were made at a very early age. Whether their lack of belief causes their lack of relation to the church or their lack of association with the church helps to form their unbelief is a matter for consideration.

The attitude of the atheists toward religion and the

church was quite varied. Four of them seemed to have a more or less anti-religious attitude. "And it's not just *the* church," said one man who was raised in the Catholic church. "Most religions I've looked at--I've looked at a few in my time--I didn't see anything good in them at all" [39]. Another depicts those who are religious as, "More or less fanatics" [5]; while still others, mentioned in a later section, were very positive about Christians they knew.

The Church was certainly not something that drew many of these men to it. "I don't like the smell of churches," said one, "I don't go to church. While I'm in church I sing my head off, but you won't get me in church" [12]. More typical of the replies was the expected, "I don't believe that you have to be a church goer to have a belief" [32].[30] He had never been to any church service on a Sunday in his life, yet he termed himself a believer and a Christian and spoke of, "A faith such as ours", seeming to refer to the expectedly outworn "Christian nation" concept. Speaking of his workmates, he added a comment which relates to many of the men, "We all believe but don't participate." Nevermind those who used to attend, today's "believer" evokes the question of whether a person can be a Christian having never once attended the central focal point of the body of Christ.

Yet there is almost a theology, besides a rationalisation, behind the non-attendance: "If he's the forgiving God that everyone reckons, he's not going to penalize you for not turning up for regular services" [32]; "I still think that it doesn't matter about going providing you know what is behind it" [19]. One has at least as serious doubts about whether these non-attenders know "what is behind it" as he does about those who do attend.

One man who did not attend church and no longer prayed showed that a specific

> church was the focal point of all what I believed, you know. It took place in there. . . . Well, that steeple there became my totem pole. Whenever I was sort of going to pray, if I could I would face that, that was what I was praying to, the steeple. Because Aston Church, I've been in a lot and I've always liked Aston Church. And that was my church and no other church had any affect on me to that extent. It was just looking at that steeple [4].

Another took pains to show just how willing a follower he was: "If it comes to got to go to church, then I'd go. . . . such as Easter or something like that. I used to go, but I don't go lately because I'm a bit tired, you know" [45]. David Martin perhaps summarizes our men's practice and attitude, "The English do not go very much to Church, but they like to have it there."[31]

Religion on a Form

What a man would fill in on a form asking for his religion may say as much about the society's view of religion as what a man believes himself. The following chart expresses the religions they would fill in on a form according to their attendance at church and their self-designation grouping:

	No Attendance Since Childhood	Sometimes Attendance	Regular Attendance
Church of England Total 27 (54%)	5 Atheists 5 Agnostics 13 Believers	1 Agnostic 3 Believers	
Roman Catholic Total 11 (22%)	1 Atheist 2 Agnostics 1 Believer	1 Agnostic 2 Believers	4 Believers
Methodist Total 3 (6%)	1 Believer	1 Agnostic	1 Believer
Christian Total 1 (2%)	1 Believer		
Others Total 7 (14%)			
+ Don't Know	1 Believer		
+ "A Don't Know Believer"	1 Agnostic		
+ Nothing, etc.	3 Atheists 1 Agnostic		
+ Non-Believer	1 Atheist		
No Information Total 1 (2%)	1 Believer		

A few feel the necessity to be consistent on the form
with their uncertainty or lack of beliefs and so give an unconventional answer or, as with other irrelevant questions on a
form, they could leave it blank. Yet by far, most people feel
that they have to put some religion on a form even if they are
not very enthusiastic. Often, they had no difficulty answering,
"Church of England" or, "Roman Catholic" even though they had
just expressed that they did not believe in God.[32]

Church of England. It appears that, "Church of England"
is not only the state religion but the common religion and the
catch-all term for those who don't attend church. Some would
designate themselves Anglicans because they do not know what else
to put or were told to put it by parents or hospital staff.
There were no regular attenders of the Church of England in the
sample, but those who attend sometimes tend to choose it as their
occasional visiting place. Colin Campbell quotes a remark
referring to British society which proves true in this sample,

"'Many agnostics are at least Protestant Agnostics.'"[33]

      Roman Catholics. The Roman Catholics--as expected--have a better percentage of attenders than anyone else. They were generally considered by the others to be more religious or devoted than the others were:. "Especially the Catholics and the Irish . . . go to church. They confess all their sins, they get a punishment of so many 'Hail Marys', they come straight out and go into the boozer again" [36]. Even so, to this man they are still true believers. Others would disagree that this is true religion.

      Yet most agree that Catholics

> are more inclined to be religious than anyone else. But if you talk about someone from the Church of England or anything of that nature, well, very, very rarely is their religion spoken about. It only comes to light in relating to a death or something of that nature. I don't think that you get religion spoken about in a family on a day to day basis unless there is something on the box [1].

When asked to clarify whether he was less religious than a workmate, one quickly replied, "Oh yes, he's a Roman Catholic like" [45]. To one man, Catholics might still respect vicars and priests, but "I don't think the Church of England would" [40].

      Many of those with a Roman Catholic background tend to hate the church and all that goes with it, but the nominal Anglican is just bored by it and accepts it as a normal part of life. The nominal Roman Catholics who do not attend church often have the view that they are wrong for not going to church. Nominal Church of England men make a point of the fact that you don't have to go to church to be a Christian: "'Cause they're [Roman Catholics] different to us in their religion. I mean, they go to church nearly every Sunday, but we don't go, do we really?" [37].

Their Views of True Believers

      When asked to delineate the difference between true believers in Jesus Christ and those who are not, the answers varied considerably. At least one in all the groupings are convinced that there is "no difference at all" between true believers and those who are not. An atheist expresses it,

> Now, I feel that I'm no different from a Christian. It is just that he believes that there is this Jesus Christ or there is God whereas I don't. But my attitude to life is no different to his--except where he believes he is going to carry on when he finishes whereas I don't [33].

An agnostic also thinks that his attitude is not much different, "I mean, I know people that go to church religiously every Sunday and I think that I'm quite as good as those, if not better in some cases" [31].[34] One in the believer grouping expresses it for two more, "To me, I don't think there is any difference at all. To me, if somebody wants to believe in God, they believe in

God and that's it. If they don't believe in God--as I say I do--
if you don't, it's up to you sort of thing" [27].

Another in the believer grouping defines the distinctions
very broadly, "I feel everyone's a Christian who does believe.
. . . It is a cut and dry line of people who believe and people
who don't" [32]. Others would find a few more complexities in
setting forth who true believers were. One felt that belief was
so invisible that "you can't really judge" whether someone is a
true believer or not [4]. Another believer describes true believers as, "People who go to church every time" [24] while a
regular attender clarifies that a true believer "not so much goes
to church, I think you can have a very good belief in God without
going to church" [11]. Others see them as, "Straight" [43] or,
"They are very honest. They don't say one thing and then say
another the next day. They're honest with God, you know" [37].
Another limited the field to a very small number indeed, "True
believers in God are people who commit themselves to him like
priests, monks, nuns and people who can turn around and say that
they haven't really committed a sin" [3].

An agnostic wanted to make a point,

I feel a lot of people who go to church can't really be true
believers cause if they don't, a lot of what I've seen from
religion, they don't follow through, you know, the forgiveness or be nice to other people or tolerance and things like
this. They just don't follow it through. They are very
intolerant of anybody [29].

A believer felt that,

In themselves, I think it would make them a better person.
If they were true Christians, not just people who say three
"Hail Marys" and think to themselves that they are going
straight to heaven. Like Dave Allen who says, "If you get
people like that in heaven, who in hell wants to go to
heaven?" [17].

Two regular church attenders spelled out the difference
according to their own views of Christianity: "I think the
believers have a different view of life really. Working for
justice and the betterment of mankind and the love of God in the
world" [2] and, "I think somebody who lets God play a part in
their life would be a true believer. . . . If you are a true
believer, I suppose you want God to plan your life or at least
ask him to or whatever" [11].

People varied enormously in how they thought or felt
about true believers. The atheist category is the most extreme
example where one man expressed,

I think that them that believe in God are fornicated people.
They don't know there is not a God. I mean their minds must
be in two ways, they must actually believe in God otherwise
they don't believe in God [15].

Another was very anti-church,

These people down on earth only want to have a good look down
on themselves. I know they say, "You involve yourself with
religion, you involve with them people." So it's them people
I'm divorcing myself from. I don't know about the churches.
God and what he is, that's a different thing. I think about
that. But the church and that, I would never get involved
with any of them [39].

On the other hand, there was the engineering student who
painted a pretty picture of the believers he knew:

What struck me particularly about my course is that there's
an awful lot of Christians and they go to Bible classes and
everything. It is the first time ever that I have met a
Christian who is down to earth. They won't push their religion on you. What surprises me is that they believe these
things and yet some of them are really clever, really scientifically informed, not to question the basis of which God is
made.

He liked their life style as well,

They seem to conduct themselves better in public for a start.
I mean I use bad language. I never heard any one of the
Christians use a bad word, never ever. They seem to be more
of a gentleman. I know that I'm not a gentleman. I'm just a
normal, run-of-the- mill, average person. But they seem
better, respect, all sorts of little things that they do.
They would seem on the whole a better person than the one who
doesn't believe, I would say [6].

Another atheist simply said, "I admire people who do believe for
instance, especially in this day and age where a lot of people
don't" [33].

Especially in the atheist and agnostic groupings, there
were many who knew no people or only one or two people they would
call true believers. When they did know one or two, these may be
Jehovah's Witnesses, Mormons, or the vicar down the road. They
often do not consider people who say, "Oh yeah, I believe in
Jesus or God," but are not devoted. With some exceptions, these
men are often looking for sincerity as a mark of the genuineness
of the belief. It is not so much the content of the belief that
is important but whether the believers really "devote their lives
to it" [19], which is evidenced in their lives.

Yet what is clear is that they know very few of these
people indeed. Even the believer grouping often found that there
were "none round here" [36] or perhaps had one or two relations
that they knew. The ones who did know true believers increased
considerably in the believer grouping. Twelve of the twenty-
eight knew "quite a few," "bags of them," or "a lot." Whether
the correlation is that believers become believers and unbelievers become unbelievers because of the contact with the same
grouping or whether, once a position has been taken, people then
stay within their groupings is not clear.

Their Views of Unbelievers

In contrast to their lack of acquaintance with believers, the men know a great many more people who they regard as unbelievers than people who they regard as true believers: "Quite a lot" [49]; "I think the majority of people I know, a very big majority as well" [29]; "Oh, hundreds" [31]; "A hell of a lot" [28]; "Bags of them, a lot, a lot" [30]. These were typical of the replies across the groupings. There were, of course, those in the believer grouping who didn't know any "atheists or unbelievers because you wouldn't like asking them if they are or not" [8] (and a similar reply in the agnostic grouping [26]) or "because we don't mix a terrible lot" [41] or those who felt, "They're all about the same as me" [40]. One thought, "There's a lot of people who say they don't believe in God verbally and yet in their mind, I think they do believe in God. They believe there is a God. I think a lot of people are afraid to admit that they do believe in God, meself personally" [27], but he was contradicted by the great majority of the sample.

Some of those in the agnostic and believer groupings had particularly strong views about those who did not believe. Two agnostics set forth their convictions, "I think a person that doesn't believe at all--full stop--is a very hard person that won't listen to any proper reasoning or anything" [46]; "The people that don't believe in Jesus Christ and if they don't believe his teachings as well, then they can't be good people" [18].

One in the believer grouping expressed it,

Well, I think those that are not have got no forgiveness at all, them sort of people. I don't agree with anybody that's got no religion at all. I don't believe in atheists because I think that's all wrong, that is. Even an atheist during the war prayed [24].

One who described himself as, "Almost a believer" said theoretically, "I think those that don't believe, I think they are selfish. I think they think more of themselves than what they do of other people." In specifics, however, his son was an atheist, "But I don't think he's any the worse for it" [44]. An older twice-on-Sunday church attender contrasted unbelievers to his already quoted view of believers, "Whereas those who don't believe in anything don't care about anything other than the material world that they're in" [2].

One young man gave an interesting test to sort out the unbelievers from the believers, and hence, a new mark of believers:

I think that you always find that atheists always tend to try and convert people. Really, you know, I think the atheists sort of sort theirselves out. I know who I know is an atheist and they make it plain. So I feel that the people who don't make it plain that they don't believe in God must believe [32].

Most people didn't know how to describe the people in-
between although they often felt a part of them. When speaking of
his own religious connection, one agnostic described himself as,
"Neither here nor there" [38] while a believer spoke in the same
vein of others, "They don't [know] whether they want to or they
don't want to. They don't know whether they're coming or going"
[36].

Their Definitions of a Christian

Instructive as to their view of the church and true
belief were their definitions of a Christian. This was particularly important in determining what they meant when they did or
did not describe themselves as such. As discussed in the previous chapter, more men could identify with the term "Christian"
than with the term "believer."[35] Of particular note is that the
believer grouping did not define the term in an appreciably
different quality to the atheists and agnostics. The only difference is that they did tend to include, "being good" a substantially higher percentage of the time and, "believing" a little
more often.

The main definitions had to do with belief and ethics.
Those defining Christianity as belief or believing spoke of these
objects of their beliefs with little explanation:
"Christianity", "God", "The teaching of Jesus Christ", "Him",
"It", "The Almighty", "Religion", "Christ", "The Lord", or "The
laws of God." One said, "It's just belief, isn't it?" [42].

Those depicting a Christian mainly in terms of ethics did
it with regard to being good or helping or following the teachings of Christ. Typical of these definitions were:

A man, in my opinion, or a lady that lives a decent life,
tries to live a decent life, keeps himself and herself to
theirselves, and leads a good life the best they can. I
mean, you can't do everything like [43].

It's what you do in your life. . . . Well, help people and
et cetera. You know, if you couldn't do anybody a good turn,
then don't do them a bad one. That's my way of thinking of
religion. That's a part of religion I think [35].

We help. A Christian helps and doesn't hinder. That's our
opinion of being a Christian. I mean we don't help to
receive help [19].

My attitudes are to help people and things, a Christian
attitude. I don't hold animosity about certain people
[26].[36]

Many had a tendency to define a Christian in terms of
either how they see themselves or how they would like to see
themselves as opposed to the term having some content from an
historical connection with either Christ or the Christian religion. A young agnostic who clearly stressed the values of honesty, tolerance, goodness, and loving others in his own life de-

fined being a Christian in the same terms [29]. He did, however, consider himself to be a non-Christian, but perhaps not on the basis of his own definition.

A young man who defined himself as a socialist and an unbeliever classes socialism as being "socially aware, knowing that we've got to make society work for everybody to be fair or else we're all going to be in very dire straits." In the next question, he defines "the perfect Christian as far as I'm concerned" as "someone who does know, who is socially aware, who does know the difference between right and wrong" [33].

Another man stressed "a good heart" several times throughout the interview and said that he "would give anybody a good turn and expect nothing for it." Although an agnostic, he called himself a Christian but "a not sure religious Christian". He defined a Christian as,

A person that's happy, not necessarily wealthy, once more got a good heart, helps people without expecting favours in return, leads a good, clean life—I don't say honest—a good clean life, and doesn't hurt anybody necessarily (both feelings or physical because sometimes you can hurt more mentally than you can physically) [22].

The atheists had the most trouble trying to define a Christian. Three couldn't come up with an answer. One started to define it, then interrupted himself, "I don't know. I can't even say that a person who has been brought up to believe is a Christian" [5]. "Everybody says, 'Oh well, I'm a Christian,' but I can't really define what that is," said one,

I suppose it has got many meanings. To me it has anyway. Some people say, if somebody was to say, "Are you a Christian?" I suppose I'd say, "Oh, well yeah, I am." But then again, I don't believe in God *really* . . . [25].

Their Views of the Bible

The questions about the Bible almost without exception took them back to school days, "the days of RE" [49], rather than having anything to do with present experience or even ready memory: "This is racking me brain from when I was at school really" [25]; "Going back now to school days" [27]; "It is going back to the teachings from school days" [32]; "You're going right back to my early childhood when I was reading Bibles, you see" [46]. One man generalized, "When school age stops, I should think that the teaching of the Bible is forgotten in about 75 percent of the people" [1]. This seemed to have almost no relation to whether they termed themselves believers or not.

No one mentioned that they currently read the Bible, although there may have been a few who did. Although no question was asked regarding whether they read the Bible, thirteen men volunteered the information that they never read the Bible now, have never read it, or haven't read any of it since school. Nine

of these (32 percent) were in the believer grouping. Any information about the Bible is "drawn from memory or the odd biblical
film you get on the TV really" [32]. One seemed to know more
than the average about the Bible because he always watched the
biblical films on the television. Another gave an interesting
twist regarding the original source of the information, "You read
the Bible and you can imagine what is actually happening as if it
was on the film" [22].

Knowledge of the Bible

Perhaps this lack of reading the Bible explains, not only
the ignorance of the basic message of the Bible, but also some of
the misconceptions and misinformation about the Bible. Many
could name no characters from either the Old or New Testaments
with the possible exception of the "disciples and those sort of
people" [19]. Most did not know the difference between the two
testaments and confused the most commonly known stories in one
with the other. Most could name only one or two and hardly
anyone could name more than four of the Ten Commandments and,
with one exception, they were always out of the six, general
ethical commandments, "Like the common sense ones, steal, kill,
covet thy neighbour's wife, and thou shall not this and the
other. Just common sense, you know what I mean" [12].[37]

Misinformation went to the extreme of thinking that,
"Jesus Christ was born through the union of Adam and Eve" [1]
and, "Jesus was born, wasn't he, on Mount Olive?" [43]. One
mentioned the story from the Bible about, "The chap that pulled
the thorn out of the lion's foot" [25] and another thought there
was a story of Jesus "about the fish and beehive [?] or something" [45].

Misconception was mainly through incomplete truth viewed
as the whole. An example was the man who

always got the impression that it was all about good.
Nothing but good. Everything that ever went on in the Bible
was always good, everything always had a happy ending. But
in life now, there's that's [sic] got a happy ending
especially how the world is now. So I think that's what's
put me off. It don't seem to be true [25].

Another thought the Bible's content was, "To just generally be
happy and to help one another" [3]. A third thought, "The Bible
is all about different people's views of the old Jewish God--
whoever he was" [17].

Truth in the Bible

Distortion. There is a prevalent view that the Bible
"grows with the telling" [4] and has been exaggerated. Many link
it to a skepticism about anything old which can't be trusted, "If
you can believe a book that's thousands of years old . . ."
[32].[38] Some have the results of a vague view of the historical-
critical approach to find which part they can believe: "I read
some of that--what is it, New Testament like--and I sort of

decide that, 'Don't believe that and believe that'" [23]. They
are certainly not agreed on which parts these are. Some accept
all but the creation account, while some think that you cannot
even trust that Jesus died on the cross. One agnostic wonders
about the central event of Christianity,

> I mean I've got no doubts that a man was crucified, no doubts
> at all of that, but was it Jesus that was crucified? If
> that's the case that he died on the cross, how did he rise
> again? That is my main problem whether he rose again. I'm
> just not sure [31].

Transcription. Many were by no means confident that the
story was written down correctly. "I see the teaching of the
Bible as a load of garbled misgivings of old priests and things
that had importance years ago that nine times out of ten has been
written down wrong" [39], pronounced one atheist. An agnostic
thought the story of Jesus was

> perhaps invented by, you know, a lot of monks or whatever who
> just had the basic idea of Christianity. I mean there might
> be an element of truth. There might have been somebody
> around like Jesus Christ who did spread the word as such,
> tolerance and peace and happiness and the like. [unclear on
> tape] exaggerated a bit [29].

One in the believer grouping didn't see the Bible as
gospel:

> The Bible itself, I believe, is a basic truth which over the
> years--like a lot of truth and myths--have got expanded and
> distorted so I wouldn't believe in the Bible as said, that
> what you read is the absolute gospel truth. I think the
> basis of it is the laws we live by and what you want to live
> by. But you know, I'm not a great advocate of the Bible. I
> think it's been, like many other old books over the years,
> you know, humans have written it and over the years, it's got
> distorted and changed and I think it's only the basic seed is
> the truth really, like many old stories [32].

Another who was an 80-85 percent believer was keen to defend God
in the distortion process:

> I think part of it is myth, but I think there is a basis of
> truth in it that has got distorted over the hundreds of years
> since most of it happened. And this is not distortion due to
> Jesus or God or anyone else. It is due to merely man passing
> the story on down through the ages [44].

Some of the men gave reasons for this distortion:

> The people that wrote about Christ, they certainly weren't
> bloody Romans. They were converted Christians or the people
> that were converted in the thirty-three years of his life, so
> all they are going to say are nice things [20].

Another used his Marxist analysis on the Bible,

I should imagine [it] has been altered slightly as well in the past thousand and a half years to suit the leaders of the day. . . . I see the Bible as being probably OK for two thousand years ago as a way to live. But certainly it doesn't hold its head above water these days. You've got to do more than what that preaches [33].

Translation. A good number link their skepticism about the Bible to changes in the translations over the years so that we don't know what the original is. The most blatant misinformation was from the man who said,

I think there's been a bit added on to line people's pockets by selling the Bibles and that. . . . Well, they made the Bibles and made them a bit larger and of course, they could sell them a bit dearer, but I don't know who done it [43].

Contradictions. Surprisingly, only a few mentioned contradictions. A few were troubled, however, "As far as stories in the Bible is concerned I don't go much into that because as you read through Bibles and testaments, they change. . . . They contradict theirselves quite a lot" [46]. One in the believer grouping was concerned about the contradictions between the Bible and modern life:

Well, to be honest with you, I don't believe in the teachings of the Bible. That's me own opinion. Because I think, "How do they know?" How do they know that these teachings of the Bible are true because the Bible, I've found, contradicts itself. It says in the Bible, "An eye for an eye and a tooth for a tooth." But it's not, is it? It is not in this world today, is it? They don't believe in killing if a man commits a terrible crime. They don't believe in punishing him, hanging him, do they? They give the man time in prison. He doesn't forfeit his life, does it? One contradicts the other, doesn't it really? . . . I disagree with a lot of things in the Bible, quite a lot of things really [12].

Overall, one Roman Catholic who attends mass regularly sums up about the Bible what was true for many who didn't articulate it, "I always classed it as a mystery really" [50]. A seventy-four year old pinpointed the critical question for all people about the Bible, "Some nice words in it and some nice verses, but is it true?" [47].

The Contradictions of Atheism

One of the interviewer's assumptions during the interviewing was not to expect people to be consistent. All people seem to live with inherent contradictions no matter what their educational level. The atheist grouping did not disprove that assumption. Although there was perhaps a stronger attempt to be consistent by them than the other groupings, their contradictions were apparent.[39]

1. **Prayer**

Whether they pray or not is usually the acid test of consistency. Would they follow the popular aphorism, "Thank God I'm an atheist"? Four of the ten men in this grouping admitted the private experience of prayer--three of them in stress or trouble asking for help and the other for forgiveness.

The most graphic self-awareness was shown by the man who quoted Brendon Behan, an Irish poet, with agreement, "'I'm a day-time atheist.' It's easy to be a day-time atheist. A night-time atheist is a different thing." He depicted a recent experience, "When my mother was ill, I think you say to yourself like, you do, you're lying in bed and you say, 'If there is anybody there, I'd like help,' you know." He had earlier explained the contradiction inside him, "With a good brainwashing you never know. You've always got that thought there, it's been planted in your mind. And you'll always think that way" [39].

Another man rather ashamedly admitted that he also prayed, "Yes, I'm afraid I do." He prays only in stress situations, but has found that in situations like praying before a job interview "about 90% of the time . . . it usually goes better than I thought it would." He stressed that it sounds "farcical" to pray, "It is hypocritical to say, 'I don't believe,' but in a stress situation to say, 'Please God.' That sounds hypocritical to me, but it is the way you are." His self-legitimation is pragmatic:

In a stress situation, it is important to believe in somebody to turn to. It seems to release a large burden from you. When you have released that burden, you feel better. But outside of stress situations, I don't think that it is important at all [6].

Another man's prayer in trouble is not so successful, "If some bloke nearly has me off the bike, the first thing I say is, 'Oh, God! Here we go again.'" When he was asked if he really meant God, he replied, "Yeah. Or something on those lines. I don't exactly know what it is. As I say, I'm not religious. A contradiction in terms." He doesn't really feel that he gets through, and besides praying at a wedding when "you ain't got a lot of choice. You can't sort of stand up and say, 'I don't believe in it'", his praying usually consists of, "'Oh God!' Splat! 'Thanks!'" on his motorbike. He summarised, "I don't believe in it, but when you are put on the spot, I suppose you need something" [49].

The other man who prayed was eighty-two and was consistent and ardent in his atheism--except for prayer. When asked about his need for forgiveness he replied, "If there is a Lord above, I've asked him to forgive me." Later, cross-checking the reply, the interaction went like this:

DO YOU EVER PRAY?
Only to meself.
WHAT LIKE?
If I've done anything wrong like to forgive.
YOU ASK GOD TO FORGIVE?

In a sense I do.
BUT YOU DON'T BELIEVE THERE IS A GOD?
No.
WHY DO YOU PRAY TO GOD THEN?
There's only one person you can pray to. But I don't
believe in God.
SO YOU PRAY TO HIM BUT YOU DON'T BELIEVE IN HIM?
No, no, no. [replying to the last part]
HOW OFTEN WOULD YOU PRAY, WOULD YOU SAY?
Once in two or three years like.
IN WHAT SORT OF CIRCUMSTANCES? WHAT PROMPTS YOU TO PRAY?
Me guilt like [15].

Six of the men in this grouping, however, said that they
never prayed at all under any circumstances. They are nearly
half of the men in the entire sample who said that they never
pray at all now.

2. Religion on a Form

If one anticipated consistency, one might expect these
men to identify themselves as non-believers when asked to do so
on a form. However, only four were willing to do so when asked.
Five of them would write in the established state religion and
one would identify himself as, "Roman Catholic", the religion he
so strongly opposed. Four of the six seemed to have no problem
with their identification, but two explained their reasoning:

I always put "C of E" because people say, you know because
when I went to a hospital appointment once, or an accident
and I went to the hospital and I said, "I don't know," they
said, "Well, we'll put you down as C of E." So ever since
then, I put, "C of E" [21].

The other brought out the family connection, "Well, me father
said that I was C of E so I would put that. I wouldn't put
atheist or anything like that. . . . It doesn't make much difference what I would put" [16].

3. The Supernatural

Three of the ten men who identified themselves as atheists also mentioned some sort of belief in the supernatural or
some higher being. One gave the extremely vague and unexplained
reply, "I believe that there is something there, but what it is I
don't know. Call it supernatural" [5]. He may have been referring to what another called an "extra-terrestrial life form":

I think that I believe in some sort of mysterial or mystic
force, I suppose they call it God. . . . I don't believe in
actual God itself. I believe that perhaps two thousand years
ago that something did come down, but I don't believe that it
was some all-fired God-giving God. . . . I believe in a
higher being, but I think that that being might have origi-
nated in another galaxy. But I don't believe in some sort of
mysterious God who is all around us [6].

The third man's supernatural was of an entirely different ilk, "I've got a definite belief in the supernatural and things like that. . . . I believe in that very strongly." He described it as, "Anything you don't know about really. Not to do with the stars or the universe type, but the more spooky side of it. Ghosts and that sort of thing." He recounted a couple of experiences which have made him quite frightened and now he "wouldn't mess with it." But this belief has quite an effect on him, "If anybody talks about the supernatural, I'm all goose-pimply and shivery", and if there was a God (which he doesn't believe) and he had a half-hour to talk with him,

> I think that I'd ask him about what's down there, if there is anything like that, like the spooks and the supernatural. That's the first thing that I'd like to know. I wouldn't ask him anything about his own, his earth or its or whatever it is. That's the main thing I'd ask [25].

The Practice of Agnosticism

Since agnosticism is usually considered somewhere in between belief and unbelief, it would be interesting to note how these men in that grouping practice their agnosticism. Does it lead them to practise it as belief or as unbelief or as something in between? It is a rather difficult question to answer from the given data, but these are the impressions:

1. Those who practise agnosticism as unbelief

Five of the twelve men in this grouping most easily fit into this category. These were the men who neither prayed nor found that belief had any influence on their lives. This is, of course, not to say that their morals were low as the man with one of the highest apparent moralities stood in this classification. He saw Jesus as a good example to follow and valued good relationships above all else, yet saw himself very much on the unbelieving side of agnosticism.

Two of these men were strongly fatalistic and one of them indicated that this is "why I don't worry a lot" [22] while the other did worry [13]. The former practiced his religion in these terms, but it did not have much relation to Christian belief. The latter was the strongest and most consistent fatalist in the entire sample and although at one time he connected fate with "God or whatever form it is that controls our lives", he was still "not sure that I believe in God." Another man who was keenly taken to the possibility of a superior race having influence or control on our planet didn't pray at all, but was open to dreams and experiences of something beyond. His "belief" side was more akin to another religion than to Western Christianity, which seems to have little influence on shaping his practice.

2. Those who practise agnosticism
mainly as unbelief but with a bit of belief

Most of the "I don't know" grouping fell in this category. They prayed to God sometimes, but considered it a contradiction in their lives which they found hard to accept: "I tell
you how stupid I am about that. Before I go to sleep every
night, I say a prayer" [18]. Another quoted a verse which he
said every night, "But does it do any good?" [47]. One prayed
seriously when his brother was in hospital and, he admitted with
embarassment, when he has gone to see his football team play. He
also went to church about ten times in the last year, but only
because of his girlfriend.

Then there was the man who was anxious to point out,

I'm not an atheist. I watch "Songs of Praise" and things
like that. I like the singing. I like to hear gospel singing. I've been to those, to these Baptist, they are more
Baptist, hallelujah and clap. All this moaning and groaning
and solemn faces is to me a load of cobblers. I like something happy and lively. . . . Alright, I'm not saying there
isn't someone up there but I'm not saying there is.

He went to church very occasionally "off my own bat", but was
adamant that he was not interested in the question of God [9].

Another's practice and belief was quite an enigma. He
prayed and has even asked his religious uncle how to pray, "I
wouldn't say that I go out of my way and make sure that I do it
every night. It is just when I just get a feeling I have to."
He has had a special religious experience which brought him out
of depression, yet he remained unsure with regard to God's existence and is skeptical toward religion and the Bible. His
classic statement: "Some of my views on religion have changed
since then [the experience]. Let's put it another way, I think
twice before I put it down" [26].

3. Those who practise agnosticism
as a true mixture of belief and unbelief

One of the informants was not only in two minds about his
belief and unbelief but also in two practices. He described
himself as, "50/50, right in the middle of the road with it." He
went to church about three times last year and always had the
service on the TV on Sunday evenings. On one hand, he said, "I
believe there is something there that we should give our whole
heart and soul to", but on the other hand he seemed to have great
reservations--even stronger than the ones of which he spoke [31].
One might speculate that he did not talk about these reservations
freely because of the powerful hold of his strong religious
upbringing. Still, there is a marked difference between his
practice and those in the category above.

4. Those who practise agnosticism
as Christian belief

As might be expected, no one practiced their middle
stance as Christian belief. Although there could have been
agnostics who were regular church-goers in this population, the
fact that our agnostics did not live as full Christian believers
gives empirical evidence to the view that Christian belief requires a commitment which is not possible to give when one is in
the state of "I don't know." Harvey Cox's maxim, "Not to decide
is to decide", is certainly born out by the agnostics in this
sample, with the man mentioned in the section above as the only
possible exception.

The Saliency of Belief in the "Believers"

What is true for many who called themselves believers in
God is that if they had never been asked specific questions about
their religious beliefs one would have never known that they
believed anything about God. They were clear that they never
talked about religion to their friends, family, neighbours, or
workmates. Over and over the statements resounded, "We don't
discuss religion"; "It's not a question that would come up"; "It
never arises". Whether this is purely the fact that, "It's a
thing you don't talk about--religion--at any time really, religion and politics, it's something taboo", or that religion truly
is unimportant is perhaps an open question.

At least, the majority of them revealed that God or their
belief in God has had no influence whatsoever on their lives. To
the question, "To what extent would you say that God or belief
in God has influenced your life?" the responses were mainly of
this type: "No, not in the slightest" [25], "They don't affect
me life, no" [37], "None at all really", [23], "No, not a bit"
[15]. Even one man who attended Mass every week replied, "Well,
I wouldn't say it influences it at all really" [50]. Slightly
less strong were, "Not a great deal, not honestly", [14] and
three who gave the possibility that God or belief in God had
influenced without them knowing it as in the response, "If God
has influenced my life, it is in some way that I am not conscious
of" [44].

Several responded that God or their belief in him had had
some influence on their lives. These were mainly in a general
sort of ethical sense, "I feel that belief in God keeps you on
the straight and narrow . . . from doing too much evil" [32], or
in a sense of their belief guiding them in life,

When you look back on your life, you can't recall on the spot
that was the cause of that. But I think that it is a guide,
it's been a guide to your life, what to do, what to think.
Regardless of what you do, I think that this is governed to a
large extent by believing in God. That's my view to God [4].

One man felt that the only moment he had been influenced
was:

At one time I was bad to me mother, not bad, but I did ask
the Lord's forgiveness for the way I treated her at one time,
you know. And I felt that my attitude to my mother changed a
lot after that, you know. I mean, God bless her, she's been
dead for twenty years now but I still miss her like [24].

Another man was influenced when God helped him through a serious
operation [45] while another thought that God "more or less
brought me together with the wife" [48]. Although agnostic about
God, one [18] was strongly influenced by the teachings of Christ
and another [3] felt the family influenced him by saying, "God
will punish you," but only fate could influence him now.

Five men, including two regular church goers, felt that
God or belief in God had influenced their lives, "quite a lot".
The two church goers used very strong words to show the extent of
the influence: "It's influenced my life to the extent to where I
am today. Where my life is today, it mightn't be much like, but
that's life like, you know" [34] and, "Well, I mean to say he has
helped us in life ever since I've been born" [30].

Perhaps not much can be made of the specific questions
regarding their trust of God and obedience to God. The more
subtle questions were more telling. Yet at least we should say
that one-fifth of all the men seemed to have no trouble saying
that they trusted and/or obeyed God and yet he or their belief in
him had not influenced their life. This is one of those human
contradictions that is very hard to explain. Perhaps there was
some vague trust in these men and some general ethical obedience
which put them in touch with the "good man" that they all seemed
to want to be, but they were honest enough to admit that the
down-to-earth practical influences of their beliefs in God were
often nil or very minimal indeed.

Four of the men in the entire sample gave protruding
evidence of the elements of Christian belief delineated in the
previous chapter. These were four of the five regular church-
goers (four Roman Catholics and one Methodist) in the sample.
Three of these men brought their beliefs out early in the interview, which may further point out the saliency of their Christian
belief to their lives.

Even with these four, however, there were elements of
contradiction and inconsistency. One man was very much involved
in gambling, "I'm wrong as regards the gambling. I know I
shouldn't be doing that" [34]. Another wasn't sure about one of
the central confessions of the Christian faith, whether Jesus was
the Son of God. "I really don't think it matters. . . . I mean
he lived the right life, the good life and his example is what
matters" [2].

Peter Hebblethwaite sees the Englishman of today as
somewhat like the working man of the nineteenth century,
described by Owen Chadwick as "somewhere between an unconscious
secularist and a Christian." Chadwick says of the working man:

He did not at all object to people who were rude about cler-
gymen and churches, but usually objected to people who were
rude about God. So far as he was an unconscious Christian,

he respected marriage in church and funerals conducted by
Christian ministers and approved babies to be christened.
. . .   So far as he was an unconscious secularist he had a
feeling that church ministers were agents of the Tory Party,
and that to attend church (except at harvest festivals) would
be a departure from the social custom of his equals, would
turn him into an eccentric, if not one liable to the accusa-
tion of trying to ape his betters.[40]

CHAPTER SEVEN

THE COMPARISON:

BELIEVERS AND UNBELIEVERS THROUGH OTHER EYES

Very few in-depth studies of people's beliefs or lack of them have been published in Britain. There are a certain number of polls, of course, surveying the general belief situation, but rarely do they touch the same issues or in the same manner as this research. Where the polls or surveys deal with similar issues, they have been documented in the footnotes of the previous chapters. The similarity in figures with the relevant data shows at least that our men are not so far out of step with the people in the polls.

A Major Discrepancy

However, one major peculiarity protrudes no matter how one looks at it. This study found that 20 percent of the men called themselves atheists while another 24 percent of the sample termed themselves some type of agnostic. A few of those who ended up in the believer self-designation category were on the borderline of agnosticism or seemed to call themselves believers as they had no language or desire to express their mixed beliefs in more explicit terms. By contrast, David A. Barrett's *World Christian Encyclopedia* registers only 8.5 percent of the United Kingdom as non-religious and 0.7 percent as atheists.[1]

Of course it is also true that only 14 percent of the men in this research would identify themselves as anything other than one of the Christian denominations or just a "Christian" if asked to enter their religion on a form. This ties in directly with Barrett's statistic of 86.9 percent professing Christians in mid-1980.[2] The divergence is not so wide with The European Value Systems Study Group's 1981 sample of Britain, but is still quite significant. They found that 76 percent believed in God while 58 percent agreed that they were religious persons.[3]

The general discrepancy between what people will respond to a casual question or write on a form and what they say when asked to speak for a longer period of time are quite significant. It points out the limited value of understanding people's beliefs by what they might put on a form. An advocate of unbelief, Szczesny sees that other than the people who are members of a group that is admittedly non-Christian and who do not belong to any Christian community,

there are many church members, the number of whom can only be
guessed at, who, while included in Christian statistics, are
not Christians in fact. But even if we take only unbelievers
and those committed to non-Christian forms of belief, both of
which groups are quite conscious of their non-Christianity,
we have a total many times greater than the ratio of dissi-
dence officially listed. The question now arises why it is
that all these non-Christians fail to exercise their freedom
of religion and of conscience, and why at least some of them,
having dared to leave the Church, should not have become
organized minorities. The only answer can be that in spite
of man's "inalienable rights," non-Christian ideological
convictions, unlike deviations from prevailing political
opinion, dare not be openly proclaimed. For this state of
affairs neither the state nor the Christian churches are
responsible, but that anonymous, yet omnipotent censor called
"public opinion."[4]

The thesis of this research is that in-depth answers are
more relevant than nominal survey questions to discover the true
motivation of the lives of men. Although perhaps helpful for
what they indicate about what people say, even Barrett's statistics for nominal and affiliated, practicing and non-practicing
appear to have little reference to life-motivating beliefs of
people. Even beyond what people say in in-depth interviews are
how they live their lives. This is the real test of their
beliefs which are very hard to examine and either quantify or
qualify.

Young People's Beliefs

One study in Britain, begun in 1974 by the Church of
England Board of Education, attempted to look at young people's
beliefs in Britain by avoiding "imposing a rigid prior definition
of belief on the respondents. We wanted *them* to tell *us* what
they believed and believed in."[5] The interviewees included both
sexes, all the main social classes and age groupings within their
thirteen to twenty-four year old definition of young people.
Some of the interviews were done in groups and some were done as
individuals. The interviews were "structured loosely around a
chronological account of each respondent's own religious upbringing or lack of it."[6] Even though there was considerable difference in both population and methodology, it is interesting to
note their findings, peppered with many good quotations, and how
they dovetail with the present research. Of particular note is
what Martin and Pluck define as "The Pattern of Belief" which is
delineated in eleven characteristics:

1. The typical position is, "Well, I suppose there might be
something in it, and then again there might not." Belief is
very amorphous and inchoate indeed, and there are no cases in
our sample of young people building up belief systems except
out of the debris of Christianity. There are no new-minted
systems only more or less agnosticism, more or less half-
hearted assent to items of theology, values, attitudes and
opinions left lying around in the wake of Protestant
Christianity. There is a widespread assent of the very
vaguest kind to the existence of God. Mostly the childhood

picture of the old man with the long white beard figures at some level, although a few more educated and sophisticated respondents had rejected an easy anthropomorphism of that kind. Quite often he is a God with neither power nor attributes: the assent to his existence is the sum total of the religious or belief response of some interviewees. . . .

2.   Belief in Jesus as divine was very much more restricted than some vague belief in a God, although few doubted that he had been an historical personage. . . .

3.   There is a persistent tendency, probably more marked in the females than the males, to select the optimistic and comforting elements in the conventional Christian package and to reject or ignore the uncomfortable. . . .

There is a section, mostly male, however, who believe there is only this life: "When I'm dead, I'm dead and that's the end of it." This makes it important not to waste time on boring and unprofitable pursuits like religion.

4.   Particularly at the lower class and educational levels there is no apparent sense of unease at combining non-prac- tice and near-atheism or indifference with institutional adherence of the type outlined in the preceding section (no. 8). This is one facet of a more general feature, that is a total absence of any drive to intellectual consistency either in the belief pattern itself or between belief and behaviour, and this despite a general conviction that you would be able to tell the "real Christian" because heart and actions would be one.

5.   This inconsistency relates to two further widespread features of the respondents' beliefs. First, childhood be- lief is breached with incredible ease on the basis of a simplistic scientism. . . .   In short, *any* sort of idea, however fantastic, will be given house room if it can be dressed up in a scientific, or more accurately perhaps, a "science fiction" garb. The difficulty religious belief encounters seems to be more one of vocabulary and ambience than of credibility.

6.   The second notable feature of the internal incoherence of belief is that while it can tolerate any degree of inconsis- tency it seems very intolerant of uncertainty. What causes unease is not an overall lack of consistency in a system but detailed factual lacunae. To the question "What would make you believe?" the typical answer is, "More facts." . . .

7.   Males are more inclined to this form of scientism in general, while females are more inclined to adopt a comfort- able and undemanding version of residual Christianity.

8.   It cannot be too strongly stressed that a universal individualism was found in the approach of these young people. What you believe is essentially private, it is your own affair, you have the right to believe anything you like. The corollary of this individualism is a strong dislike of having other people's beliefs pushed on you. . . .   One boy

went so far as to liken mission efforts to recruiting drives for a football club. "It's like saying everyone should support Arsenal 'cause it's a good side." . . . Involvement, getting it out of proportion, being intrusive, these are to be avoided as an embarrassment and a threat. . . . In general the view is that if you are going to believe you'll believe, and if you're not then no amount of effort on anyone else's part nor of will power on your own can possible [*sic*] "force belief on you". It blows in the wind like Fate, it is emphatically not something you should be expected to work at.

. . . the individualism takes the form of keeping yourself (and your belief) to yourself. It is so exclusively your own affair that you never articulate it to yourself at all until you are asked to do so by an interviewer. When you are meeting with your friends you don't discuss, you just *do* things. Meaning in fact is mediated through customary action far more than through talk. No wonder we find both individualism and startling inconsistency here.

9. Going along with this individualism and privacy of belief is an equally strong and universal insistence on one's own open-mindedness. . . . It is noteworthy that while one takes pride in having come to one's own belief system independently, other people, and especially foreign or exotic or historic religions, are seen as the product of the environment-- "they didn't (or don't) know any better." . . .

10. There was a widespread use of "belief", "prayer" (and in some cases a would-be use of "vicars") for individual comfort and for contact in moments of loneliness. This was especially a female characteristic. . . . God, Jesus and the priesthood seem to be viewed as instant social workers: the ideal religious contact seems to be something like confession without either confession or penance.

11. One might summarize the pattern of belief by saying that hardly any of our respondents regarded it as having any *social* relevance at all. It was an essentially private thing, unconnected with everyday life, practical decisions or habitual value judgements. It made no demands but offered a cushion of comfort against mildly distressing disruptions of life. It existed at the level of personalised emotional life and bolstered a sense of self-worth and of identity.[7]

Beliefs Firmly Fixed by Time of School Leaving. What is surprising perhaps is how similar Martin and Pluck's pattern of belief is to the findings of this research. Since their population was only young people, it causes one to theorize further on the supposition that beliefs are firmly fixed by the time the person has left school. The answers of our interviews reveal only slightly more mature responses but are no more enlightened and are without any fewer prejudices and cliches than the examples given in the *Young People's Beliefs* study. The fact that the men have not been to church, nor read the Bible, nor discussed or often even thought about their beliefs gives credence to the fact that these men's beliefs are thoroughly settled by the time they leave school and not intended to change for the rest of their lives. Like their knowledge of English or history, their religious and probably ethical education is completed. Crises may shake them for a moment and perhaps cause them to re-evaluate, but they all appear to come back to those beliefs decided upon in childhood.

Class Distinctions? The similarity in the two studies may also make one wonder whether there are *major* differences between the beliefs of the classes. Indeed, it *may* be that the higher classes go to church more often,[8] but it is possible that there is little difference in the actual beliefs except for the literary sophistication with which they articulate them.

After surveying the "Demographic Correlates of Values" in Britain for the European Value Systems Study Group, i.e. looking at attitudes to religion, sex, family, patriotism, work, and property from the point of view of age, gender and social class, Mark Abrams concludes:

> From the data presented it would be reasonable to conclude that broadly all three social classes in this country hold the same value systems; all three contain much the same proportion of traditionalists, anti-traditionalists and ambivalents, and the only distinctive differences between the classes are those of occupation, income, residential tenure and educational background. However, these latter four differences generate class differences in life-styles that are often more important than values in generating and sustaining class divisions.[9]

David Martin points out that there are similarities be-tween the elite and the proletarian:

> On two points the attitudes at the extremes of the social spectrum are identical: in equating religion with conduct and in regarding one's beliefs as inappropriate for general dis-cussion. Religion is equivalent to decency, and in the one case this may include attending church or running one of its organizations, and in the other case not. The universal reticence which goes with this emphasis on decency is partly a fear of ridicule, partly a wish to avoid any hint of con-tamination by religious fanaticism. The fear of ridicule is related to a masculine ethos which regards religious practice as appropriate for children and women, along perhaps with all the gentler arts. The English male is supposed to live up to an ideal of psychological opacity and culture philistinism, and it may even be that this ideal is quite frequently at-tained.[10]

Where Are the Real Differences? The third matter for consideration is more serious. The fact that the study on young people's beliefs could find a pattern of belief among the variety of their interviewees makes one wonder how various the findings of this research actually are. We have been careful at this stage to keep the men in their self-designations, but only rarely have we been able to tell the difference in their replies as to who was atheist, agnostic, or believer. Conservative or liberal moral views seemed to coincide more consistently with believer and unbeliever respectively along with a few major Christian stances like belief in God, but there are also some instances of unbelievers holding to more traditional beliefs, on their own wrongdoing for example, than to which believers held. This will, however, be discussed more thoroughly in the next chapter when exploring the boundaries between believer and unbeliever. At this stage, however, the similarity of beliefs between believer and unbeliever is the striking matter, especially for those concerned with what has been termed the "radical" message of Jesus and his followers.

Hidden Religion in Workers?

Looking from the context of German workers, Tilman Winkler sees beyond the apparent lack of anything religious in these men at all. He finds religion hidden in the everyday language--in curses, greetings, and humour. Winkler believes that behind their non-religious comments are latent religious questions, such as their feeling of no significance. Since the workers don't read the Bible, they have no theological language with which to discuss it. The Church language is too beautiful and they can't tell you what is said there. His thesis is that you have to go by a religious assumption and look for the hidden religiosity. Since the worker doesn't put such a value on language as the higher classes, everything they believe, hope, fear, and feel comes out in different forms: in their behaviour, in their casual talks and trite expressions, and in their language hide 'n seek games.[11]

One of our sample, when asked to clarify why he uses the phrases, "God bless. Good night", replied: "I don't know really. It feels if I'm giving them a bit of security by saying it. You don't really think about it, but by saying it, it gives them that bit of security. 'God bless,' he's looking after you like" [46].

One can feel affinity with Winkler's thesis and its application to British workers. Although one can never be content with what people tell you about their beliefs when their actions contradict it, it seems that we must also take seriously what these British workers unequivocally wanted to say: "We are not religious! We may have some beliefs, but they are not very important. They do not influence our lives. They are our private thoughts." They said this both about themselves and about what they thought other men to be like.

Existential and Religious Questions. It is true that they may sometimes have to deal with existential questions, but the existential questions, although overlapping, are not identical to the religious questions--or at least the men do not identify them that way. Most of the men are, at some point in their lives, forced to ask at least some of the basic questions of existence, usually at a crisis point, but they are not plagued with the more literary classes' "search for meaning." Such thoughts would be far too lofty for their concrete minds.

Yet in the existential dimension, the religious answers--
even the preceding questions--have been pushed out of the arena
very early in life. Often, because they feel that these questions cannot be answered, they are no longer even asked. If they
could be answered, in their view they would still be irrelevant
to the concrete life of the working man. If the religious questions are related to eternal values, life after death, God, they
are not interested.

Winkler sees that the talk in the pub about banalities is
an attempt to gain acceptance. If the pastor can also talk about
these trivialities, they feel, "He understands me." But explicit, existential--non-religious--questions are not the talking
point of the working man. These questions are not discussed in
the local pub, rather they are worked out in daily life--if at
all. His need for acceptance, love, achievement--although perhaps initiated in public--is largely worked out in private.
"Wearing ones feelings on one's sleeve" is one of the mortal sins
for working class families as well as for their higher class
distant neighbours.

Swearing at a Real or Absent God. It is true, as Winkler
says, that their swear words are God words (and sexual words).
But what do they mean by this? Do they denounce him by doing
this? Are they swearing at the God who exists and who does
nothing, where the curse at his existence is a wish that he did
not? Or is their cry that he does not exist a wish that he did?
The answers to these questions from this research are not forthcoming, but at least we must take seriously the fact that they
say that they are not bothered about God or life after death.
However, they are troubled by the suffering in this world and
most of them relate that in some way to God or the lack of God.

The Gamble Prayer. Their prayer, although by no means
universal, is significant. But what does it mean? Why do they
pray since they often expect nothing from God?

For the working man who prays, prayer is a stab in the
dark, a gamble. It may even be regular like filling out the
football coupon each week without fail. It is not hope of the
expectation variety, but a long shot gamble at being relieved of
the misery which is inevitable, imminent or both. There is less
than a chance in a million that his number will come up at
Littlewoods, but he does it "just in case." Or perhaps, in
trouble, he had his one-time big flutter hoping against hope for
a godsend. It does not come nor does God send it. Yet he carries
on hoping and praying, "just in case".

Today's working man neither follows the law in order to
receive God's approval nor believes in a gospel of no works,
reliant on someone else for salvation. He is alone and hence
needs approval only from himself or those in his extended self
(family). He often receives neither, so the existential (and
religious) drama goes on unresolved and unresolvable. He comes
to terms with it in the routine of daily life--his only existential. It is not surprising that the contemporary, psychological
mood, yet to become popular in the working classes, stresses the

need for self-acceptance above all.

We must, at least, take both the working man's words and actions seriously. He does not need God, but he prays. He does not discuss God, but he swears. He is not religious, but puts a religion on a form. He may believe in God, but God does not order his life.

Concrete Expressions of Belief. Where is concrete Christian belief demonstrated? Most who say they believe show nothing different in their concerns, motivation, and action from those who do not. Their own particular concrete expressions do not reveal a following of the Man from Galilee.

Middle-class conceptual belief has an excuse--its style claims no need for overt expression. It remains conceptual along with much of the rest of middle-class life. The middle-class who claim belief discuss their religion but do not live it. The working-class style, however, is to live their beliefs and pass on their stories. If true Christianity is believed by these working masses, it has yet to seat itself in its cultural home. "We all believe but we don't participate," almost a sort of working class article of faith, is perhaps a self-indictment that they do not really believe since working class conviction in anything else is shown by its participation. Alternatively, perhaps it simply shows the nature of what there is in which to participate, which does not take into consideration working-class values.

The Working-Class Unchurched and the Church

Tracey Early's comments on the 1978 Gallup Poll of the Unchurched need to be considered here:

If we reflect on the Borough of Manhattan, in which the survey results were first announced to the world, we are struck that residents have access to almost any kind of church they might want, from the most rigid fundamentalist to the most humanistic, with worship from the highest Anglo-Catholicism to the most unbuttoned storefront holy rollerism, and social justice concern scaled from 100 to 0. So whatever complaints Manhattanites may have about churches in general, they can easily find a church free of those "defects." Yet church attendance in Manhattan is lower than in many other places. We can further observe that many of the Manhattan worship services that are well attended function in large part as rites of ethnic self-affirmation.[12]

It is also true that for many years the church has not been a part of British working-class "rites of ethnic self-affirmation." David Martin describes further the working-class problem with any voluntary association:

One aspect of working-class styles especially important for participation in church life is the widespread resistance to any kind of major involvement in voluntary associations, trade unions included. With every step up the status scale active participation in voluntary association of every kind increases. These are somewhat differently distributed as between the churches themselves: the Free Churches maintain their own integrated network of association whereas the Church of England is uniquely linked with a number of generally available associations, often of a charitable kind, usually run by high status persons, such as upper-middle-class women. By contrast the working-class style is based on kin and neighbourhood and only emerges for the pub, the cinema and the football match. Indeed, so far as women are concerned not even this minimal emergence is likely.[13]

He also points out the contradiction in the working-class which both criticizes the church for its incomprehensible, foreign language, yet also wants the church to be the stalwart of ancient customs.

It may be suggested that what goes on inside a church is out-of-date mumbo-jumbo. This puzzlement at liturgical complication is very genuine and particularly concerns the Church of England, in which every new ritual quirk or even reform devised by clergy only deepens the conviction that this is not designed for people "such as us". It might also be said that if an attempt were made to bring the services up to date and if parsons were to step outside the prescribed role of persons with cultured voices who do not understand the mysteries of the working man's way of life, then resentment would be even greater than it is.[14]

Martin further states that

The English working class remains one of the most unrevolutionary and one of the most irreligious in the world. As we have seen it "believes" in Christianity after a fashion, but it will be enticed into church only with great difficulty. That is why one must rely on an explanation based on the cultural rather than the political chasms.[15]

He continues to point out that "the most important single focus of it all is gesture and voice. 'Them' and 'us' are distinguished by enunciation."[16] Os Guinness shows that F. G. Downing criticizes apologists

for bias towards abstract modes of thinking at the expense of more concrete modes. "Apologetics has recently, and I think for a long time, flattered the abstracters into thinking that they were by that fact mature, and has made visualizers feel primitive." One problem is the same that we have seen before: accommodation easily becomes assimilation. "The codes we use always have the effect of fitting the faith to the literate upper classes, who are not nicer, more loving or even more intelligent: just more lettered and more leisured". Similarly, C. S. Lewis urged that vernacular English "simply has to be learned by him who would preach to the English; just as a missionary learns Bantu before preaching to the Bantus."[17]

These cultural matters must be carefully considered when moving toward communicating the gospel to the working classes and

seeing what kind of a church these working-class men would make
if they could use their own cultural forms. However, the pit-
falls of the homogeneous unit principle of the church growth
schools are just as significant among the working classes in
Britain as among the middle classes in the USA. Yet even if one
gets that far, one still cannot forget that a move of the church
to accommodate herself to the working class or a new attempt to
make them into a more "clubbable class" is not a sure recipe for
success. These men show that there is a problem not only of
culture but conversion, not only background but of belief.

J. Russell Hale has done a far-reaching study of the
unchurched in the United States. His conceptualization of the
types that he found is purposely given in non-technical terminology. Although the approach of my research was not weighted
toward the unchurched nor did it attempt to delve seriously into
attitudes toward the church, there may be some relevance in some
of the types found; even though the church situation and therefore responses to it are quite different from that in the USA.
He found ten classifications:

1. The Antiinstitutionalists
2. The Boxed In
3. The Burned Out
4. The Floaters
5. The Hedonists
6. The Locked Out
7. The Nomads
8. The Pilgrims
9. The Publicans
10. The True Unbelievers[18]

The main difference, however, is that Hale's unchurched
tend to have been to church and have something to which to respond. My believers and unbelievers always look at the church
from a distance with their only experience of church being a
little bit of Sunday School and a few experiences of churches
based on birth, marriage, and death. These have mainly been
negative or indifferent experiences, so these men have had no
reason either culturally or experientially to return.

Summary

A. H. Hasley summarized the findings of the European
Value Systems Study Group:

In short, though by no means outlandish from the European
culture to which they belong, the British are to be seen and
see themselves as a relatively unchurched, nationalistic,
optimistic, satisfied, conservative, and moralistic people.[19]

CHAPTER EIGHT

THE FRONTIER:

MARKING THE BOUNDARIES BETWEEN BELIEVERS AND UNBELIEVERS

The last chapter questioned whether there was enough qualitative difference between those who called themselves believers and those who termed themselves unbelievers to make many conclusions. Be that as it may be, it is necessary to try to make a distinction between belief and unbelief, as we have already done from a biblical base in chapter three, and now to make a distinction between believers and unbelievers from more practical and partly empirical bases.

Not so many people like to mark boundaries between groups of people today. There are so many barriers of race, class, status and religion that divide and destroy. Religion especially was cited by a number in our sample as the cause of many wars and a scandal to either true religion or the possibility of the validity of any religion. It is easy to see why the question is better left alone.

In certain parts of the the modern ecumenical movement, even so-called "natural" boundaries have been questioned, redefined, and blurred in an attempt to make "one church" and further, "one world." The traditional chasm between believers and unbelievers is being bridged by a variety of creative thinkers and reconcilers, some of whom have already been discussed in chapter two. Dialogue not only brings together Christian diversities but now brings together groups as diverse as Christians and Marxists, Christians and Jews, Christians and Buddhists, Christians and atheists.

However, some dialogue, including certain meetings initiated by the World Council of Churches, not only brings out the similarities of belief but sharpens the differences between partners in dialogue. It is to this aspect of our own dialogue between belief and unbelief, believers and unbelievers that we must now focus our attention.

At times boundaries have been artificially drawn by the church from the inside or by atheists from the outside,[1] but we would do well not to disregard the fact that differences are seen in both those who call themselves believers and those who call themselves unbelievers. Those who have made the shift from one major grouping to another confirm that their shift is genuine, at least from their perspectives. Conversion seen phenomenologically is difficult to disregard.

Even more so, we would not be wise to disregard the words of Jesus and the writings of the New Testament on the nature of the distinction. That Jesus draws a line between those who "believe in me" and those who do not is clear. It is not always so clear to us, however, precisely where he draws the line. The Lukan sayings of Jesus, "He who is not with me is against me" (11:23) and, "Whoever is not against you is for you" (9:50) typify the nature of the contemporary dilemma in trying to clarify the distinction. The history of Christian denominations could be seen as a history of people trying to draw the line between "true believer" and "unbeliever" at different points.

Who Marks the Boundary? God, Man, or Both?

Is this a problem that man should consider at all? Is it not best left up to God Himself to pursue what is not a problem to him at all?

Matthew records the well-known words of Jesus on judgement forbidding any ultimate decision about a man's final and eternal destiny (7:1-2). Yet the Johannine Christ discerns those who believe and those who do not believe, the only qualification for beginning eternal life (John 3:15). He sees that, "'There are some of you who do not believe.'" John explains, "For Jesus had known from the beginning which of them did not believe and who would betray him" (John 6:64). It is also noted that, "From this time many of his disciples turned back and no longer followed him" (6:66), indicating that unbelievers are those who do not follow. These men who turned away, with little doubt, still believed in God but they did not accept the "hard teaching" of eating his flesh and drinking his blood.

In another instance, the Johannine Christ speaks to "the Jews *who had believed in him*": "If you hold to my teaching, you are really my disciples" (John 8:31). He goes on to make judgements regarding them, including that they are slaves to sin, children of the devil, do not belong to God, and are deaf. He further focuses upon these apparent "believers" in still another incident following the healing of the man born blind, "'If you were blind, you would not be guilty of sin; but now that you claim you can see, your guilt remains'" (John 9:41). Although Jesus' *purpose* in coming to earth was not to judge (John 12:47), it was, in fact, necessary (John 8:16).

Matthew records Jesus asking people to discern whether this new belief to which he calls them is present in themselves. In the Sermon on the Mount, Jesus says that the new life of faith (= righteousness) is not like the religion of the scribes and Pharisees or like the religion of the pagans. He further calls for critical evaluation of the way in which the righteousness of the scribes and the Pharisees is inadequate, what hypocrisy is, who "dogs", "pigs", and "false prophets" are (that they are not to "give to", "throw pearls to", "and watch out for").

Jesus' hearers are called to make some level of evaluation of the presence of this belief, if for no other reason than to know what *not* to be like. The evaluation presupposes that people without this "new" faith can properly be called unbelievers. Although faith has objective manifestations, one must never make an ultimate judgement. That is the prerogative of God alone. The end of the sermon warns the hearers that not everyone who gives the confession of faith, "Lord, Lord" will enter the kingdom of heaven--although this judgement appears largely a matter for Christ himself rather than for others.

The Apostle Paul exhorts the Corinthian Christians to deal with both moral and "legal" matters themselves: "What business is it of mine to judge those outside the church? Are you not to judge those inside? God will judge those outside. 'Expel the wicked man from your number'" (1 Corinthians 5:12-13). Paul knew who was inside and who was outside and he appeals to the Corinthians to deal with those inside. He sees the need to put some who were inside out, in order that they might understand the nature of the inside from the out. Is the distinction between those who are inside and those outside the same as the believers and unbelievers? This becomes the classic problem of the visible and invisible Church. Paul does not appear to know anything about believers outside of a local Christian congregation, although he takes account of those "who do not have the law [who] do by nature things required of the law" (Romans 2:14).

We proceed in exploring the frontier between believers and unbelievers with trepidation, knowing that no man is the ultimate judge in this matter, and yet men need to have some way of discerning believers from unbelievers.

How The Men Divided Themselves

First of all we must look at the empirical evidence to see where, if at all, it corresponds to the biblical elements of belief and unbelief. There was no unanimity in the characteristics of belief and unbelief in the sample, but it is interesting to note where the self-designations actually divided and took on their own characteristics. Even the areas which separated the the men were by no means absolute, but these six areas stand out for consideration:

1. **Cognitive Belief in God.** Most of the men, seemed to consider cognitive belief in God as the single criteria for being a believer, whether or not that was the characteristic they gave when asked what a true believer was. As already shown, those who believed were often very vague indeed and some of those classified as believers also described themselves as low as 60 percent belief and 40 percent "the other way", and some confessed their own belief to be rather hypocritical or inauthentic.

For many their conception of God had more in common with deism than with Christianity. They wonder a great deal more about creation--and that often being what man creates--than the Creator. Perhaps some could bear the definition of the Eighteenth Century deist defined by his critics as, "'A person who is not weak enough to be a Christian and not strong enough to be an atheist.'"[2] Nevertheless, some sort of cognitive belief in God, however slippery or woolly, was a demarcation between the "believers" and the "atheist/agnostic" double grouping.

2. The Person of Jesus. They also divided on who they believed Jesus to be. There was a great deal of uncertainty, but those who called themselves believers were naturally much more likely to think of Jesus as some kind of Godly or messianic character. Even many of the believers, however, gave answers with little conviction. The answers resembled more cognitive statements about a vague ancient person than a confession of faith.

3. The Afterlife. Belief in some kind of life after death was also an issue of separation. The atheists stood firmly against it, the agnostics mainly didn't know, while the believers divided. The believers were almost equally divided between those who didn't know (43 percent) and those who thought that there was some kind of afterlife (39 percent). The remainder were certain that there was no afterlife at all (18 percent). There was, however, little to show that their beliefs about the afterlife had its source in the biblical tradition, but at least there was some distinction in the way the groupings thought about the afterlife.

4. The Results of Prayer. Among those who prayed, the believer grouping tended to have some kind of results or answers to their prayers much more often than those who prayed in the agnostic grouping (very few in the atheist grouping prayed at all). Even though there was strong uncertainty about how to express these answers, or whether they were answers to prayer at all, they still reported it more often. They were also more likely to feel that something happened to them when they prayed.

5. Views on Abortion. Although there was very little difference in the groupings with regard to how they came to their moral choices, there was a striking agreement on the way in which they viewed the ethics of abortion. 76 percent of those who called themselves believers viewed abortion as always wrong or mainly wrong while 71 percent of the atheists and agnostics thought that abortion was acceptable and a matter of the right of the individual to decide. It would have been interesting to have found out how they fared on other moral issues. It appears that closer identification with Christianity and more conservative stances on moral issues may be a social rather than a religious pattern, but at least it must be noted that this was a point of separation among the groupings.

6. Their Own Wrongdoing. How they viewed their own wrongdoing was perhaps the most interesting of the findings which divided the groupings. The believers were much more prone to say that they had done no wrong in their lives while three-quarters of the atheists and a few less of the agnostics were keen to admit their wrongdoing.

With Jesus standing so firmly against self-righteousness, one would wonder in what tradition these believers stand. In Christian tradition, only the holiness doctrine of sinless perfection would give any remote credence to their view and no one appeared to espouse this view. The centrality of the death of Jesus in New Testament theologies and its necessity for forgiveness of sin makes it clear that many of these believers do not have a close connection to this same *kerygma* and *kerygmata* of the early apostles.

This "anti-element" of true belief makes clear what was suspected through the "woolliness" of the other distinctions, that is, that their definition of "believer" is very different from the Biblical ones. This makes one call into question whether the men are able to meaningfully classify themselves as believers or unbelievers without any understanding of the biblical meaning of the belief/unbelief distinction. "If we claim to be without sin, we deceive ourselves and the truth is not in us" (1 John 1:8). It asks further whether one can be a true believer in the good news of Jesus without awareness of one's own sin.

Comparison With the Elements of Biblical Belief. Even though these distinctions, by self-designation, are so vague, in their best forms (with the exception of the wrongdoing), they could have some reference to the elements of biblical belief delineated in chapter three.

Belief in God, in the person of Jesus, and in an afterlife are related to the second element, confession/belief that. Their belief in life after death could also be related to the fifth element, hope/belief for the future, although it seemed to move that far only in a very few men. What happens when they pray could also have some correspondence in some with hope and perhaps the third element, trust/belief in. The ethics of abortion could then be related to element number four, obedience/belief in action.

The Elements in Believers and Unbelievers

At least the atheists cause us no trouble in looking at this frontier. They do not number themselves among the Christian believers. For someone to call them an "anonymous Christian" is at best an anomaly and for some an insult. The agnostics stand in various stages of unknowing for a variety of reasons already discussed. They, too, can for all practical purposes be ruled out of this discussion. They define themselves as riding on the wide line between unbelief and belief, with most tending to verge nearer to the former in their practice as we have already described.

The most interesting topic for our discussion are those twenty-eight men (56 percent of the sample) who call themselves believers of one stripe or another. It is not so simple as to merely accept their designation since it differs so sharply at points from biblical views of what a believer is.

Francis M. Tyrrell in pointing out the dialectic of belief-unbelief, "omnipresent in the human species", shows that

unbelief is an attribute, not of some, but of all. It seems to be present more conspicuously in those who outwardly reject Christian faith. Actually genuine unbelief is more discernible in those who outwardly accept Christian faith, for there the deviations from authentic faith stand out in bolder relief.[3]

These men are not perhaps the men Tyrrell had in mind, but their claim to some kind of Christian belief allows us to examine them to see if their claims correspond with the elements of Christian belief already explained.

1. **Choice.** It is clear from the interviews that only a few have any awareness of making a choice to follow Jesus. On the whole, their lives are not marked by a decision about belief which has any of the characteristics of a major life choice. Totally lacking is the seriousness or importance involved in normal decisions like getting married or changing vocations. However, this is also true with regard to beliefs and values about those who term themselves atheist and agnostic and may be a nearly universal attribute among these men.

Their decisions about who Jesus is and even whether they believe in God--if consciously considered at all--are made by the time they leave school. There is no searching to see whether the assumptions on which they base their lives are true or false. They imbibe the presuppositions of their society, family, etc. in their various pluralistic forms. The atheists often felt that they had choice in the matter while the believers felt that their cognitive belief was something that blew in the wind. It was not something that they should find out about, expose themselves to, or search out. If it was genuine and they should believe it, it would come to them. It had nothing to do with logic, choice or even emotion.

It is not by their settled choice that they are either believer or unbeliever. It is more like one of those "givens" of society, such as the social security system or job opportunities or the type of food in the shops or the schools available to which to send their children. It is just one of those cultural phenomena over which they have *no* choice. To believe is given or not given through a sort of religious genetic code.

The problem in this type of belief is not so much that they might have slipped into believing at an unknown point, but that there is *now* no conscious awareness of following Jesus/God in their concrete lives. Surely those who are true disciples of Jesus must find the point or points where God has touched their lives and they have responded to him--however small or insignificant these points may be. At least followers of Jesus need to be aware at some level of trying to follow him in the daily routine of life. This appears to be a necessary qualification of a Christian believer/disciple.

2. **The Necessary Quality and Quantity of Belief Content.** *What* people believe is the subject of controversy among many Christians. The content of the faith has been a major dividing force as early as the New Testament and was the motivating force for most of the great ecumenical creeds.

Even for those in this sample who called themselves believers there was little interest in sorting out anything more than the bare belief that God and Jesus existed. The Bible--or anything written for that matter--is not a part of their oral, or, perhaps more correctly stated, audio-visual, culture. And even if it were, the Bible, or even the church, would not be the means by which to solve creedal disagreements so remote from the concrete world in which they live. "Science" or "reason" or "common sense" would be the decisive basis on which these matters are judged if the men were to be involved at all.

These men call us not so much to continue the task of defining precisely what Christian faith is, but make us ask, "What is the *minimum* content necessary then for one to be included as a Christian believer?" Their vague, undefined beliefs hardly have a corpus of belief at all, nevermind arguing over the specifics.

At the very least, we must call for some kind of confession of faith in our men based on the distinctiveness of Jesus Christ. There must be a sound connection of the historical figure of Jesus to the exalted Christ, Son of God, Lord. Working class men may well want to make their own creedal formulae to spell out the relevance to its particular situation in the world in which they live. Dunn's application challenges them to do just that:

> The fact is, quite simply, that *confessions framed in one context do not remain the same when the context changes. New situations call forth new confessions.* A Christianity that *ceases to develop new confessional language ceases to confess* its faith to the contemporary world.[4]

Yet a non-Christological faith, advocated by some both at the popular and intellectual level, is not *Christian* faith. The often found vague sense of a "God somewhere," although perhaps an honest confession, may be amply found in biblical literature but is still not the biblical faith of Israel nor is it the faith which Jesus Christ reveals in the New Testament.

Although the confessions of these "believing" men were not explored carefully enough to be conclusive, one gets the impression that many were not really making a confession of faith about a man who was exalted Messiah, Lord, and Son of God, as much as they were repeating a title not unlike sir, lord, or prince of a more earthly nature. There was a distinct lack of connection between the past and the present. The future was mostly not even considered.

If one were judging by Glock and Stark's "index of orthodoxy" (i.e. belief in: 1) the existence of a personal God, 2) the divinity of Jesus Christ, 3) the authenticity of biblical miracles, and 4) the existence of the devil)[5], these men are indeed very unorthodox in the content of their belief.

3. **Subjective Trust as the Essence.** The element which most clearly exhibits the nature of biblical faith is, at the same time, the most difficult element for which to test. It is

like life itself, describable but undefinable. Physical life, however, is perhaps easier (for humans!) to test for than spiritual life animated by trust. It is known by "imperceptible signs" discussed below, yet because of the human frailty of the "testers" and the "makers", it has also been copied.

However, without the "belief in", as described in chapter three, there is no biblical faith.

4. Discipleship/Obedience: Full Marks or One Mark?
Most of the men in the sample were well aware that there was little to commend them being a true believer. They were good enough in their ethics on one hand, certainly in contrast to those who go to church all the time, yet on the other hand, there was a standard of living that they had not reached which true believers--however few there were--did reach.

The element under consideration here is not so much ethics as discipleship--a walking relationship with Jesus which issues in obedience to the demands of Jesus. The New Testament's emphasis is never simply following the ethic, for example, in the Sermon on the Mount. The ethic arises from the relationship. Discipleship is the prelude to ethics and is only bifurcated from it at the cost of the ethic itself. The ethic becomes truly human when touched by the Human in the Man-God.

There will always be those who do good actions which are deemed vital in any society and which may have eternal dimensions. They may even be the "righteous" sheep who, in the Matthew account, Jesus separates from the goats in the final judgement and identifies their actions of kindness to those in need with service toward himself (Matthew 25:31-46). There is ultimate judgement by which Jesus is able to see things which neither believers nor unbelievers are given the ability to see.

Be that as it may regarding ultimate judgement, there is no indication in the New Testament that those who attempt to be "Christians without Christ" can properly be called *Christians*. One in the sample, "a Christian, but agnostic all the same", because he follows the teachings of Christ, is representative of one stream of this view:

God Himself has never influenced me at all, but Christ, the teachings of Christ has. We don't know whether there was a God, nobody knows. But we certainly know that there was Jesus Christ. And if everybody followed his teachings, this world would be a great place, well, would be a much better place [18].

Although one can have empathy with this man's genuine conviction, there is little biblical precedent for calling him a Christian believer. "Christian" has come to be used as an adjective rather than a noun in our day, devaluing its content and minimizing its relevance to the belief/faith we have stressed.

Jesus did not separate himself from his teaching. The synoptics indicate what is further spelled out in John, "The work of God is this: to believe in the one whom he has sent" (John

6:29). Dunn's warning of separating the teaching of Jesus from
the man is in the context of the difference between the kerygma
of Jesus and the kerygma of the first Christians:

> In the meantime we should recognize and underline the
> most obvious difference between the pre-Easter proclamation
> and the post-Easter proclamation--and that is *Easter* itself,
> belief in the resurrection of Jesus. This needs to be said
> in view of the still strong tendency to try to return to the
> pre-Easter kerygma, to sum up Christianity in terms of the
> Sermon on the Mount or the parable of the Prodigal Son. But
> *there can be no going back to the proclamation of Jesus as
> such.* The kerygmata of Acts and Paul, and in a different way
> of John, demonstrate that *the first Christians were not
> concerned simply to reproduce the message of Jesus.* In the
> view of the earliest churches a decisive development had
> taken place which *itself* became the good news *par
> excellence*--that Jesus had been raised from the dead and
> exalted to heaven. It is this new development which forms
> the distinctive essence of the post-Easter proclamation,
> which gives it its distinctively *Christian* character. As
> Paul explicity [*sic*] states, a kerygma without the
> proclamation of Jesus as risen or exalted would not be
> Christian proclamation, it would cease to be valid as gospel
> (I Cor. 15.14-19). In short, *the Christian Church is built
> round the post-Easter kerygma, not the teaching of the*
> historical Jesus.[6]

Obedience and the Body of Christ. It is perhaps easy to
point out the deficiencies in any man's discipleship whether
professed or unprofessed. One must be careful of this overcriti-
cal response which leaves no one in the believer category at all.
Yet one huge discrepancy in many of the men who called themselves
believers is their relationship to other believers. It is easy
to understand historically but difficult to justify biblically
how true believers are to avoid that particular call to become a
part of the body of Christ.

Emil Brunner expresses it this way:

> The witness to Christ in the Word creates the faith that
> binds the individual to the Ekklesia as the fellowship of
> believers. The Word of Christ takes the isolated man out of
> his solitariness and binds him, when he becomes a believer,
> to the congregation of believers, *ek pisteos eis pistin*, from
> faith to faith. It is therefore in fact impossible to speak
> of faith without at the same time speaking of the Ekklesia
> from which alone faith comes and in which alone it finds its
> realization. For only *that* faith counts which shows itself
> effectual in love. The isolation of the believer, Christian
> individualism, is a contradiction in terms. Faith is exis-
> tence in fellowship, as it is also at the same time personal
> existence. On the other hand, it is not existence "in the
> Church", since mere existence in the *institution* of the
> Church is neither fellowship nor personal existence. Church
> membership is no guarantee that our life is a life "in love",
> Therefore, aloofness in relation to the Church institution
> and unwillingness to co-operate with, the so-called individ-
> ualism of the unchurched, is understandable.[7]

Jesus did not simply call individuals to relate singly to himself but called a group of disciples *together* to become an example of what, anachronistically speaking, a church should be. While full of failures, they were still to be a body with the mark of discipleship: "All men will know that you are my disciples if you love one another" (John 13:35).

H. Richard Niebuhr in his move toward a definition of Christ himself connects being a Christian with belonging to a community of believers:

> A Christian is ordinarily defined as "one who believes in Jesus Christ" or as "a follower of Jesus Christ." He might more adequately be described as one who counts himself as belonging to that community of men for whom Jesus Christ--his life, words, deeds, and destiny--is of supreme importance as the key to the understanding of themselves and their world, the main source of the knowledge of God and man, good and evil, the constant companion of the conscience, and the expected deliverer from evil.[8]

Although certainly without perfect models of what Jesus' church should be, the men in our sample almost totally rejected Jesus' call to be a part of the body of Christ. Their attempts at community--if considered at all in their individualism--are through the nuclear family and perhaps some social relationships, but they make no conscious attempt to be a part of anything which might be narrower in terms of believers or wider in terms of universality. Of course, much of the blame rests clearly on the churches which have little that draws these working class men.

It is interesting to note, however, that the teaching and example of Jesus and the pattern of the early churches which so clearly stresses the necessity of being a part of the body of Christ is unequivocally ignored by those who claim to believe. Yet this private individualism in religion is found not only in working class, unchurched men. It is a substantial part of most expressions of the body of Christ themselves.

Evangelicals advocate an individualism in relationship with God promoting this "private religion" conception which contributes to their own downfall in building the body of Christ and reaching out to others. The more mystical conception, prevalent in the generally catholic and high churches, emphasizes the same from a different tradition. Both of these emphases, along with clericalism, tend to isolate people from any idea of what the body of Christ could be in theory, never mind in practice. The community of believers becomes irrelevant to working-class men when it is only a conglomeration of private prayers, private songs, and private listening for private application, all of which they can quite happily do in private at home. J. Tiller describes this as "that privatised religion which is the peculiarly English heresy and which fits so neatly and so dangerously into the wider privatisation of life today."[9]

Already noted is the example of one man who ardently calls himself a Christian and a believer, yet has never in his life been to *any* meeting of the Christian Church except for the family celebrations. Others in the sample appeared to have been to a few meetings of the church more by accident than design. The biblical data questions whether it is possible to be a disciple without working out one's own discipleship with others in some sort of conscious coalition.

This is only one example of the sorts of questions which one must ask about the element of obedience working out in practice.

5. **Hope.** A certainty about the eternal of any kind is present in only a few in the sample. The presence of this element marks a certain type of believer, perhaps one who understands more of the eternal or simply believes "beyond" without any questions. That Christian faith has an eschatological dimension is without question. Some theologies are based entirely on one or another aspect or view of eschatology.

Yet there have always been believers with little hope (as well as little faith itself). Hope perhaps touches the psychological state of the believer as much as any other element. The personalities in the biblical literature give us ample variety exposing people with such diverse psyches as Elijah and Abraham, Amos and Hosea, Paul and Peter, John and Judas. Their moods, and sometimes linked states of hope, are equally various. It is Paul who gives one of the best records of a paradoxical state of hope and of not-quite-hope at the same time: "We are hard pressed on every side, but not crushed; perplexed, but not in despair; persecuted, but not abandoned; struck down, but not destroyed" (2 Cor. 4:8-9).

As a subjective element, hope, like trust, is difficult to test. It has its expressions deep in the personality of the individual and an hour interview perhaps touched little of it. The general impression, however, was that these men lived with little hope in anything which had a decidedly Christian mark of eschatology. Their fears were related to their most imminent concrete eschatology, the possibility of a nuclear war. They sometimes shrugged it off because of their powerlessness and rarely seemed to relate it to hope in a Christian God. Their "concrete eschatology", although bearing some similarities to the Apocalypse, is not understood in a Christological context. Very few had anything approaching certainty of afterlife as a dimension of hope.

Substantial Evidence of the Elements

What then is the relation between these five elements in potential believers? Is one to be found with the ultimate expression of all five before he can be considered a true Christian believer? Or is one out of five enough? Or can one even be a believer without *any* of these elements characteristically marking his life?

Biblical demands call for an authentic faith. It is not enough to claim faith, there must be genuine qualities in Christian faith. Jesus was always willing to point out both the inauthenticity in quality of religion as opposed to true faith,

as well as the lack of quantity of faith necessary to truly live
the life to which he was calling them.

Although it is difficult or perhaps impossible to define
the exact quantity, or even quality of faith necessary to be
considered a true believer, there must be *substantial* evidence of
faith in the life of the true believer. What one finds in believers in churches is usually an emphasis on one or the other
elements of belief or a combination of certain ones. This makes
for varieties of believers, sometimes claiming that their particular combination is authentic Christian belief while others are
not. The New Testament gives us no lead to do such. There are
varieties of Christian expression stemming from the actual prop-
erties existing in the faith itself. This is true in the early
churches documented in the New Testament as well.

From another context, the Second Letter of Peter describes our elements, as well as the qualities that it wants to
bind together:

> For if you possess these qualities in increasing measure,
> they will keep you from being ineffective and unproductive in
> your knowledge of our Lord Jesus Christ. But if anyone does
> not have them, he is nearsighted and blind, and has forgotten
> that he has been cleansed from his past sins (1:8-9).

Perhaps one could view an increasing measure of the elements of
biblical belief as a marking point between those who only claim
to believe and those who are actually believing, but this is, of
course, not so easy to ascertain in practice.

It is difficult to make any of these elements a priority.
They stand or fall together. One may, of course, make normative
statements from people one knows or from empirical studies, but
this would probably prove problematic for the nature of true
Christian belief.

"Imperceptible Signs"

Ignace Lepp in *Atheism in our Time* gives perhaps a rather
inadequate basis for our purposes but he perceives something of
the essence of Christian belief: "The true believer is distinguished by almost imperceptible signs. There is 'something' in
his way of speaking, of living, of working--and even of sinning--
that does not deceive."[10]

However, what are those "imperceptible signs"? To ask
the question is almost to be impertinent.

On the Borderline. Occasionally in the course of interviewing the men, there was a spark of something which gave hints
of a latent faith. Even though there was little content, no
clear decision (even decision not to follow God's call in one
case), little evidence of more than inherent ethical norms rather
than conscious obedience, and only a faint glimmer of hope, it
still gave one an inkling that "something" was present, yet it
was never quite substantive enough to be considered true faith.

It probably related more to subjective trust than any of the other elements but could not be considered full-blown "trust *in*" Jesus, especially since there was often a conscious desire not to follow God's direction for their lives. In some instances, the "signs" were hidden even from those closest to him and only an outside interviewer seemed able to touch any faith that was buried there. The men's relation to God was a distant nearness, perhaps only a memory that they may have once felt lovingly toward God.

I sometimes wondered whether these signs had more to do with personality than with true faith. These men were a little softer, a little more open, sometimes with scars from wounds distant or near. Perhaps those with hints of "imperceptible signs" were more akin to Tillich's "ultimate concerns" than biblical belief, but it struck an existential note that made the interviewer wonder whether there was more hidden below which had not yet surfaced. Those were the borderline men.

The Border of the Border. Others were on the border of the border. There was not enough evidence of the elements for them to be considered as "near" as the borderline men, but there appeared some impulse to believe--in one instance through a background which made Christianity more understandable and, therefore, possible for the person to respond to the call of Jesus if he desired. These men had a sort of proleptic faith, which could have sprung in action at any point. These few were, evangelistically speaking, ripe for conversion, perhaps more so than those who were actually living on the border.

One man in the believer grouping was a mixture of simple cognitive belief, cultural skepticism, common religion, and un-certainty:

> We've all got to believe that, ain't we? But how do we know it's true? All I know is looking at the television and reading books, don't we? Because we haven't seen a man. But they've seen him, haven't they, in Palestine was it, and Nazareth and Bethlehem. . . . I don't know what to think. I think God's true. Not Jesus [37].

There was little evidence of the elements in this man except some marginal trust and belief content, but he was a prime example of those who are easily influenced by our culture's skepticism, society's uncertainty, and the church's ineptitude.

The Others. It is easier to disbelieve some of the others who called themselves believers, assuming the data is accurate, since there is almost nothing substantitive in the evidence. For them, cognitive belief in a vague conception of God and the historical personage of a man who may even be termed "Son of God" is not the biblical faith for which we are looking. In the majority of the believer self-designation grouping, belief boiled down to a more or less firm conviction that God exists. We must not devalue this in itself, but it cannot be termed Christian belief as we have described it (Cf. James 2:19). Al-though it is difficult to define the precise combination of the elements necessary, we can at least state that cognitive "belief that" alone is not sufficient.

Some of those in the the believer grouping might best be termed "Secular Pharisees." They had a self-professed goodness with a prescribed pattern of living and a vague conceptual belief in God, but their life was ordered without reference to God. The fact that these men had no impression of their own sinfulness--"I always think that I've been on a good path, a good life and I've never done nothing wrong in my opinion" [48]--poses the question whether one can be a believer without even a basic comprehension or appropriation of two central doctrines of Christianity: the universal sinfulness of man with its personal application and the necessary forgiveness of Jesus Christ.

There were also some who had a sort of general trust in God for well-being in life: "He give me a good life up to now and the wife's alright and you know" [45]. Yet beyond the statement this type of trust appeared little different from its secular counterpart of trusting the natural order of things, a deistic Nature.

The Bare Minimum

If we have to choose a bare minimum for Christian belief, we must find some aspect--however tiny--of subjective trust. Ideally, the subjective element should issue from some sort of objective assurance of the historical God-Man, yet it is often the other way round. The subjective actually becomes primary while the content is contingent on the trust step.

Tyrrell says the intellectual dimension of faith "has to do with what we believe as distinguished from the one we believe in. It is subsidiary to the personal dimension inasmuch as we have faith-in-an-assertion because we have faith-in-a-Thou who makes the asssertion."[11] This is true once someone has "seen" the historical Jesus and made a continual response of trust, which moves him back to the content issues of the faith. The content is often previously irrelevant until one is living one's life on the basis of one's relation to another Man.

The Crucial Question

Even after all these attempts to understand the believer self-designation grouping, one must sympathize with Martin and Pluck in their *Young People's Beliefs* study: "The major problem was not which sub-categories of belief to employ but whether to categorise any of it as belief at all."[12]

Conclusions

My judgements on the men may seem harsh, ruling out so many who claim some type of belief from being anything resembling true biblical belief. If this is so, it is also one aspect of the men's own judgement of themselves and more particularly their judgement on others who were like them. They knew few people who they would term true believers and my assumption is that the people who knew them did not count them as one of their "few", rather considered that with regard to believers, there were "none round here".

The general view also ties in with Jesus' own expectation that it is a small number rather than a large number who walk the narrow path of faith toward a small gate. For Jesus and for potential analysts, this is not something to be *guarded* for the exclusive "few" but proclaimed to the larger group for inclusion. Noah was numbered among the few but preached among the many. This "few" mentality, of course, has destructive dangers of self-righteousness and its related family. But neither the potential dangers of the "few" nor the compassion for the "many" give us reason to draw back from the conclusions which are readily apparent.

D. Gerard in his chapter on "Religious Attitudes and Values" explains it this way:

The Christian call to perfection, the very notions of, "holiness" (i.e. difference) and of "church" (i.e. those "called out") which are employed; Christ's own reference to the hostility of the world to His teaching; and the many instances of rejection of its implications in the Gospels suggest that fully committed Christians will be a minority group. Similarly, the notion of Christians as the "light of the world" and the "leaven", by definition, imply "darkness" and "dough". Yet the invitation remains for all mankind. As indicated in the introduction, the level of response and intensity of commitment vary within and between cultures, reactions foreshadowed in the parable of the sower (Mark 4:1-20).[13]

He concludes similarly from an empirical base,

It supports the view that convinced Christians are a minority (less than one-fifth of the population), and raises the possibility that they will become fewer still, particularly as religious faith was not regarded as a priority as far as imparting values to children was concerned. Yet complete rejection of belief in God is confined to a tiny minority--about 2 per cent of the population--and personal attachment to Christian moral teaching remains high, particularly as expressed in the moral commandments of the decalogue. The impression remains of an enduring but partially absorbed Christianity, to use Martin's phrase (Martin 1967), varying in intensity according to age and generation, sex, family background and, for women, occupational status.[14]

Now we return to the Lukan sayings of Jesus from where we began this chapter. We do not have a right to say that when someone is not a part of our particular grouping and yet exhibits evidence of the elements of belief that he is not a believer, that is, "Whoever is not against you is for you." Yet we must call people to a radical belief that shows a clear stance on the side of Jesus. A positive move to follow Jesus must be taken if one is to be considered a believer/disciple. It is not simply those who decide *against* but those who do not decide *for* Christ that are also without this Christian faith. Harvey Cox's maxim, "Not to decide is to decide" corresponds well with Luke's record of the words of Jesus, "He who is not with me is against me."

The wobbly line which I have drawn between belief and unbelief, which tends to divide believers from unbelievers, is not definitive; it may state too much or too little. It is only an attempt to think seriously about the nature of a group of men who live in a very uncertain setting--uncertain of themselves, others, and of God. Yet they are not unusual. They are representatives of humanity today. No one stood out as other than the man next door--if you live in the right area. They are our fathers, our sons, our brothers, our workmates, our repairmen, our friends. In short, they are us.

A Parable of Men and Soils

When trying to draw the lines between various believers and unbelievers, one is drawn to Jesus' own summary of how men respond to his words. It may be worth attempting to reinterpret my fifty men through Jesus' famous parable of the soils.

Most of the men had some contact with the word of God through church or school or hearsay. The words they heard may not have represented the full quality of the Word, but it must be acknowledged that most people hear the Word through distorted words.

The atheists are like the path. They heard the word while they were quite young, but the word took no solid root in them and was taken away completely.

The main group of "believers" are like the rocky places. Most of them had something of belief spring up in them when they were very young, but when they grew up and saw more of life, it died while they still retained the memory that belief had sprung up. This group often lived on the legacy of past belief, thinking that it was still present belief when in reality it did not root deeply enough to survive, live and produce. They "believed" when it was essential or convenient but at other times did not live from a rooted source.

The agnostics are like the soil which has thorns growing along with the grain. They try to let belief and unbelief grow together without making a decision about which to uproot. They live in the uncertain land between belief and unbelief, which makes for an unproductive life. Unbelief, being the stronger, tends to motivate the direction of their lives.

A few of the believers are like the good soil. They hear the Word through the words, accept it and produce a crop of varying quantity and quality.

The "Few True"?

We are perhaps treading on even more dangerous ground when we try to identify the few true believers than when we rule

out those who do not have evidence of biblical belief, but in
order to relate to the concrete nature of these men and address
the frontier, it is a necessary task.

With the considered exception of those on the borderline,
discussed above, only four of the fifty men substantially evidenced the elements for which we were looking. All regularly
attended a church and found some sort of meaning among the other
believers--however variously this was expressed. It was not
presupposed that church attendance would be a necessary quality
of the "few" even taking into account the previously discussed
questions. One who regularly attended church gave no convincing
manifestation of biblical belief. Yet even these few had glaring
contradictions in their lives and theology (compare chapter six).
One man's theology was extremely mixed-up but firmly stated--
along with his certainty about the controlling power of fate.
Another defined being a Christian at least incompletely and to my
way of thinking mistakenly: "Good living, that's a Christian"
[30] while another was not sure about one of the central confessions of Christianity, that Jesus is the Son of God. He did,
however, see Jesus as the focal point of his life.

Even with these major diversions, these men evidenced
substantial elements of biblical belief. For all, God was a high
priority in their thoughts and motivations. They had a trust in
him which, although frail in part, was intrinsic to their lives.
God related to their past, present and future in some ways. They
reported that he did not simply exist "somewhere", but that their
own existence in some way depended on him.

In short there was a mark of genuineness about their
obedience, although imperfect. There was a mark of decisiveness
about their conviction, although some had never believed anything
else. The content of their faith, although sometimes muddled,
included connection to a historical yet exalted Jesus Christ.
Their hope had a positive belief for the future, even though
still troubled about many of the concerns which the other men
faced and still they had few concrete answers. Nevertheless,
overarching all was a trust which manifested some imperceptible
signs.

It is best to let one of the men himself suggest an
aspect of a true believer contrasted with one who merely pro-
fesses:

> I think somebody who lets God play a part in their life would
> be a true believer. It's alright saying you believe in God.
> You say, "I believe in God and that's it," and you go about
> your business and don't give it a second thought. If you are
> a true believer, I suppose you want God to plan your life or
> at least ask him to or whatever [11].

Another Model

In contrast to the catholic model of frontier, Walter
Hollenweger suggests a different model based more on the Reformed
tradition. He suggests that the gospel is like a light with a
clearly identifiable centre. The centre is the historical person
of Jesus Christ of Nazareth. Like the sun, this light is very

far reaching, theoretically into the whole universe. Some people are nearer and some are further from this light and nobody is outside of the range of this light. It is, of course, possible to be so far that the light has very little or almost no influence on the person.

This is a model about the grace and love of God. There are no boundaries to God's grace and love and hence no frontier. Yet there are still those who believe and do not believe, i.e. those who receive and do not receive God's love. The truth is that God's love is important even to those who do not believe because it is reality whether one receives it or not.

PART   THREE

COMMUNICATION:

RELATING   THE   GOSPEL
IN   A   CLIMATE   OF   UNBELIEF

CHAPTER 9

APPROACHING POPULAR UNBELIEVERS TODAY

Prominent Characteristics

When thinking of communicating the gospel of Jesus with these men, one is drawn to several prominent characteristics which must be addressed.

1. **Inability to articulate.** One gets the general impression of the men that they do not know how to talk about their beliefs or lack of beliefs. They talk to no one about these beliefs and so are bereft of words when asked to discuss these matters. They seem to have some vague convictions, but no language with which to express them. Although theirs is, at least in background, an oral culture, religious beliefs are something that they do not--and cannot--articulate.

2. **Uncertainty.** As already stated, among all the groupings there is a general uncertainty about life and in particular about religious beliefs. The agnostics typify this in obvious ways, but the atheists and "believers" express the same uncertainty. Three phrases: "I don't believe. I don't disbelieve" [46]; "I just believe just a certain amount, you know, not a lot" [41]; "'I'm a day-time atheist'" [39] exemplify the uncertainty of agnostic, "believer", and atheist respectively. There are, of course, exceptions, but uncertainty and a characteristically English kind of skepticism is a common denominator of the sample. Gerald Priestland explains that, "We are in a transitional culture which can't make up its mind whether it wants a God or not."[1] "In Durkheim's phrase, '. . . the old Gods are growing old or already dead, and others not yet born.'"[2]

3. **No conception of the transcendence of God.** Most of the men had no conception, much less experience, of the transcendence of God. Their idea of anything beyond human limits was mainly gained through fairy tales, science fiction, or through a child's conception of a Sunday School interpretation of miracles. Fabro suggests of Hobbs something which may be true of many of these men: "For always, side by side with his repeated assertions of God, there is his materialistic sense-perceptionism that does not permit of an ontological and therefore transcendent notion of the Spirit."[3]

4. **Apathy.** Generally there was no interest in things religious. It was marginal or optional to their lives. There was little sign of hostility or antagonism against God or even the church. Their unbelief was of the *apatheia* variety. Colin Campbell notes that "there has been considerable discussion of the tendency for the a-religious response to have gradually supplanted the anti-religious response as the primary form of irreligion in British society."[4]

Harry Blamires makes an important distinction between those who accept the finitude of humanity and those to whom it is not an issue. The former are usually the objects of Christian communication.

What is common to believers, uneasy questioners, and indeed to many thoughtful and earnest unbelievers, is a certain attitude to the finite. Finitude either has been, or is, a problem to them. They may or may not feel themselves to have solved the problem of finitude, but they have all, in some manner and measure, faced it. They may have faced it with the minimum of intellectual activity, or they may have tussled with it in learned researches of the philosophical or scientific order; but they have all alike been aware of it. This awareness may have come upon them as an abstruse intellectual problem or as a crude piece of primitive reasoning-- Who made everything? What happens when we die? On the other hand, it may have come as a barely articulate, largely emotional response to some shattering fact of personal pain or bereavement. It may have come in sorrow or in joy; in response to the death of a child or to the birth of a child; in response to the cruelty of Nature or to the beauty of Nature; to the human refusal of love or to the human granting of love.
What is common to those who lack any interest in religion is a failure to recognize the finitude of the finite, and especially failure to accept man's own finite status for what it is. This failure is the source alike of moral evil and of intellectual confusion. All forms of moral evil have their roots in a tacit denial of human finitude--of the contingent and wholly dependent nature of man's existence. Pride in all it's forms is always an implicit rejection of finitude. Man behaves as though he were not a dependent creature with a limited and temporary existence in a limited and temporal universe.[5]

Blamires continues to specify

that failure to accept the finitude of the finite is the Highest Common Factor in the varied states of mind which breed indifference to the religious issue. The man of learning who is too interested in his specialized research to think about religion, the labourer who is too interested in darts and beer, the clerk who is too interested in football pools, the statesman who is too interested in party policy, the shop-girl who is too interested in films, the company director who is too interested in high finance--they all have this common element in their prevailing mental visions, that man's finitude is not present to them as a realizable fact. This does not mean that they have each and all failed to take a particular philosophical view of the human situation. It means rather that they have failed *in any kind of way* to absorb into their mental systems the sense of humanity's imposed limitations.[6]

Arthur A. Cohen sees unbelief and disbelief as distinct entities with unbelief less prevalent and less serious than disbelief:

> The disbeliever affirms that God no longer counts, that He is ineffective, meaningless, trivial. The cruelty and suffering of history, the solitude and despair of individuality, the anguish of the lonely ego cannot be mitigated by this burned-out God. Disbelief is real and tragic.
>
> Unbelief is rather different and far less terrifying. The unbeliever is simply not interested--God is an amusing or grand hypothesis, but little more. The fact of historical belief is a curiosity to unbelief or else a mere possibility among innumerable possibilities. . . . Unbelief is not the doctrine of significant minds, for serious thinkers know the history of unbelief and the grounds on which it was affirmed sufficiently well to disbelieve. They do not put away belief with boredom and disinterest. No! For the thinker there is belief or disbelief. Unbelief--the condition of being unaware--is the situation of those who do not think deeply at all.[7]

Although we agree with Cohen that in his terminology, unbelief is more casual than disbelief, it is not less serious. The assumptions and presuppositions which fill an age to such an extent as to be unquestionable are worthy of most serious attention and are often very sinister indeed.

Blamires continues to point out the problem of Christian communication to the men in our sample, who are more often in Cohen's "unbelief" category:

> People to whose consciousness the fact of finitude is daily present do not find it easy to conceive of states of mind from which the fact is habitually absent. And this presumably is why Christian apologetic is invariably directed towards the questioners and those vocally hostile to the Faith. For the questioners and the vocal enemies of the Church share with believers this common mental state of sensitivity to the fact of finitude. The indifferent, the uninterested, and the apathetic belong to another category altogether. Since they are habitually unaware of man's finitude, they can hardly be expected to respond to persuasions and exhortations which presuppose a fundamental sensitivity to man's finite status as the common inheritance of all mankind.[8]

There is no opposition from these men. Christianity is acceptable to them *in its place*--which is an arm's length away from them. Of an earlier age, R. J. Campbell concurs, "The ordinary working man is not hostile to Christianity; he just lets it alone, because it seems to have nothing to do with his life."[9] At first sight, what may look promising as an audience ripe to hear the kerygma is in reality a disinterested audience or perhaps no audience at all.

This research does not share the optimism of A. H. Halsey regarding recent values research in Britain, "The evidence of tenacious religious belief, albeit unchurched, constantly renews the promise of religious revival."[10] Nor does it see with a common viewpoint that there is a "terrible spiritual thirst evident." Drought, yes, but there is no general, conscious thirst. If there is going to be a spiritual renewal, these men are going to have to be shaken or shocked out of their apathy by God or man to even look at the Christian message.

5. No desire to believe. One gets the strong impression from the men in this sample that they do not want to believe. We have already quoted David Martin who shows that there is a resistance to making the church more up-to-date and relevant. Although working-class people complain about the church, they expect it to be a foreign institution. A few of the men commented informally after the interview that they would like to see the church become more lively, like the "more baptist, halle- lujah and clap" [9] type of churches. Yet when one gets more specific, one finds that they do not really want to be involved with that either.

One also finds that they can use a profound truth--for example, that people follow God because of God not because of themselves--in order to keep them away from God, i.e. "I'm afraid fate has decreed that I shouldn't take much interest in it [i.e. Christianity]" [22].

Pseudo-religions are used in some cases as a substitute for a more authentic religion. In a few cases, the language of science fiction seemed to be a new secular, religious language. The followers of this "religion" are able to be in touch with sources beyond human perceptions, but it is a finite beyond. This "science fiction religion" gives an apocalyptic taste, but no substantial eschatological nutrition. It is mystery without meaning, apocalyptic without ultimacy, interest without purpose, stimulation without motivation, extraterrestrial without God.

The most pressing question is, "**Why** do they not want to believe?" Three suggestions can be made at this point:

a. They do not want to be faced with their own religious and existential void. Their lack of articulation not only showed that they did not have a language with which to express the convictions which were there, it also revealed a religious and existential void--an unfilled space in their lives. They revealed that they thought little about death, but they also thought little about the meaning of life.

The privitisation of religion keeps this religious void at bay--it can do little harm when it is "in it's place". Not only does this privitisation reduce conflict between people (e.g., "We never really brought it up . . . in case there's a few arguments over it") it also reduces conflict within one's self. It may be that a counselling service which gets people to talk about their hidden religious voids may be as liberating in the religious and human sphere as Freud's psychotherapy was in sexuality.

b.   They have *no* confidence that man can know anything *about* God much less *know* God in any meaningful sense.   Rapid changes in knowledge, truth, wisdom, and ultimately epistemology leave these men with a skepticism which exalts doubt above cer- tainty.   From a more intellectual standpoint, Os Guinness points out that the passwords today are "ambiguity" (never certainty) and "reflection" (never revelation).[11]   These men do not articulate from this perspective, but the loss of certainty in the intellectuals has created a crisis of popular, unspoken epistemology so that our non-intellectuals could never speak of certainty in these matters even if they were privately convinced. Like Levin and the majority of his contemporaries in *Anna Karenin*, they are "in the vaguest position in regard to religion. Believe he could not, and at the same time he had no firm convic- tion that it was all untrue."[12]

c.   They do not want to let go of their newly found autonomous, secular nature.   Since man's autonomous stance is still in its adolescent stage, it does not yet stand with confidence.   These men do not want to let anything get near enough to threaten its permanence.   "I'm not prepared to let myself believe in religion. I think it's a weakness" [49], revealed one young atheist.   They also stand shocked by the absence of God as an explanation, realizing that they are on their own.   Martin Marty comments,

> I think we are overlooking what is still the basic feature of
> the culture of unbelief, and that is the first event in the
> West, the death and disappearance of the God of explanation
> which begins at least with Copernicus. . . . If one should
> make a study of the vast majority of people who have taken on
> the culture of unbelief, I would surmise that this comes
> about, because they have never overcome the shock of the
> disappearance of spatial transcendence when they got a new
> physical world view.[13]

What are the Causes of these Characteristics?

Although very difficult to verify, one has to discover something of the causes of these prominent characteristics in these men. We have to agree with Tracey Early's comment on a USA study: "Unfortunately, however, knowing ever so much about the 'unchurched' does not automatically provide sufficient insight for reaching them."[14]

One may not need to go further than the church and the men to find the causes.   John Mahoney states his "frightening question" for the church:

> And the Values Study with its findings on religious
> values, raises for the Church in an acute form the frighten-
> ing question to what degree the apparently widespread lack of
> belief in the fundamental tenets of Christianity is to be
> viewed as a justified dismissal of a badly conceived and
> wrongly presented portrayal of Christian beliefs, and to what

extent it would be an evasion for the Church to write off
such disbelief as reluctance to accept the personal implications of the Gospel.[15]

Bonhoeffer observes,

The real trouble is that the pure Word of Jesus has been
overlaid with so much human ballast--burdensome rules and
regulations, false hopes and consolations--that it has become
extremely difficult to make a genuine decision for Christ.
. . . It is just not true that every word of criticism
directed against contemporary preaching is a deliberate
rejection of Christ and proceeds from the spirit of Anti-
christ.[16]

The degree of responsibility of the church and of the
"hearers" themselves is difficult to pinpoint. However, the
responsibility of the church is not for the response of the men
but for the portrayal of the gospel. It may well be that most do
not respond to the gospel because they are avoiding the responsibility implications of *metanoia* and so miss its privilege implications as well. However, before we can confirm this, we must be
sure that the gospel is both presented and understood in the
local, cultural dialect where it has a realistic opportunity for
becoming an indigenous (or contextualized) gospel and eventually
an indigenous church and theology.

Charles Kraft lists six propositions regarding indigenous
theology, which are relevant to the sub-culture of these working
class men and which prepare the way for developing an approach
for communicating the Christian gospel:

1. Indigenous theology must be formulated "in the
language of the people," not merely in terms of the words and
sentence structures used, but in terms of culturally founded
conceptual categories and/or imagery.
2. Indigenous theology must also use a methodology, that
is a logic and a set of procedures which make sense in the
cultural context. Think, for instance, of the vast gulf
between the rabbinic argumentation of Paul and the
Hellenistic logic of the patristic theologians (and all of us
since!).
3. Indigenous theology must address itself to issues
that are real to the people for whom it is done. It should
resolutely ignore questions that do not emerge in the
context, so as to avoid irrelevance. . . .
4. Indigenous theology must use literary forms and
genres that are culturally appropriate to the formulation of
the most serious religious discourse. This may be poetry, or
mythology, or some other narrative form, or a "wisdom" type
of text; or it may find appropriate philosophical forms
within the culture. but whatever form it adopts, theology
must always remember its true vocation, to serve the people
of God; and it cannot serve its purpose unless it is
intelligible to them.
5. Indigenous theology must emerge from the community of
believers. As Nyamiti has said, ". . . the making up of
African theology is not the task of theologians or religious
people alone, but all members of the People of God have to

participate in it." . . .
    6. Indigenous theology must be such as to invite the
Christian community to participate actively and integrally in
the life to which it gives verbal formulation.[17]

    Mahoney observes about the church that, "There is no
inherent necessity for its growth throughout the world to be
identical":

Herein lies the challenge to the British churches to discover
a Church for Britain today, not nostalgic for dwindling
heritages but building upon present particular strengths and
aspirations in a society which is also impoverished and
challenged socially, racially, economically and culturally.[18]

    However, it is impossible to find those strengths without
going back to the source of the strengths Himself. Whenever the
church has been successful in any true sense, it has never built
on its human strengths, but on the sole strength of God. The
real challenge for the Church is to rely on that strength while
secondarily discovering the human transactions necessary for
communication.

What is Redeemable in Their Religion?

    A Christian communicator must always look not only for
what is unconverted in a man, but what in practical life and
knowledge is already positive, prepared by God for conversion, or
genuinely good:

In the message of the missionary, whether we are willing to
admit this or not, to be able to make use of the knowledge
which the pagan, unconverted, man already possesses plays a
decisive part. No missionary work has ever been carried on
in any other way, and it can never be done in any other way.
. . .

The non-believing hearer--above all the presumptive hearer--
is already affected by a definite "spirit of the age"; that
is to say, his views of life and its problems, and of his own
nature, are all coloured by a definite outlook which claims
to rival the Christian view of life. The total sinfulness of
the natural man does not consist in the fact that all that he
thinks and believes is false, but in the fact that he is
wholly unable to distinguish between the true and the false
in his understanding of himself or of life. Therefore one to
whom the truth of Christ has been granted has the task of
making this distinction, and in so doing he has to explain
the meaning of the Christian message. And this is the task
of "missionary theology", the positive aspect of Eristics.
The first part of the Pauline statement [2 Cor. 10:4ff.]
described the first, negative, task; the second part describes the positive task. Missionary theology is an intellectual presentation of the Gospel of Jesus Christ, which
starts from the spiritual situation of the hearer, and is
addressed to it.[19]

    Several items inherent in both the Christian gospel and

in these men's approach to life stand out as needing to be exploited in order to move them closer to the gospel:

1. **The privacy of a man and God in prayer.** They are not like the Pharisees of Jesus' day who flaunt their prayers on the street corner. When they pray, they are aware that if it matters at all, it matters between the man and his God alone.

2. **A need for God.** They have existential experience of feeling the need for God when they are in trouble and distress. They often see this as hypocrisy, but at least they know that they turn to God--whoever he is--when there is personal trouble.

3. **An awareness of "sin".** Although they would not term it sin, the atheists and agnostics were more certain of their wrongdoing than those who called themselves believers. Consequently they also felt a need for human forgiveness more often.

4. **An awareness of an unknown God.** In some, there was an awareness of a God who was unknown but present. They are perhaps similar to the fifth century Germanic nations who eventually conquered the Roman Empire. The Germanic nations had a number of gods, which were not all-powerful. But above everything, even above the gods themselves, they saw an unspeakable power. It was even above the gods themselves. It had no real name, but they alluded to it as "giscapu" (the making), "werdendi" (the becoming), or "wurd" (that which became, fate). Over against this fatalism, the Christians declared to the Germanic nations that their God was the God who made everything and there is no unmentionable fate behind him. He is the one who has revealed himself clearly in Jesus Christ. The missionary presentation of the Christians showed that there was a way out of the fatalism of the Germanic nations. Jesus had come to overcome all the powers of fate. He was like one of their military heroes, yet far more powerful. The Germanic people could understand and accept this message.[20]

This kind of redemption of people's present beliefs is useful in proclaiming the gospel of Jesus. Paul also used this method in Acts 17.

The Context of Communication

We have already expressed that true believers are in Peter Berger's term a "cognitive minority." Berger explains that

> whatever the situation may have been in the past, *today* the supernatural as a meaningful reality is absent or remote from the horizons of everyday life of large numbers, very probably of the majority, of people in modern societies, who seem to manage to get along without it quite well. This means to those to whom the supernatural is still, or again, a meaningful reality find themselves in the status of a minority, more precisely a *cognitive minority*--a very

important consequence with very far reaching implications.[21]

Gerhard Szczesny views it from the opposite perspective, "'Unbelief' is no longer the prerogative of an especially enlightened minority. It is the fate of a contemporary type of Western man who may actually be in the majority, or who at any rate is frequently encountered."[22]

Plausibility Structure. Because of the fact that true believers are clearly a minority, for anyone to enter the context which we have described is to find the plausibility for true Christian belief very low indeed.[23] Paul Pruyser adds his point, "Thus in modern times, at least for some people, the negative term "unbelief" is no longer a term of disapprobation. *The vantage point is shifting from belief to unbelief as the natural or normative condition.*"[24] Szczesny sees this as a slow but widening process:

> Though modern "unbelief" is a deep-reaching, collective phenomenon, the process from which it results is still immature, which in turn limits individual apostasy. It is a gradual thing. The transformation of a "believer" into an "unbeliever" does not threaten to upset the individual's psychic equilibrium, as a rule, since it comes about insensibly from a gradual widening of the consciousness. The process is occurring everywhere.[25]

A transcendent conception of God as a meaningful conception in everyday life is far removed from the men in our sample. There is almost no social and psychological structure for belief expressed in any cultural significance. In this context, the question of whether one's conceptions of reality are actually true may well never become an issue. Plausibility upstages credibility.[26]

Both plausibility and credibility are important issues for the church. "Without a feel for the social dimension of believing, the church is like a person paralyzed from the neck down--quite insensible to the further damage being inflicted on her."[27] Without both a credible kerygma and kerygmata, there is no body at all.

Understanding the plausibility context in which one finds oneself is essential for the necessary task of opening the plausibility structure itself to Christian faith.

Choice. Related to the plausibilty structure in which they live is the issue of choice. In many cases, the men felt that they had no choice about their belief or lack of it. Religiously, they were determined by an abstract fatalism. Sociologically, they were controlled by their upbringing and social environment. Their range of choice was limited by the state, the economy, and their class. They may have been pushed about by the gaffer, the management, the social security, or the police (and perhaps even the wife, the children, and the mother-in-law). It is no wonder that so many saw their choices as so limited. One man expressed his powerlessness in doing anything about the problems in the world:

> What could I do? Nothing. It is impossible as an
> individual to do anything, I think. I think that an
> individual has got to be born or, you know, born to become,
> shall I say, famous or in the political world or even things
> like that. You've just got to be born into it. [22]

On the other hand is the overwhelming religious choice
which pluralism brings. Unprepared for this choice, they choose
not to choose: "Pluralisation reduces the necessity of choosing
at all. In other words the extension of choice leads to the
evasion of choice. . . . having too many choices leads either to
a sense of vertigo or to a yawn."[28] Vertigo is frequently the
response of the more articulate classes, while the working class
adopts the "I can't be bothered" yawn, leaving it to the more
intelligent to settle the question. Although even if the
religious question was settled absolutely, in today's context,
these men would still want to preserve their independent
decision--a contradiction of the fact that they cannot decide.
An agnostic responded about his belief in God:

> There again, I don't know. This argument has come up lots of
> times and I've thought about it. And I think to meself,
> "Supposing I'd been born in the jungle and never had seen a
> church, never saw a chap in a dog collar,
> would I have been a less evil man or a better person as a
> Christian, or you know, Christianity?" There's thousands of
> people in the jungle, they worship the sun, the wind, the
> moon. They're not any less evil than the rest of them [22].

There are some areas where the range of choice is very
slim indeed, but the choice is neither as limited as our men's
fatalism would suggest nor as insignificant as their view of
pluralism intimates. It is necessary to find ways of helping the
men to realize that there are some choices which they *can* make.

Approaches in Communication

At least we can be sure that most of the men are not
hearing the message that churches or even individual Christians
are speaking. With only a few possible exceptions, they have no
intention of exploring the meaning of true Christianity any
further. They may be forced to do so by some unexpected
experience in their lives, but it is not on their agenda of
secondary matters, never mind in their diary of ultimate
significance. One waits in vain for them to come to church, much
less to Christ himself.

What way forward is there through the sad revelation of
so much unbelief in these working class men? What approaches
need to be made in order to make the gospel understandable and
relevant?

We will consider it through the four general categories
of doing, thinking, feeling, and articulating. Whatever their

particular emphases, biblical theologies agree that man must be reached at the core of his existence: from where the motivating force for all his action, thought, emotion, and speaking springs--his heart.

It is probably true that the majority of steps toward Christian conversion of others have centred on an approach to the feeling aspect of man. This is, of course, an important *part* of man, but it is only a part. For the men under consideration here, it may be that this is, on the whole, a futile approach. Their perception of this feeling approach is that it is largely a female way in, which leaves them no relevant doorway.

Whether the feeling approach *is* more female is not the point. The crucial issue is the perception of the approach. The fact that churches are more successful in reaching females heightens the fact that men perceive that the message is for females--and children.

In evangelical circles, appeals (as well as explanations and preaching) are mainly given in feeling (as opposed to entire heart) terms, which men especially find easy to discard as irrelevant. Although not highly emotional in "the appeal" (using only silence and no music in the "decision time"), the *Mission: England* stadium meetings give evidence of the response of women to the approach. Of the 26,181 people coming forward to make some kind of inquiry or decision at the Birmingham meetings (30 June to 7 July, 1984), 62.2% were women and 37.8% were men.[29] Since there is evidence that women in Western culture respond more often and highly to anything religious, our approach needs to be considered with a bias toward men.

Men indeed have feelings, which need to be captivated, channeled, and converted but in British culture these may be better reached indirectly rather than directly. Men will need to expand their openness to expressing feelings, but it may not be a primary way to reach them. On the other side of conversion, sorting out their feelings will be extremely relevant and, for some, tapping their present feelings will be central to reaching them, but many churches appear to have overemphasized the ability of men to relate initially on the feeling basis.

When men are reached largely through feeling approaches, it often paralyses their further witness to other men because they have no categories through which to explain their experiences or feelings. Their speechlessness surfaces and reveals unexplainable contradictions with the world in which they live. Doubt sets in and what began as faith begins to fade.

If, however, communication of the gospel is initiated in a way which touches their normal cultural categories of doing and thinking, the feeling channel is also likely to be opened. On acting out and considering the content of faith, they are then more likely to express their faith to other men (and women) in terms which can be further contextualized. Doing and thinking are two essential poles of life, which may be relevant starting points to discover the meaning of Life.

Doing

Walter Hollenweger tells the story of a church building burning down in a mining village in Wales. Very quickly, the whole community rallied round. The men gave their work at great sacrifice and the church was built again. All the men (and women) came for the church dedication, then they stayed away from church again. The vicar asked them, "Why don't you come to church since you were so involved before?" They replied, "We have done our job. The church is standing there. It doesn't need us. If it burns down again, we will come again." Previously, the men were able to do something. They spoke with their hands.

This story could be told over and over again in different contexts. It is typified by one man in our sample who had *never* been to a church service in his life except for rites of passage. Speaking for others, he said, "We all believe but we don't participate" [32]. The real evangelist must find a way for people to respond to the invitation of the gospel by doing something.

Jesus formed a group of men into a band of disciples by asking them to do something. "Come and follow me," were his words to working men. They actually had to leave their boats, their collaborating tax collecting tables, their insurrectionist political action, and do something physical to show their discipleship.

In all the gospels Jesus is recorded asking people to do something physical preceding many of the miraculous events. The Gospel of John represents this well, "Go, wash in the pool of Siloam" (John 9:11); "Fill the jars with water" (John 2:7); "Get up! Pick up your mat and walk" (5:8); "Take away the stone" (11:38). Jesus did not find it difficult to ask people to do something even though they were not believers in him. He often asked them to do things in order that they might learn, expand, and eventually put their trust in him. He did not ask them to come to meetings, but to act in some way relevant to learning. Discipleship was a self-perpetuating relationship. A disciple was a learner who passed on what he learned, often by doing.

With Jesus and the early church, repentance and baptism were actions more than spiritual conceptions. Repentance often meant restitution for wrongdoing, e.g. Zacchaeus (Luke 19:8) and the soldiers who came to John (Luke 3:12-14). It encompassed a turn around in the whole of life. If repentance was man's action to reverse all aspects of everyday life, baptism was God's action in a microcosm. Baptism, as seen in the whole New Testament, is not merely a spiritual event robbed of its physical power, nor is it a ceremonial sacrament robbed of it's down-to-earth action. The action of the baptized here is not the dominant feature, rather the baptized is acted upon. His only action is his openness to receive what God does in baptism.

Participating in the Story. Evangelism may also want to ask men to participate in the telling of the gospel itself. In the synoptics, Jesus asks his disciples to feed the hungry multitude (Matt. 14:16 and parallels). Their awareness of their inability to do something along with their participation in the miracle itself helped Jesus to begin to reveal who he was.

The things unbelieving men are asked to do by Christians have often not been helpful in telling the story or moving men to faith. Men have not been significantly reached by the old voluntary association methods. We have already seen that the working class do not readily involve themselves in these voluntary associations. Added to this is the fact that many of the voluntary association chores have appealed more to women than to men, and to middle and upper class women rather than working class women. Even so, leading Scouts, teaching Sunday School, helping with the Boys' Brigade, or organizing fund raising events for charity does not give much evidence of helping men to explore unknown areas of faith. It is also true that Jesus did not generally ask men to be leaders and teachers, but to learn how to be followers.

Roman Catholics have created their own social club networks embodying some working class sports and pastimes, yet these appear to provide more of an ethnic identity than ways for men to experience the nature of true faith in shared action. In some cases, the strength of the ethnic identity is a hindrance rather than a help to the gospel.

The church's task is to discover a variety of meaningful expressions of the gospel that involve learning by doing. I suggest four ways for consideration, which may have various degrees of relevance to some working class men.

1. **Creative projects like building, maintaining, etc.** In construction and maintenance projects at church buildings and in other good causes, men may have opportunity to meet the believers they say they do not know. Ways of incorporating learning activities must also be explored lest it end up only a building and not a church as in the example above. Without stretching beyond natural bounds, one may encourage the men to think about the significance of what they do and feel. Biblical ideas, which could be explored, are activity concepts like building (e.g. Nehemiah, Peter) and body (Paul), and the nature of ministry and giving in the context of what the men are doing. It may also be possible to explore areas of wonder like baptism and communion. The cross and other symbols which might be in the church building may prompt their questioning if the work project is based there. Many of these opportunities will come spontaneously when believers are aware of their role in the gospel, but planning may be essential in many cases.

2. **Drama, role plays, music, and dance.**[30] In a secular, working class setting, this may have more appeal than one might expect. The challenge to act out and learn something while doing it may be just the stimulation that some men need. Homes should be considered as a possible venue, especially for capturing initial interest. It would also make an excellent place for discussion about the meaning of the play or music. It goes without saying that the media used must have relevant cultural content. It is essential that the communicators have some clear

experience and teaching goals in mind lest the experience be wasted.

   3. Prayer. Since many of the men prayed at some time or other in their lives, experimentation with prayer by unbelievers should be encouraged. As one of the areas where these men ventured closest to faith, prayer could be approached from the angle, "One of the things most of us do at some points in our lives is to pray. Why can't we do it more often and with more benefits for us and our friends?"

   Prayer is one of the areas with regard to which the men in our sample were the most positive and yet their view of prayer was incomplete and misinformed.[31] They need help in exploring its full potential. Prayer in stress was the most often reported reason for prayer, which leaves the doorway open in those difficult times as well as expanding the reasons for prayer. Helping them to feel unashamed of their prayer would be a good service in itself.

   In an extremely stressful environment, Bonhoeffer speaks for unbelievers in their need of prayer and Christians for lack of response to that need:

> But when all's said and done, it is true that it needs trouble to drive us to prayer, though every time I feel it is something to be ashamed of. Perhaps that is because up to now I have not had a chance of putting in a Christian word at such a moment. As we were all lying on the floor yesterday, someone muttered, "O God, O God"--he is normally a frivolous sort of chap--but I couldn't bring myself to offer him any Christian encouragement or comfort.[32]

   In situations where reconciliation is needed, prayer together could break open the way. This has proved especially helpful in Northern Ireland and in other places where hatred is less dramatic. Prayer as a way of letting God touch the human and bring peace may be an important step in the conversion process. Physical and emotional healing may also be areas for prayer with and for non-Christians. In these prayer experiences one could also gradually add group prayer to their private conception of prayer.

   Prayer is usually seen by believers as exclusively for themselves. Its already widespread usage should cause us to reconsider prayer as an evangelistic method. It is important, however, that it includes elements of doing and is not just talking. Touching, the next method, may also be considered as an important aspect of prayer which Jesus, the disciples, and Christians throughout the centuries have used. Perhaps, if prompted, some men would echo another disciple's words, "Lord, teach us to pray." However, we must also consider Paul's question: "How can they call on the one they have not believed in?" (Rom. 10:14). "Unbelieving prayer" may have limited efficacy, so this type of prayer must be used to tap into what little belief they might have and expand it.

4. Touching. Although people often want to touch and be touched, there is resistance in British culture to touching another person. This is especially so for men. Incorporated with other methods, touching may be seen as a way of sharing love and conveying the power of God among those who do not believe. Touching is also an indirect way to open up the area of feeling, which eventually must also learn to trust. It should be noted that there is a sort of acceptable male touching in the football crowd, the pub, etc., which should not be ignored in this consideration.[33]

Thinking

Working class men like to think through what they believe and act on. They are not, of course, trained in the sophisticated disciplines of logic, philosophy, and science, but they have their own methods of thinking things through.

The problem is that the issue of belief, for reasons stated above, is no longer considered a worthwhile object to think about. For the men in our sample, the Bible was mainly discarded as a child. How can one encourage men to use this most important category of life, thinking, to look at Christian belief?

Bible studies, as traditionally conceived and practiced by the church, are attended only by the committed, quite interested, or argumentative. The bulk of the men in our sample would not be enticed to a Bible study. A few might consider learning something about certain topics from the Bible in the non-threatening environment of their own home; this should not be ignored.

One of the important aspects of collecting the data for the research was the effect that the interviews seemed to have on the men themselves. They prompted the men to reflect on questions which they had not considered for many years or had never considered. The interviews themselves became an experiment in the aspect of pre-evangelism which gets men to consider their own lives and its relation to faith.

"You do ask some good questions" [7], was one man's thanks for helping him to consider important issues. Although there were exceptions, many seemed to genuinely enjoy the stimulation of their thinking. The fact that the interviews were conducted in ostensible neutrality, wanting only to hear from them, accentuated the necessity for them to come to terms with their own belief and unbelief. In some cases, the interviews may have changed their self-understanding.

One man who called himself an "average Christian" volunteered, "I haven't thought about these things for a long time." Exploring his reaction, he was asked, "How has it affected your thinking about these things?" He replied, "It hasn't really. It's just reminded me that I haven't thought." This cautions us that helping men to reflect is not a complete answer.

Even so, true evangelism must explore men's capacity for evaluation of "Who do you say I am?" (Matt. 16:15). Bonhoeffer

explains the ministry of listening in a way that is applied to
unbelievers as well as Christians:

> The first service that one owes to others . . . consists in
> listening to them.   Just as love of God begins with listening
> to His word, so the beginning of love for the brethren is
> learning to listen to them. . . .
>
> Many people are looking for an ear that will listen.   They do
> not find it among Christians, because these Christians are
> talking when they should be listening.   But he who can no
> longer listen to his brother will soon be no longer listening
> to God, either; he will be doing nothing but prattling in the
> presence of God, too. . . .
>
> Christians have forgotten that the ministry of listening has
> been committed to them by Him who is Himself the great
> listener and whose work they should share.   We should listen
> with the ears of God that we may speak the Word of God.[34]

One man could not have understood the biblical conception
of preaching when he used the secular term, derived from an
outsider's perspective of the church: "You always get the impression that they are preaching all the time to you" [40].   He
points out that the church has often forgotten that listening is
the prelude to speaking our own faith.   Brunner sees it in the
form of a conversation:

> Missionary theology takes the form of a conversation between
> a Christian believer and an unbeliever.   The Christian be-
> liever enters into the questions raised by the unbeliever; he
> gives full weight to all the truth and insight the unbeliever
> already possesses.   But he shows also how his knowledge, and
> therefore also his questions, ignore the very thing which
> brings light and true knowledge.   Missionary theology is, so
> to say, pastoral work in the form of reflection, just as
> dogmatics is witness in the form of reflection.[35]

Articulating

Not only was the interview process (and perhaps what
followed) important in helping them reflect, it was also important in helping them to articulate their beliefs and doubts.   The
speechlessness of these men has been recorded above.   These men
live in what could be described as a post-literary, audio-visual
culture.   They still value their oral culture, but opportunities
seem to be limited by the prominence of external input like
television and stereo in their homes and even in the pubs and
clubs they used to visit in order to talk.   One man feels that
his work environment has affected his articulation.   Speaking of
the interview, he said:

> I'm enjoying it.   You see, when I had a better job, I used to
> like talking.   I used to speak a darn sight better.   But when
> you get back to transport and things like that, factory work,
> you tend to do as the Romans do and you forget.   In actual
> fact, you forget how to talk properly and think properly,
> educationally, or what you would like to think about it

clearly and define that thought as you would have   wanted
to do [22].

There is no desire here to bring these men to the middle
and upper classes' type of articulation, but these men find it
difficult to talk about beliefs even in their own language. The
vocabulary is often absent. One of the tasks of pre-evangelism,
then, is to discover ways to help men to put their thoughts,
feelings, hopes, and fears into a Christian context. What ways
can we suggest?

1.   **Dialoguing beyond their own framework.**[36]   As with
most social groupings, these men do not often talk beyond their
own framework. Like the classes "above" them, they are locked
within only to cast a fleeting scornful look outside to other
frameworks of thought. They do not naturally meet true believers
and the plausibility for them becoming such themselves is, by
their own admission, very low. The shift to becoming a true
believer is almost too great for them to contemplate, much less
actually make. On that basis, there must be consciously motivated importation of other Christian frameworks into their setting.[37]

The environment for dialogue must be in their own cultural setting, while the range of Christian thinking must be
conspicuously different from their own perspectives. If actually
motivated to do so, the men would have both something to give to
and something to receive from dialogue with true believers.

2.   **Bible Study.** As already mentioned, motivation to
traditional Bible study will be very difficult indeed. However,
it is essential for these men that they return to the primary
source of Christianity. Ways must be found to look at the biblical content in a way consistent with their oral culture's thought
forms.

Their preconceptions will in many cases be a hindrance to
hearing the biblical witness, but many of their objections would
be silenced if they were to hear first hand the authenticity of
the earliest Christian records. It would also be a benefit to
the church to have the men's fresh perspectives on primitive
faith.

3.   **Liturgy.** Liturgy incorporates something to do as
well as something for them to articulate. Evangelical churches,
with their emphasis on the spiritual, have often missed out the
rich experience of the action of the more liturgical churches--
although it is important to note that it is the meaningless
liturgy about which the men most often object.[38]   This prompts
the necessity for exploration of new forms of "articulate action"
or "active articulation". In an article on "Experimental forms
of Worship", W. J. Hollenweger states, "The celebration we have
in mind cannot happen unless liturgy becomes an event of the
whole people of God and even of those who believe they do not
believe."[39]

a. Prayers. Prayers said together in groups must strike a cord of meaning and cultural identification for these men. They need to be able to say, "That's what I want to say," when they hear a prayer. It is essential that the men can recognize their own hopes, fears, failures, beliefs, and doubts both in liturgical set prayers and spontaneous prayers. The language must be simple yet not degrading their natural intelligence. There must be no sense that formal education or enunciation is a necessary qualification for spontaneous prayer. Working class men who pray in church services often help to bring a fresh wind of the Spirit into shared prayer.

b. Confessions of faith. Again it is important to have both set liturgical confessions and spontaneous ones. The record of a fisherman asked by Jesus to make his confession (Mark 8:27-30 and parallels) gives us an example to follow in encouraging the men to make their own confessions of faith.

Tilman Winkler suggest that the "good man" is the nearest thing to a confession for his working class with latent religious belief.[40] This is worth consideration as it has some precedent in the gospels and invokes trust in the working-class man. A good man, for him, is one that will stand with you in a time of trouble. Whether one can fill this term with the full christo-logical content necessary to distinguish *the* Good Man as the God-Man is not certain. The fact that some use, "Jesus is *only* a good man" as a popular excuse to avoid the claims of Jesus also raises doubts,[41] but this may be a middle-class excuse.

A number of early confessions of faith were coined partly to combat heresies of the day, e.g. "Jesus has come *in the flesh*" (1 John 4:2) as a wedge against docetism. For our working men, we would suggest for consideration a confession such as, "Everyday Life-Giver", which would give Jesus a concrete relevance as well as touching on the divine and human interplays. The words have no particularly negative religious categories and they could help to bring religious language out of its own separate class. From a quite different perspective, one of our men termed Jesus, "God of all G(g)ods" [28], which should also be given considera-tion as worthy of wider usage.

Nothing, however, can replace those classic biblical confessions, "Lord," "Son of God," and even "Christ/Messiah," the latter of which keeps the continuity with a God who promises and keeps his promise. Additional confessions, however, must be discovered by the men in a dialogical relationship between the biblical records, the world in which they live, and the object of the confession himself. As men become believers in Jesus, they will formulate these confessions from within the community of believers themselves; they cannot be imposed from outside. Charles Kraft quotes Daniel Von Allmen regarding indigenous the-ology:

> Any authentic theology must start ever anew from the focal point of the faith, which is the confession of the Lord Jesus Christ who died and was raised for us; and it must be built or re-built (whether in Africa or in Europe) in a way which is both faithful to the inner thrust of the Christian

revelation and also in harmony with the mentality of the person who formulates it. There is no short cut to be found by simply adapting an existing theology to contemporary or local taste.

Kraft continues, "If we are to be true to the dynamism of the early days of the Christian movement, we should be involved both in producing new theological formulations and in encouraging others to do the same."[42]

     c. We must also leave room for the enjoyment of "spontaneous liturgies", which include homespun stories from the men's own experience often containing profound truth. Testimony will be another aid to articulate what they believe and disbelieve.

     d. Hymns in relevant language and music which can clearly communicate to unbelievers, who the believers are worshipping and why, are also important. However, just because hymns are modern in words or music is no certainty that there is communication to unbelievers. (This attempt to clarify will do no harm to believers in working out their own theology!)

     e. Silence is an untapped area of importance for these men in their world of noisy homes, factories, transport, and social life. Providing a place of quiet could be a service which would allow them to discover something both of God and themselves never before touched. The men, indeed, could theoretically be quiet at home, but just like much of their prayer, this does not appear to happen very often. It is also true that silence has a dimension in community which it does not exhibit in solitude (Rev. 8:1). Perhaps only when there is silence within will they be able to speak without.

    4. Individual and group discussions in homes. We must not fail to mention the need for meeting a man on his own turf at home. Because of the inability to articulate and the accompanying inferiority, it may be best to talk initially on an individual level. The peer pressure in the plausibility structure may make groups more difficult--at least initially. Even so, groups should not be ignored since social links can often be a means to spreading both the word and practice of the gospel. There may already exist informal groups free enough to talk together, which can then be networked for expansion.

    Besides enabling the men to articulate their beliefs, they also need to learn another lost art, that of listening. They should learn from the example of the one aiding their own articulation, to listen even as they have been listened to. Even more they need to know the theological basis from which he speaks. As Bonhoeffer says it, "The basis upon which Christians can speak to [others] is that each knows the other as a sinner."[43] This will probably be shown more in the nature of the interaction than in the ensuing explanation.

Audio-visual Media

The men receive much of their information about the Bible and the present day church from the television. Although their information is often mistaken, theoretically the audio-visual should be helpful on the informational level and may also stimulate some feeling. However, it is largely impotent to touch the two areas of reflection and action which we find so necessary to stimulate, create, or mobilize faith in these men. This media also appears to militate against helping them to articulate their beliefs and concerns.

On a deeper level, one wonders whether the audio-visual media has the capacity to communicate a message of faith, which has a personal--not limited to private--essence. God himself did not take the audio visual option of dramatic event, e.g. earthquake, wind, or fire (although these are used elsewhere) for his word in the last days (Hebrews 1:1-2). Rather the Person is the chosen media for the personal message, which addresses individuals as well as societies and institutions. Although it can move us to tears or cause us to laugh hysterically, neither two-dimensional nor 3-D film have demonstrated themselves capable of communicating the fully personal dimension of the Christian faith.

It is evangelicals in the USA who exploit television and radio to the full extent of the freedom of their airwaves. However, because of the nature of the media itself, they often end up exporting an even more privitised version of faith than they would wish to those on the other side of the screen and speaker because of the nature of the media itself.

The audio-visual media may be considered as an aid in changing the plausibility structure of belief and conveying facts, but it is probably unrealistic, because of the media's limited nature, to expect it to "do the work of an evangelist" (2 Timothy 4:5).

Conclusions

We must not minimize the importance of those who will discover ways of tapping the valuable yet unused ranges of emotion--good and bad--in these men. The British popular press evokes emotion with its huge headlines, which draw men and women to read the appertaining scandal. The emotions which it stirs, however, are often the emotions of confrontation and controversy. Christian liturgy and approach in communicating the gospel may need to tap into the limitless emotional reserves of those it seeks to influence, but it must stimulate the fruit of the Spirit rather than the works of the flesh (Galatians 5). Yet even the uncovering of evil emotions--inherent in all people--need to be brought to the surface by the Spirit in order to be touched by God.

The gospel must touch all the areas of a man's life, but, initially, helping the man to articulate where he stands and helping him to learn and experience through doing and thinking may have priority over the much used area of feeling, which has been largely unsuccessful with the working classes. Certain groups of Christians will be more at home with one approach than with others and so are likely to reach a certain group of men more easily.

J. Russell Hale sketches the "Word and Witness" programme of the Lutheran Church in America and mentions that

Austin Shell, a professor of pastoral care and writer of one of the texts used by the laity, has developed the rationale for communication. He speaks of the need to bring "three stories" together--the story of the other person, the correlating story of the evangelist, and the "intersecting" story of how God deals with his people in history.[44]

These stories are best approached through the general areas of articulating, thinking, doing, and feeling, which, of course, does not leave many areas remaining.

All the areas of approach must be considered with fresh imagination. These are men who think that they have heard the message of Jesus and are largely apathetic. Os Guinness sketches G. K. Chesterton's approach as an apologist:

The problem he faced as an apologist was one of apathy and prejudice. He therefore contended that, whereas the best judge of Christianity is a Christian, and the next best judge would be someone sufficiently different, like a Confucian, the worst judge of all is the most ready with his judgements: "the ill-educated Christian now turning gradually into the ill-tempered agnostic . . . blighted with a sort of hereditary boredom with he knows not what, and already weary of hearing what he has never heard". Chesterton's solution to this problem was to "invoke the most wild and soaring sort of imagination", and his intention was deliberate. "In order to strike . . . the note of impartiality, it is necessary to touch the world of novelty. I mean that in one sense we see things fairly when we see things first."[45]

Our task in approaching these men is to get them to see Christianity (as if?) for the first time.

The Challenge and Strategic Significance of Reaching Men

Although the church is largely male dominated in hierarchy and clergy, her body is more female than male. Although it may sound philosophically sexist, it is empirically true that more women than men are involved in the church. Perhaps it is not accidental that the church is usually termed "she".

Those of us in the church would in no way decry the accomplishments of women or wish for less of them. On a human level, there would be little or no church without them. But whether one likes it or not, reaching men with the gospel is a crucial challenge for today's church. They are the most unbelieving and irreligious. Because of that, when vitally touched by the gospel of Jesus, their changes may be the more far-reaching.

It is my general impression that there is also a strategic significance in reaching men with the gospel of Christ. Although the influence of women is widening rapidly into areas once entirely male dominated, the influence of men is still wider in scope than that of women. It is my impression that men are more likely to influence other men and often women as well. David Martin sees it as an "almost universal fact that in modern industrial societies religious practice is largely transmitted through the female",[46] but present religious practice and belief shows the failure of that transmission, "Hence, the religious male may easily be accused of effeminancy."[47]

With plenty of exceptions, it has become almost a general rule that if a man becomes a believer, his wife will follow, but it does not work the other way around. Men--however weak or silent--remain a central direction agency in the British nuclear family. Although the maternal influence is in many ways the greater and does pass down the religious beliefs, it is most likely that fathers have a greater influence in the absence of religious beliefs (at least in sons).

Without in any way disregarding women in the evangelistic enterprise, it is crucial that the weight of attention shift toward the unreached men. In a day of economic uncertainty which especially effects the working class men, they should be a prime consideration for the direction of witness and mission.

Essential Content to Communicate

Via Mahoney and Tiller, we find some helpful words of Jürgen Moltmann to the effect that "the church always belongs *within the context of the world* . . . but the context is not *the text*, and we must never allow it to become so. The church's context is society. But its text is the Gospel of Jesus Christ."[48] We have already attempted to describe the context in which this gospel is lived and spoken. What could be given as the necessary elements of this "text" which is to be spoken whenever there is opportunity?

1. Christ as Central

Our data has already showed that those men who did believe in God mainly had a very vague conception of him. Central for our men's understanding of God is a clearly proclaimed message of Jesus as Christ, Lord, and Son of God. He is the concrete revelation necessary to explain to them who God is.

Following Pauline and Hellenistic Christianity, "Christianity is Christ" is W. H. Griffith Thomas' way of proclaiming the centrality of Christ to Christianity. He quotes F. J. Foakes-Jackson to emphasize his point:

The relation of Jesus Christ to Christianity differs entirely from that of all other founders towards the religions or philosophies which bear their names. Platonism, for example, may be defined as a method of philosophic thought from Plato; Mohammedanism as the belief in the revelation vouchsafed to Mohammed; Buddhism as the following of principles enunciated by Buddha. But Christianity is in essence adherence to the Person of Jesus Christ.[49]

Following James Dunn, as quoted in chapter three, the Christ who is confessed must have an unbroken connection between the earthly Jesus and exalted Christ. Without this connection of who Jesus *is*, it cannot be the Christ of Christian faith.

2. Universal Sinfulness of Man and the Offer of Forgiveness in Christ

In the preaching of the early evangelists recorded in Acts, there is a strong emphasis on the universal sinfulness of man and its accompanying judgement by God (Acts 10:42). This is especially relevant for a high proportion of men in our sample who had no idea of their own wrongdoing. Many who were painfully aware of their own wrongdoing had not deepened this conception to personal sin.

These men do not hear Puritan style hell-fire sermons, but this is a mixture of blessing and bane. Hearing a message of forgiveness becomes irrelevant until one at least acknowledges one's own sin. The need for forgiveness is foreign to him, like trying to sell a scientific laboratory to a bushman. It is as contrived, yet as common, as the modern selling institution trying to create a non-existing market for a product. The Pauline pattern derived from Romans is to begin with expounding God's wrath toward man's sinfulness, *then* he moves to the promises of God.

C. S. Lewis speaks of the moment that "Christianity begins to talk":

Christianity tells people to repent and promises them forgiveness. It therefore has nothing (as far as I know) to say to people who do not know they have done anything to repent of and who do not feel that they need any forgiveness. It is after you have realised that there is a real Moral Law, and a Power behind the law, and that you have broken that law and put yourself wrong with that Power--it is after all this, and not a moment sooner that Christianity begins to talk. When you know you are sick, you will listen to the doctor. . . . Of course, I quite agree that the Christian religion is, in the long run, a thing of unspeakable comfort. But it does not begin in comfort; it begins in the dismay I have been describing, and it is no use at all trying to go on to that comfort without first going through that dismay. In religion, as in war and everything else, comfort is the one thing you cannot get by looking for it. If you look for truth, you may find comfort in the end: If you look for comfort you will not get either comfort or truth--only soft soap and wishful thinking to begin with and, in the end, despair.[50]

Jesus, however, does not usually approach men initially with their sin. He simply approaches them. His presence--and radical difference--makes men aware of their own sin in the same way in which the Prophet Isaiah knows his uncleanness when he encounters the presence of God (Isaiah 6:5).

Although there were plenty of self-righteous people in Jesus' day, his audience was mainly steeped in the Law. When people know the Law, they are aware of their own sin; it is only a question of whether or how to deal with it. Our men, however, do not know the Law and are steeped in a progress myth which only believes in mistakes and perhaps a structural evil for which they are not responsible. How to raise the awareness of the unbeliever's sin is a challenge for today's sharing believers. A necessary precondition of hearing the joyous Word is some understanding--however it comes--of personal sin. Jesus, of course, had a forerunner preaching repentance in order to prepare his way to preach the love of God. It should be noted, however, that Jesus also preached repentance combining it with need for belief: "Repent and believe the good news" (Mark 1:15).

3. Promises of God

God's open offer of forgiveness (and it's fuller statement, salvation) to any who will receive it naturally follows the words of sin and forgiveness. Our men have shown, not surprisingly, that they have no conception of the biblical idea of being saved (note chapter six). There is a great need for translation and incarnation in order to communicate the idea of forgiveness and salvation which is dependent on God alone.

4. Response of Men

The message of Christ is good news, but it is mainly--if not exclusively--to those who believe. The Johaninne Christ (John 3:14-21) and Paul (Romans 1:16-17) especially emphasize this connection between belief and escape from condemnation.

Throughout the biblical literature, God requires a response to his message. The first Lukan sermon in Acts requires this response, "Repent and be baptized, every one of you, in the name of Jesus Christ so that your sins may be forgiven. And you will receive the gift of the Holy Spirit" (Acts 2:38). A necessary element in the content of the gospel message is that the hearers know the necessity of making a response to God.

The Sermons in Acts

Luke highlights these four elements throughout the sermons which he records in the Acts of the Apostles. The hearers of the sermons are responsible for the death of Jesus (3:13-15a; 4:10-11; 5:30; 7:52, 10:39; 13:27-29). It is their sin which crucified him, often followed by showing the contrast with God's validation of Jesus in raising him to life again (3:15b, 5:30-31,

13:30-37). There is a promise of forgiveness of sin, a coming time of refreshing, and the gift of the Holy Spirit (2:38; 3:16; 9:17; 10:43; 13:38-39; 19:2) for those who respond by faith, repentance, and baptism (2:38,41; 4:4; 5:14; 6:7; 8:12-14; 8:37-38; 9:18; 9:42; 10:46-48; 11:21; 13:12; 13:48; 14:1; 16:15; 16:33-34; 17:4; 17:12; 17:34; 18:8; 19:5-6).

John Stott compares early sermons recorded in Acts with each other and with the beginning of 1 Corinthians 15, showing, in slightly different terms than our own, that the good news contained at least the following four elements: the gospel events, the gospel witnesses, the gospel promises, the gospel demands.[51]

A message clearly proclaimed to these men is important to get rid of ignorance (*agnoia*) and declare all excuses invalid (3:17; 17:30; cf. also Romans 2:1ff). The kerygmata, besides taking note of the kerygma, must be declared in an understood context which we have already discussed.

Word and Event

Another way of looking at both the message and the proclamation, the kerygma and kerygmata, is through the terms, "word" and, "event". Both were essential in the early church's proclamation of Jesus. The Word is Event told while Event is the Word lived. Word needs Event to demonstrate it. Event needs Word to explain it.

The prologue to John's gospel aptly demonstrates the christological example. Jesus is the Word (1:1) who becomes Event (1:14). Jesus teaches by sermons, parables, and reprimand--using words. He also lives with authority: a sinless life, healing, loving--using events. *The* Word uses words. *The* Event lives events.

Matthew records Jesus sending out the twelve disciples to the lost sheep of Israel. They are to follow the same pattern Jesus used: "As you go, preach this message: 'The kingdom of heaven is near'" (10:7)--Word. "Heal the sick, raise the dead, cleanse those who have leprosy, drive out demons. Freely you have received, freely give" (10:8)--Event.

A later apostle, Paul, asks others to follow his example as he follows the example of Christ (1 Corinthians 11:1). Although the passage is in the context of events, it also relates to words. Paul lived the Word and knew the Event. In the *Acts of the Apostles*, "*word*" is used over fifty times.

Matthew's last recorded words of Jesus (28:18-20) are the commission of mission, which can be seen in terms of word and event:

Go	Event
Make disciples	Word & Event
Baptising	Event
Teaching	Word
Obey	Event
Commanded	Word
I will be with you always	EVENT

John's record of Jesus' commission bases the sending of disciples by Jesus on the sending of the Son by the Father. The commission to witness by (and to) Word is given with the promise of the Event of the Holy Spirit (20:21-22).

The content of the message is not only expressed in both words and event, it *is* Word and Event. This requires that both the voices and the lives of witnesses be authentic.

Clyde Fant, an expert in pulpit preaching, draws the distinction between a voice and the Word:

The Scripture tells us that John the Baptist was a voice crying in the wilderness. His voice was as unique as his ministry. He preached the gospel of the preparation of Christ. In one sense, the ministry of John is without parallel in either the Old or the New Testament. His voice was crying out in a real wilderness between the prophetic age which was past and the gospel age that was to be. But in another sense, the authentic voices in each period of Christian history always prepare the way for the coming of Christ. Their message is essentially the same, "Behold, the Lamb of God." And eventually every preacher must also say to his disciples as did John, "He must increase but I must decrease."

But long after the authentic, original voices have left the scene of their own particular ministry, the wilderness is filled with echoes. Crying in the wilderness is no special virtue, but that fact always seems to elude the inevitable imitators of notable Christian voices.

The echoes of the heralds of God always miss their message as thoroughly as they copy their style. The echoes of great preaching merely duplicate the outward mannerisms of the original voices of a preceding age of Christian preaching without the slightest notion of the true sense of the power of preaching. They are like Delilah plying Samson to learn the secret of his strength. They always imagine that some external characteristic is responsible for God's power. And so they do the most ridiculous things in a futile attempt to capture the secret for themselves, little suspecting that without the Spirit of God they are powerless indeed.

Every age of Christian preaching produces a hundred echoes for every true voice. The true voices of preaching hear the word of God and try to speak it. The echoes hear the words of these preachers and try to imitate them. The voices listen to the cry of the multitudes and try to respond to it. The echoes listen to the applause of the crowd and seek to gain that. The voices clearly point the way of Christ, but no one can track an echo. It is now here, now there. The true voices of proclamation confront culture with the gospel while caring deeply for both. The empty echoes lose the gospel in culture while caring truly for neither.[52]

This brings us to the next point regarding the interrelationship of Christ and culture.

Christ and Culture

H. Richard Niebuhr gives us a classic exposition of the problem of, and hence dialogue necessary between, Christ and culture:

> Given these two complex realities--Christ and culture--an infinite dialogue must develop in the Christian conscience and the Christian community. In his single-minded direction toward God, Christ leads men away from the temporality and pluralism of culture. In its concern for the conservation of the many values of the past, culture rejects the Christ who bids men rely on grace. Yet the Son of God is himself child of a religious culture, and sends his disciples to tend his lambs and sheep, who cannot be guarded without cultural work. The dialogue proceeds with denials and affirmations, reconstructions, compromises, and new denials. Neither individual nor church can come to a stopping-place in the endless search for an answer which will not provoke a new rejoinder.[53]

Typical Answers

Nevertheless, Niebuhr gives us five "typical answers" or "stylized patterns" to this "enduring problem". The first two are the black and white extremes while the last three attempt to identify the shades of grey. Niebuhr introduces the greys:

> If Christ and culture are the two principles with which Christians are concerned, then most of them will seem to be compromising creatures who somehow manage to mix in irrational fashion an exclusive devotion to a Christ who rejects culture, with devotion to a culture that includes Christ.[54]

1. **Christ Against Culture.** This answer is "the one that uncompromisingly affirms the sole authority of Christ over the Christian and resolutely rejects culture's claims to loyalty."[55] In the New Testament, this is seen most clearly in Revelation and 1 John. Early Christianity's greatest representative of this type is Tertullian while Tolstoy is a classic example of a more modern age.

2. **Christ of Culture.** Niebuhr explains this grouping:

> On the one hand they interpret culture through Christ, regarding those elements in it as most important which are most accordant with his work and person; on the other hand

they understand Christ through culture, selecting from his teaching and action as well as from the Christian doctrine about him such points as men seem to agree with what is best in civilization.[56]

The extreme attitude, which interprets Christ wholly in cultural terms and tends to eliminate all sense of tension between him and social belief or custom, was represented in the Hellenistic world by the Christian Gnostics.[57]

More modern exponents of this pattern were Abelard and A. Ritschl.

3. **Christ above Culture.** This third grouping understands Christ's relation to culture similarly to the second type:

Yet there is in him something that neither arises out of culture nor contributes directly to it. He is discontinuous as well as continuous with social life and its culture. The latter, indeed, leads men to Christ, yet only in so preliminary a fashion that a great leap is necessary if men are to reach him or, better, true culture is not possible unless beyond all human achievement, all human search for values, all human society, Christ enters into life from above with gifts which human aspiration has not envisioned and which human effort cannot attain unless he relates men to a supernatural society and a new value-center.[58]

Niebuhr's representatives of this type are Clement of Alexandria and Thomas Aquinas.

4. **Christ and Culture in Paradox.** This dualistic, typical answer finds its greatest advocate in Luther following a similar motif in Paul and Marcion. His dualism, however, is not in a Manichaean sense of light and darkness; rather the conflict is between God and man, between the righteousness of God and the righteousness of self. His starting point is the miracle of God's grace.[59]

5. **Christ the Transformer of Culture.** Those who advocate a fifth type of answer to the problem of Christ and culture "understand with the members of the first and the fourth groups that human nature is fallen or perverted, and that this perversion not only appears in culture but is transmitted by it."[60] Christ, then, is seen to be necessary as the converter of man and his society. Augustine offers the great outlines to this answer while John Calvin attempts to make it explicit.

Niebuhr gives both theological commendations and condemnations of each position, concluding that the problem is indeed enduring: "It must be evident that neither extension nor refinement of study could bring us to the conclusive result that would enable us to say, 'This is the Christian answer.'"[61] We are left to sort out the problem of Christ and culture in the presence of Christ in the midst of culture.

In my view in considering the communication of the gospel to the men to whom we are referring, we must reject both extremes. Both confrontation and accommodation are necessary--and biblical--at various points.

Confrontation

Confrontation is necessary, as Charles Kraft, explains

because human culture, like human personality, is an intimate mixture of the divine (God's image, God's creativity reflected in human genius, God's character reflected in human conscience) and of the demonic (the image marred by the Fall). But the point of crucial confrontation will differ from society to society, and even from individual to individual.[62]

Confrontation, of course, sometimes means that unbelievers will be offended by the gospel. Niebuhr comments,

Ancient spiritualists and modern materialists, pious Romans who charge Christianity with atheism, and nineteenth century atheists who condemn its theistic faith, nationalists and humanists, all seem to be offended by the same elements in the gospel and employ similar arguments in defending their culture against it.[63]

Niebuhr follows Gibbons's *The Decline and Fall of the Roman Empire* in seeing three specific, timeless reasons for unbelievers being offended by the gospel: Firstly, "Christians are 'animated by a contempt for present existence and by confidence in immortality.'"[64] This is similar to Blamires' argument about the infinite. Another common argument against Christ is that, "He induces men to rely on the grace of God instead of summoning them to human achievement."[65]

The offense Niebuhr mentions last may be especially relevant in our pluralistic culture:

A third count in the recurring cultural indictments of Christ and his church is that they are intolerant, though this does not occur in the Communists' complaint, for it is not the objection which one intolerant belief raises against another but rather the disapproval with which unbelief meets conviction. Ancient Roman civilisation, says Gibbon, was bound to reject Christianity just because Rome was tolerant.[66]

We must also agree with Niebuhr that, "Not only pagans who have rejected Christ but believers who have accepted him find it difficult to combine his claims upon them with those of their societies."[67] This brings us to accommodation.

Accommodation

It is well known that Christianity has flourished most when it has accommodated itself to certain popular ways of life as culturally divergent as the Roman Empire and the USA:

> Berger suggests that in America the churches have maintained a position of central symbolic importance because they have accommodated themselves to, and support, the American Way of Life, have "modernised" and marketed their products, adapting it to meet the needs of their constituents. Consequently church involvement has remained much higher than in Europe where "internal" secularisation and the process of adjusting to the demands of the wider society has proceeded much slower.[68]

Also speaking of Berger, Os Guinness makes a similar observation:

> Following Luckmann and Herberg, he [Berger] sees European secularisation as being "from without" (with religiosity being strongest and secularisation weakest on the margins of society), while American secularisation is "from within" (with the churches occupying a more central symbolic position, but at the expense of being secularised themselves). Thus, despite differences, he can say that these are "two variations on the same underlying theme of global secularization". In Europe, secularisation has decisively altered the church's social location; in America, it has transformed its inner universe of meaning.[69]

It appears easier to "baptise" the pagan gods (e.g. nationalism and materialism) than to "baptise" the gods of secularised societies. A sort of "Christian secularism" led by Dietrich Bonhoeffer, John Robinson, and Harvey Cox has not been successful in inducing a thorough-going Christianity among secularists.

Yet it is necessary that Christian communication follows the Pauline example of becoming "all things to all men so that by all possible means I might save some" (1 Corinthians 9:22b). As Von Allmen says,

> Putting it provocatively, one may say that the heretics in the New Testament are not those who preach the Gospel by becoming Greeks with the Greeks but rather the conservatives who, because they hesitate to win a new culture for the service of Christ, run the risk of being drowned by that very culture.[70]

Worldviews are a particular area of interest for accommodation. Christians through the centuries have shown that they have been able to accept widely divergent worldviews while retaining Christian faith. Kraft explains,

> It is highly probably [*sic*] that the biblical message will over time, along with other external influences, bring about a change in the worldview of people. But it is not legitimate to require people to change their worldview in order to become Christians in the first place; this would be, even in the case of assumptions and attitudes incompatible with the Gospel in its fulness, putting the cart before the horse.[71]

A Dynamic Model

We find that one infinite and one huge, but limited, complexity exists--God and man, Christ and culture. Niebuhr says, "When Christianity deals with the question of reason and revelation, what is ultimately in question is the relation of the revelation in Christ to the reason which prevails in culture."[72] It is that essential relationship that must be under constant consideration when communicating the gospel to the men in question:

What we have termed absolute, supracultural Truth exists--outside culture and beyond the grasp of finite, sinful human beings. But God provides revelation of himself *within* the human cultural context. Much of this, including detailed records of his supreme revelation in Jesus Christ, has been recorded and preserved in the Christian Scriptures. To the understanding of this revelation a variety of Spirit-led human beings apply a variety of culturally, psychologically, disciplinarily, and otherwise-conditioned perceptions. On this basis they develop theologies appropriate to their own insights and experiences, and instructive to others of similar and dissimilar backgrounds.[73]

This divine and human interchange of Truth and culture gives credence to Kraft's suggestion of a dynamic model:

I suggest that we work with a more dynamic model which sees Gospel and culture as meeting in the midst of a trajectory of change, and from the moment of contact mutually affecting and altering each other. We can visualize this as the confluence of two streams, one bearing pure water, the other containing various impurities. The two run along for a while downstream of the confluence, initially maintaining their separate identities, but gradually becoming merged into a single stream.
The hope is that the Gospel would over time transform the culture and its bearers; the reality has too often been in all societies, that the Gospel has been tamed by the incompatible culture. In the history of western Christianity, there was initially a powerful flow of the Gospel into Hellenistic culture; but after Constantine the pagan culture in many ways polluted the Gospel water. As later cultures in turn flowed into the mix, the initial input of Gospel was gradually contaminated and diluted. It was perceptions of this process that gave rise to the several reforming movements starting well before the 16th century, movements which had as their expressed intent precisely to restore primitive Christian faith and practice.[74]

We cannot, and will not, give up Christ and his confrontation to the demonic in our culture; neither can we give up sensitivity to culture because we are human and do not exist without culture. Only a model of dynamic interchange will allow a gospel of change to affect the life of men. If there is a choice, however, we must always choose Christ, looking as far beyond our cultural conceptions of Christ as possible. For the Christian communicator, the authentic voice speaking the Word will always pledge his allegiance to God, not men.

Toward the Church

Our study of fifty working-class men reveals not only the poverty of the men but the poverty of the church. The church is poorer without them. They have their objectionable qualities and sins (whether acknowledged or not), but they also have a wealth of culture to bring--some of which more nearly appropriates the gospel than the present church.

In some working-class men there is a remarkable honesty with little pretence. Of course, in some it is simply *another* pretence, but at its best the honesty of working men is infectious in whole churches.

The culture of working-class material values is in many ways similar to certain teachings of Jesus. They have no trouble living from week to week without storing up for the future in the institutions of the world. My intuition from experience is that at the lower income end of the working class, the giving without expecting anything in return is evident. The men in this sample, no longer poor and mainly on higher workers' incomes, did not reveal that they were very liberal in their giving. Rather extreme in reply but, I think, typical in action was the man who explained:

Oh, I give to charities. I don't make it important, but you know if somebody rattles a box under me, I'll willingly put. I wouldn't go out of my way to do it, but I wouldn't go out of my way to avoid it either. If it's there I put. [40]

However, in the background of their background is a willingness to give generously expecting nothing in return and not to worry about tomorrow. They do not, of course, start from the biblical basis, "Seek first his kingdom and his righteousness" (Matthew 6:33), but there is an untapped resource of giving present.

A backhanded virtue is that these men do not praise the church, religion, or even God for its own sake. If it has no value to them, they say so. This openness to criticism is greatly needed in the church where we are often too near the situation to see it clearly. Of course, their openness is not usually to self-criticism but to other-criticism, which would need expansion once they were inside.

The sadness is that some--perhaps many--of these men will never come to Christ. Their riches will be squandered by their co-inciding poverty.

The Whole Church

If anything, this study visualizes how much we need the whole church. People in various sub-cultures and cultures have appreciation for areas of the gospel where other groups are closed. We need others to help us hear a bigger--but not an-other--gospel. Some sections of the church (often lumped into denominations) have an emphasis on one or another of the elements of biblical belief. We need others to "help our unbelief" and expand our belief. Because of their biblical, cultural, or psychological stance, some churches reach certain unbelievers that others do not--and cannot. We need others to help us communicate.

Wherever the church exists, there must be Christians who both listen and speak--hearing the unbeliever from our unique vantage point of belief (and remaining aware of our own unbelief) and giving Christ by word and event. Wherever this happens, the church will understand in experience these words attributed to Emil Brunner: "**A church exists by mission as a fire exists by burning.**"

APPENDICES

Appendix 1

INTERVIEW SCHEDULE

1.1. If you look at the things in which you are involved in your life, what would you like to do more often?

1.2. What would you like to do less often?

2.1. When you think back over your life, what period of your life would you have liked to have made longer? Why?

2.2. What period of your life would you have liked to have made shorter? Why?

3.1. What sorts of things do you normally *think* about on the weekdays?

3.2. Is it any different what you *think* about on the weekends?

4.1. In the last week, has anything really important--good or bad--happened to you?

5.1. Who have been the really important people who have helped you in the past? in crunch situations?

5.2. In what way did they help you?

6.1. Can you tell me about the really important experiences or turning points in your life, things that changed your direction or turned your world upside-down?

7.1. Can you describe some times when things went wrong for you?

7.2. How did you feel then?

7.3. What did you do about it?

7.4. Did it help? Why or why not?

7.5. Why do you think that this happened?
Is there any other reason?
Was the reason altogether to do with you?

7.6. Would you have done things differently if you had your time again?

8.1. If you think ahead ten years, what do you expect of (your) life?

8.2. [For younger interviewees] If you imagine yourself to be about 70, what do you think that your life will be like then?

9.1. Do you have any worries about the future of the world? Could you tell me what they are?

9.2. Do you have any worries about your own personal future?

9.3. Why does that worry you?

9.4. What do you do about that worry?

10.1. Would you say that your life is more of a success or a failure?

10.2. What is success and failure in life to you? i.e., What does it mean to succeed or fail in life?

11.1. When you are alone and thinking beyond the day-to-day problems, what do you consider to be the most important thing or things (or concern or concerns) of your life?

11.2. Why is it so important?

11.3. What do you do about this concern?

11.4. [rarely used] Do you talk with any other people or groups of people or organisations to share these concerns?

11.5. [rarely used] Could you tell me which people, groups, or organisations these are?

12.1. A lot of people talk in different ways today about sharing possessions and giving money. Do you believe that sharing your possessions and money with others is important?

12.2. Do you share your possessions and money with others?

12.3. In what way? or Could you give me a few examples?

13.1. What do you feel about the fact that you will die one day?

13.2. Have you thought about the sort of funeral which you would like to have? What sort?

13.3. What do you think will happen to you after you die?

13.4. Is it the same for all people?

13.5. How certain do you feel about your answer?

13.6. What would you *like* to happen to you after you die?

13.7. How do you know if you are right about these sorts of questions, i.e. questions about life and death?

13.8. What do you do to learn more about knowing what is right and wrong about these sorts of things?

14.1. Do you think that abortion is right or wrong? Why?

14.2. How do you know if it is right or wrong? (or) What proves to you that it is right or wrong?

14.3. How do you decide if other things are right or wrong?

15.1. Do you ever feel that you have done something wrong?

15.2. What do you do about it?

15.3. When was the last time that you felt that you had done something wrong?

15.4. Would you mind telling me what you did about it then?

15.5. Did you feel a need for forgiveness?

15.6. If yes: From whom?

15.7.   From God?

15.8.   How would you go about receiving their/God's forgiveness?

15.9. If no, Have you ever felt a need for forgiveness of any kind?

16.1.   In a difficult situation, who do you go to for advice?
16.2.   Why?
16.3.   [Perhaps suggest possibilities] Social workers, solici-
        tors, priests, friends, ministers, astrologers, clairvoy-
        ants, etc.

17.1.   Do you believe in the existence of a power beyond man or
        a higher being? (Or God?)
        If yes: What would you call it?
17.2   If yes: What do you think this power/God is like?
17.3.   What kind of power does it have?
17.4.   Are there things that it/He cannot do?
17.5.   Does it/He have feelings? What sort of feelings?

18.1.   Who or what do you trust?
18.2.   Do you put trust in God or the power/higher being?
18.3.   When do you consider God and whether you will trust Him?
        Why then?
18.4.   Was there a period of your life when you thought (more)
        about God and whether you would put any trust in Him?
18.5.   Have you changed your mind or considered changing your
        mind since that time?
18.6.   If no: If anything did cause you to change your mind,
        what would it be?

19.1.   Can God help you in any way?
19.2.   If yes: In what way?
19.3.   If no: Why not?

20.1.   Do you every pray? (or)
        Do you ever call on (or draw on) this power?
20.2.   In what circumstances? On any other occasions?
20.3.   What happens?   To the situation?   To you?

21.1.   To what extent would you say that God or belief in God
        has influenced your life?
21.2.   In what way does God or belief in God influence your life
        now?
21.3.   Would you say that you obey God?
21.4.   If yes: In what way?

22.1.   Have you ever had an experience which you would call
        religious or spiritual?
22.2.   If yes: Could you describe it for me?
22.3.   Listed below are a number of experiences which people
        have reported having. Have you ever had any of these
        experiences and how sure are you that you had it?

                    SHOW CARD WITH
                    __Yes, I'm sure I have.
                    __Yes, I think I have.
                    __I don't think I have.
                    __No, I definitely haven't.

a. A feeling that you were somehow in the presence of God or in contact with something holy or sacred.
b. A feeling of being afraid of God.
c. A sense of being saved by Jesus Christ.
d. A feeling of being punished by God for something you had done.
e. A sense that God truly loved you?
f. A feeling of being tempted by the devil or something demonic.
g. A sense that you were healed or someone was healed of an illness in an unexpected way.
h. A sense of the presence of supernatural evil or something demonic.

22.4. If answer is no to *all* of the above:
Do you think that it is possible for anyone to have any kind of genuinely religious or spiritual experiences?

22.5. If yes to 22.4.: Why have none of these experiences happened to you?

22.6. If no to 22.4.: Why do people say that they have had these experiences?

23.1. Assuming for a moment that there is a God and you had half an hour to talk with Him, what would you want to say to Him?

24.1. How would you feel if your a) family, b)workmates/colleagues, c) friends knew all you thought about God?

24.2. Do any of them share your views about God?

24.3. Do you think that you are more or less religious than your a) family b) workmates/colleagues, c) friends?

24.4. Does your being (more or less) religious lead to any conflict or problems with any of them?

25.1. Would you like for your children (or grandchildren) to grow up to believe the same things as you do?

25.2. How important to you are your beliefs about religion?

25.3. Have you always believed the same as you do now?

25.4. If yes: Why do you stay with these same beliefs all your life? (or)
Why have you not changed your beliefs?

25.5. If no: What caused you to change?

26.1. What is the difference between those who are true believers in Jesus Christ and those who are not?

26.2. Have you ever met anyone that you would say is a true believer in Jesus Christ?

26.3. If yes, what showed you that he/she was a believer?

26.4. How many people do you know who you would consider to be true believers?

26.5. How many people do you know who you would consider to be unbelievers?

26.6. What is a Christian?

27.1. How would you describe yourself in terms of beliefs or lack of beliefs in the Christian faith?
If terms are needed: A Christian or a non-Christian?
A believer or an unbeliever?
An atheist, agnostic, humanist, etc.

27.2. Would you (strongly) agree or (strongly) disagree with the following statements:
a. Jesus Christ is the Lord of my life.
b. I have a desire to follow God's direction for my life.

27.3. If (strongly) agree: Was there a point in your life when this was not true?

27.4. If (strongly) disagree: Was there ever a point in your life when you could agree with those statements?

28.1. Describe for me in a few sentences what the teaching (or content) of the Bible is all about?

28.2. Tell me the story of Jesus Christ in a few sentences.

28.3. What do you make of this story?

28.4. Who do you believe Jesus was?

28.5. How can it be that a man who was crucified has influenced the world so much?

28.6. What do you think the Christian faith is really all about?

28.7. Do you have a favourite story or event out of the Bible-- or perhaps just one that you remember more than the others?

28.8. Could you name a few characters out of the Old Testament for me?

28.9. Could you name a few characters out of the New Testament for me?

28.10. If you were asked, do you think that you could name the Ten Commandments? Could you just name a few for me?

29.1. When you were growing up, did you ever attend any sort of Sunday School?

29.2. From what age until what age?

29.3. How often did you attend during that time?

29.4. Did you attend the Church services?

29.5. From what age until what age?

29.6. How often did you attend?

29.7. What sort of experience was Sunday School and/or Church for you while you were growing up? If needed: Good, bad, indifferent?

30.1. How many Sundays out of the last four have you attended a church service of any kind?

30.2. Over the last year, how many Sundays have you attended a church service?

30.3. Are you a member of a church?

30.4. If yes: Which one?

30.5.   For how long have you been a member?

30.6. If you were filling out a form and it asked for your religion, what would you fill in?

30.7. How have your experiences of Sunday School and Church over your whole life affected your beliefs or lack of beliefs?

30.8. Would you have liked for your experience of Church to have been different?

31.1.   What is your age?
31.2.   Are you single, married, divorced, separated, or widowed?
31.3.   Do you have any children?
        If yes: What are their ages?
31.4.   At what age did you leave school?
31.5.   Do you have any qualifications of any kind?
        CSE, "O" levels, "A" levels, indentured papers, diplomas,
        certificates, etc.
31.6.   Are you one of the fortunate ones to be in work at this
        present time?
        If no: What is your normal work?
        If yes: What is your work?
31.7.   Could you tell me in which of these categories your
        present income would fall before deductions?   (Show Card
        with graduations.)
31.8.   If married: Does your wife work?
                    What category does her income fall into?
31.9.   What was your father's job?
31.10. What was your mother's job?

Appendix 2
Religious Experience Of Interviewees

22.3 No.	a. presence	b. afraid	c. saved	d. punished	e. loved	f. tempted	g. healed	h. evil	22.1.
1.	4	4	4	3	4	1	4	4	No
2.	2	4	1	4	2	1	2	3	No
3.	1	3	1	1	2	3	3	4	Yes
4.	1-2	1	2	3	1	3	1	4	No
5.	4	3	4	4	4	3	4	-	No
6.	4	2	4	1	3	1	3	4	No
7.	4	4	4	4	1	4	4	4	No
8.	1	3	3	3	1	1	1	3	Yes
9.	-	-	-	-	-	-	-	-	No
10.	1	4	-	3	3	1	-	4	No
11.	1	4	4	3	1	1	3	4	Yes
12.	1	4	1	2	4	1	3	1	No
13.	4	2	4	4	3	2	3	1	Yes
14.	3	4	3	4	3	4	4	4	No
15.	4	4	4	1	4	4	1	4	No
16.	4	4	4	4	4	4	4	4	No
17.	2-3	4	3	1	1	4	4	4	Yes
18.	2	1	2-3	3	4	1	3	4	No
19.	4	4	1	4	2	4	1	4	No
20.	4	4	4	4	4	1	4	4	No
21.	4	4	4	4	4	4	4	4	No
22.	4	4	4	3	2-3	4	4	4	No
23.	4	4	2	3	4	3	4	4	No
24.	-	-	-	-	-	-	-	-	No
25.	4	4	4	4	4	4	4	1	Yes
26.	1	4	4	2-3	4	2-3	1	-	Yes
27.	4	4	3	4	2	4	4	4	No
28.	-	-	4	1	4	2	4	4	No
29.	4	4	4	4	4	4	4	4	No
30.	1	4	1	4	1	4	4	4	No
31.	1	4	1	4	-	2-3	4	4	No
32.	4	4	4	4	3	2-3	4	4	No
33.	-	-	-	-	-	-	-	-	No
34.	1	1	1	1	1	1	1	1	?
35.	1	4	1	4	4	4	3	4	No
36.	4	4	1	4	1	4	1	-	Yes
37.	4	1	4	4	4	4	1	4	No
38.	2	4	4	4	4	4	4	4	No
39.	4	4	-	-	-	-	-	-	No
40.	3	4	4	4	4	4	4	4	No
41.	4	4	4	4	4	4	4	4	No
42.	1	4	2	1	2	4	1	4	No
43.	4	4	2	4	2	4	?	4	No
44.	4	3	3	4	3	1	2	3	No
45.	4	4	1	4	?	4	4	4	-
46.	4	3	?	1	?	4	3	1	Yes
47.	4	4	4	3	4	4	4	4	No
48.	3	4	2	4	4	4	-	3	No
49.	4	3	4	4	4	2-3	4	2	No
50.	4	4	4	4	4	4	1	4	No

1 = Yes, I'm sure I have.   3 = I don't think I have.   - = No answer given
2 = Yes, I think I have.   4 = No, I definitely haven't.

ENDNOTES

ENDNOTES FOR CHAPTER ONE

[1]Michael Hare Duke and Eric Whitton, *A Kind of Believing* (London: General Synod Board of Education, 1977).

[2]*Toward A Sociology of Irreligion* (London: Macmillan, 1971), pp. 25-26.

[3]*Ibid.*, p. 32.

[4]Johannes Baptist Metz, "Unbelief as a Theological Problem", *Concilium* VI (June, 1965), 32.

[5]"Introduction" in *The Culture of Unbelief*, ed. Rocco Caporale and Antonio Grumelli (Berkeley: The University of California Press, 1971), p. 3.

[6]*Who Are the Unchurched?* (Washington D.C.: Glenmary Research Center, 1977), p. 38.

[7]Rene Padilla, "The Contextualization of the Gospel", in *Readings in Dynamic Indigeneity*, ed. Charles H. Kraft and Tom N. Wisley (Pasadena: William Carey Library, 1979), p. 304.

[8]"Foreword" in *The Culture of Unbelief*, ed. Caporale and Grumelli, p. xi.

[9]*Ibid.*, p. x.

[10]Rocco Caporale, "Introduction", in *The Culture of Unbelief*, ed. Caporale and Grumelli, p. 3.

[11]"Toward a Definition of Unbelief" in *The Culture of Unbelief*, ed. Caporale and Grumelli, p. 148.

[12]E. Vogt, "Objectivity in Research", in *Readings in the Sociology of Religion*, ed. Joan Brothers (Oxford: Pergamon Press, 1967), pp. 124-125.

[13]Robert A. Stebbins, "The Unstructured Research Interview as Incipient Interpersonal Relationship", *Sociology and Social Research* 56 (January, 1972), 174,175.

[14]*The Sociology of Belief: Fallacy and Foundation* (London: Routledge and Kegan Paul, 1980), p. 114.

[15]Campbell, *Toward a Sociology of Irreligion*, pp. 118-123.

[16]John V. Taylor, *The Go-Between God* (London: SCM, 1972).

ENDNOTES FOR CHAPTER TWO

[1] *Notizen zum Westöstlichen Divan* quoted in Joseph A. Magno and Victor S. Lamotte, *The Christian, The Atheist, and Freedom* (New York: Precedent Publishing, 1973), p. vii.

[2] Jean Lacrois, *The Meaning of Modern Atheism* trans. Garret Barden (Dublin: Gill and Son, 1965), pp. 14-15.

[3] *Ibid.*, p. 17.

[4] Harold Tonks, "Faith, Hope, and Decision Making" (Ph.D. Thesis, University of Birmingham, 1981), p. 101.

[5] "Unbelief as a Theological Problem", *Concilium*, VI (June, 1965), p. 32.

[6] Joseph A. Magno and Victor S. Lamotte, *The Christian, The Atheist, and Freedom* (New York: Precedent Publishing, 1973), p. 10.

[7] Lacrois, *The Meaning of Modern Atheism*, p. 16.

[8] "Variations in Perspective on Secularization and Unbelief", in *The Culture of Unbelief*, ed. Rocco Caporale and Antonio Grumelli (Berkeley: The University of California Press, 1971), pp. 101-102.

[9] "On the Development of Unbelief", *The Culture of Unbelief*, ed. Caporale and Grumelli, p. 181.

[10] "Response to Glock", in *The Culture of Unbelief*, ed. Caporale and Grumelli, p. 125-126.

[11] "Belief, Unbelief, and Religion", in *The Culture of Unbelief*, ed. Caporale and Grumelli, p. 37.

[12] "Foreword", *The Culture of Unbelief*, ed. Caporale and Grumelli, p. xiii.

[13] *Ibid.* Note also Richard Machalek and Michael Martin, "'Invisible' Religions: Some Preliminary Evidence" *Journal of the Scientific Study of Religion*, 15 (1976), 311-321, and David A. Snow and Richard Machalek, "On the Presumed Fragility of Unconventional Beliefs", *Journal for the Scientific Study of Religion* (March, 1982).

[14] "Belief, Unbelief, and Religion", in *The Culture of Unbelief*, ed. Caporale and Grumelli, p. 37.

[15] "The Historical Background of Unbelief", in *The Culture of Unbelief*, ed. Caporale and Grumelli, p. 39-43.

[16] "Variations in Perspective", in *The Culture of Unbelief*, ed. Caporale and Grumelli, p. 91-92.

Chapter Two Endnotes

[17] *Dogmatics*, Vol. 3: *The Christian Doctrine of the Church, Faith, and the Consummation*, trans. David Cairns (London: Lutterworth Press, 1960), p. 140.

[18] (New York: Harper and Row, 1970), p. 228.

[19] Peter Berger, "Forward," in *The Culture of Unbelief*, ed. Caporale and Grumelli, p. xiii.

[20] "Variations in Perspective," in *The Culture of Unbelief*, ed. Caporale and Grumelli, p. 99.

[21] "Belief, Unbelief, and Religion", in *The Culture of Unbelief*, ed. Caporale and Grumelli, p. 36.

[22] "Religious Attitudes and Values", in *Values and Social Change in Britain*, ed. Mark Abrams, David Gerard, Noel Timms (London: Macmillan, forthcoming).

[23] *Between Belief and Unbelief* (New York: Harper and Row, 1974), p.54.

[24] "Toward a Definition of Unbelief", in *The Culture of Unbelief*, ed. Caporale and Grumelli, p. 146.

[25] *Ibid.*, p. xiv.

[26] "Program and Prolegomena for a Sociology of Irreligion", in *Actes de la X Conference Internationale* (Rome: Conference Internationale de Sociologie Religieuse, 1969), pp. 160-161.

[27] "Variations in Perspective," in *The Culture of Unbelief*, ed. Caporale and Grumelli, p. 93.

[28] *Ibid.*, p. 95.

[29] Robert Bellah, *Beyond Belief* (New York: Harper and Row, 1970), p. 228.

[30] "Variations in Perspective," *The Culture of Unbelief*, ed. Caporale and Grumelli, p. 99-100.

[31] *Ibid.*, p. 100.

[32] "The Case Against God", BBC Radio 4, 18 November, 1984.

[33] "Anonymous Christians," in *A Rahner Reader*, ed. Gerald A. McCool (New York: Seabury Press, 1975), pp. 211-214 as quoted in Shane Womack, "Encounters With Atheists at a State University: Personal Interviews and Theological Reflections" (M.A.R. thesis, Emmanuel School of Religion, 1983), p. 52.

[34] Quoted in Ignace Lepp, *Atheism in Our Time* (New York: The Macmillan Company, 1963), pp. 9-10.

[35] *Does God Exist?*, trans. Edward Quinn (London: Collins, 1980), p. 339.

[36] *Ibid.*, p. 568ff.

Chapter Two Endnotes

[37]*Notizen zum Westöstlichen Divan*, this time as quoted in Brunner, *Church, Faith, Consummation*, p. 140.

[38]*Church, Faith, Consummation*, pp. 150-151.

ENDNOTES FOR CHAPTER THREE

[1]Paul Tillich, *The Courage to Be* (New Haven and London: Yale, 1952), p. 40.

[2]Francis M. Tyrrell, *Man: Believer and Unbeliever* (New York: Alba House, 1974), p. 282.

[3]O. Becker, "Faith" in *The New International Dictionary of New Testament Theology*, ed. Colin Brown (Grand Rapids: Zondervan Publishing House, 1975), I, pp. 587-588.

[4]*Man: Believer and Unbeliever*, p. 285.

[5]*Ibid.*

[6]*Dogmatics*, Vol. 3: *The Christian Doctrine of the Church, Faith, and the Consummation*, trans. David Cairns (London: Lutterworth Press, 1960), p. 187.

[7]"Faith", in *A Dictionary of the Bible*, ed. James Hastings (Edinburgh: T. & T. Clark, 1898), I, p. 836.

[8]"πιστεύω κτλ. ", in *Theological Dictionary of the New Testament*, ed. Gerhard Friedrich, trans. and ed. Geoffrey W. Bromiley (Grand Rapids: William B. Eerdmans Publishing Company, 1968), VI p. 208.

[9]*Ibid.*, p. 209.

[10]*Ibid.*, p. 210.

[11]*Ibid.*, p. 212.

[12]*Ibid.*, p. 213.

[13]"Faith" in *The New International Dictionary of New Testament Theology*, ed. Brown, I, pp. 600-601.

[14]Tyrrell, *Man: Believer and Unbeliever*, p. 283.

[15]*Does God Exist?*, (London: Collins, 1980), pp. 575-576.

[16]Note James D. G. Dunn on the act of faith and the gift of the Spirit. *Baptism in the Holy Spirit*, Studies in Biblical Theology, Second Series, no. 15 (London: SCM Press, 1970), p. 96.

[17]*Church, Faith, Consummation*, pp. 174-175.

[18]Rudolf Bultmann, " πείθω κτλ. ", in *Theological Dictionary of the New Testament*, ed. Friedrich, VI, p. 1.

[19]O. Becker, "Faith" in *The New International Dictionary of New Testament Theology*, ed. Brown, I, p. 591.

[20]Bultmann, " πείθω κτλ. ", in *Theological Dictionary of the New Testament*, ed. Friedrich, VI, p. 7.

Chapter Three Endnotes

[21]O. Becker, "Faith" in *The New International Dictionary of New Testament Theology*, ed. Brown, I, p. 587.

[22]*Baptism in the Holy Spirit*, p. 91.

[23]*Christ and Culture* (New York: Harper Torchbooks, 1951, 1956), p. 242.

[24]*Ibid.*, pp. 243-246.

[25]*Ibid.*, p. 246.

[26]*Ibid.*, p. 24.

[27]*Church, Faith, Consummation*, p. 156.

[28]*Varieties of Unbelief* (New York: Holt, Rinehart and Winston, 1964), p. 33.

[29]*Church, Faith, Consummation*, pp. 160-161.

[30]*Ibid.*, p. 161.

[31]*Ibid.*

[32]*The Tests of Life* (Edinburg: T & T Clark, 1909; reprint ed., Grand Rapids: Baker Book House, 1968), chapters 9-11.

[33]James D. G. Dunn shows that "Jesus is Lord" is "undoubtedly *the principle confession of faith for Paul and for his churches.*" *Unity and Diversity in the New Testament* (London: SCM Press Ltd, 1977), p. 50.

[34]*The Theology of the New Testament*, trans. Kendrick Grobel (New York: Charles Scribner's Sons, 1951), I, p. 318.

[35]Dunn, *Unity and Diversity*, p. 69. Also note the rest of this section on "Tradition in the Pastorals".

[36]*Ibid.*, p. 369.

[37]*Church, Faith, Consummation*, pp. 174-175.

[38]*Ibid.*, p. 168.

[39]*Unity and Diversity*, pp. 57-58.

[40]*Ibid.*, pp. 56-57.

[41]Walter Hollenweger has sketched some of the significant moments of its formulation in "The 'What' and the 'How': Content and Communication of the One Message", *The Expository Times* 76 (11), pp. 322-328.

[42]"Response to Bellah" in *The Culture of Unbelief*, ed. Rocco Caporale and Antonio Grumelli (Berkeley: The University of California Press, 1971), p. 120.

Chapter Three Endnotes

[43]"Belief, Unbelief, and Disbelief" in *The Culture of Unbelief*, ed. Caporale and Grumelli, p. 208.

[44]*Between Belief and Unbelief* (New York: Harper and Row, 1974), p. 11.

[45]From a different perspective, Peter L. Berger says, "When everything has been subsumed under the relativizing categories in question . . . , the question of truth reasserts itself in almost pristine simplicity. Once we know that all human affirmations are subject to scientifically graspable socio-historical processes, *which affirmations are true and which are false?* We cannot avoid the question any more than we can return to the innocence of its pre-relativizing asking." *A Rumour of Angels* (London: The Penguin Press, 1970), p. 57.

[46]"Theological Reflections on Religo-Sociological Interpretations of Modern 'Irreligion'", *Social Compass* 10 (1963), p. 260.

[47]*Theology of the New Testament*, I, p. 319.

[48]*Ibid.*, II, p. 135.

[49]"Belief, Unbelief, and Disbelief" in *The Culture of Unbelief*, ed. Caporale and Grumelli, p. 208-209.

[50]*Unity and Diversity*, p. 27.

[51]*Belief and Unbelief* (London: Darton, Longman and Todd, 1966), p. 19.

[52]Johannes Behm, "καρδία", in *Theological Dictionary of the New Testament*, ed. Gerhard Kittel, trans. and ed. Geoffrey W. Bromiley (Grand Rapids: William B. Eerdmans Publishing Company, 1968), III, pp. 611-612.

[53]O. Michel, "Faith" in *The New International Dictionary of New Testament Theology*, ed. Colin Brown (Grand Rapids: Zondervan, 1975), I, p. 595.

[54]B. B. Warfield, "Faith" in *Dictionary of the Bible*, ed. Hastings, I, p. 828.

[55]Tyrrell, *Man: Believer and Unbeliever*, pp. 289-290.

[56]Dietrich Bonhoeffer. *Letters and Papers From Prison* (London: Collins/Fontana, 1953), pp. 123-124.

[57]Warfield, "Faith" in *Dictionary of the Bible*, ed. Hastings, I, p. 827.

[58]Pace J. M. Ward's statement: "Believing/trusting does not necessarily involve the ethical commitment of the believer to the object, or the evocation of a deep or lasting emotional response. *True* faith *in God* entails these things, as the OT affirms, but this is a religious conviction and not a meaning inherent in the word "believe" itself. There is no more hidden theological or ethical significance in the Hebrew word than in

Chapter Three Endnotes

the English equivalent. ‎ל'אֲכָה means simply to be certain in the mind (Barr)." "Faith, Faithfulness in the OT," *The Interpreter's Dictionary of the Bible*, ed. Keith Crin (Nashville: Abingdon, 1976), Supplementary Volume, p. 329.

[59]"Faith" in *The Interpreter's Dictionary of the Bible*, ed. George Arthur Buttrick (Nashville: Abingdon Press, 1962), II, p. 222.

[60]Warfield, "Faith" in *Dictionary of the Bible*, ed. Hastings, I, p. 829.

[61]*Ibid.*

[62]*Ibid.*, p. 830.

[63]*Ibid.*, p. 831.

[64]*Church, Faith, Consummation*, p. 174.

[65]O. Kirn, "Faith", *The New Schaff-Herzog Encyclopedia of Religious Knowledge*, ed. Samuel Macauley Jackson (London: Funk & Wagnalls Company, 1909), IV, p. 269.

[66]Warfield, "Faith" in *Dictionary of the Bible*, ed. Hastings, I, p. 832.

[67]E. C. Blackman, "Faith" in *The Interpreter's Dictionary of the Bible*, ed. Buttrick, II, p. 222.

[68]C. Robert Wetzel, "The Existence of God: An Analysis of Epistemological Presuppositions" in *Essays on New Testament Christianity*, ed. C. Robert Wetzel (Cincinnati: Standard Publishing, 1978), p. 148.

[69]Os Guinness, *In Two Minds* (Downers Grove, Illinois: InterVarsity Press, 1976), p. 128.

[70]Dietrich Bonhoeffer, *The Cost of Discipleship* (New York: The Macmillan Company, 1963), p. 69.

[71]*Ibid.*, pp. 63-64.

[72]Rudolf Bultmann, *Jesus and the Word*, trans. Louise Pettibone Smith and Erminie Huntress Lantero (London: Collins/Fontana, 1934, 1958), p. 61.

[73]Bultmann, " πιστεύω ", in *Theological Dictionary of the New Testament*, ed. Friedrich, VI, pp. 205-206.

[74]Bultmann, *Theology of the New Testament*, I, p. 314.

[75]Note H. Richard Niebuhr's critique in *Christ and Culture*, p. 23.

[76]O. Michel, "Faith" in *The New International Dictionary of New Testament Theology*, ed. Brown, I, p. 604.

211

Chapter Three Endnotes

[77]"Faith" in *Dictionary of the Bible*, ed. Hastings, I, p. 834-835.

[78]Jürgen Moltmann, *Theology of Hope*, trans. James W. Leitch (New York: Harper and Row, 1967), p. 44.

[79]Harold Tonks, "Faith, Hope and Decision Making" (Ph.D. thesis, University of Birmingham, 1981), p. 172.

[80]*Calvin's Institutes* (reprint ed., MacDill AFB, Florida: MacDonald Publishing Company, n.d.), III.2.42, p. 307.

[81]*Ibid.*

[82]Moltmann, *Theology of Hope*, p. 20.

[83]*Ibid.*, p. 16.

[84]*Church, Faith, Consummation*, p. 268.

[85]Warfield, "Faith" in *Dictionary of the Bible*, ed. Hastings, I, p. 835.

[86]*Ibid.*

[87]*Ibid.*, p. 836.

[88]*In Two Minds*, p. 286.

[89]Warfield, "Faith" in *Dictionary of the Bible*, ed. Hastings, I, p. 834.

[90]Bultmann, *Theology of the New Testament*, I, p. 319.

[91]Moltmann, *Theology of Hope*, p. 20.

[92]Bultmann, *Theology of the New Testament*, I, p. 320.

[93]"Faith" in *The New International Dictionary of New Testament Theology*, ed. Brown, I, p. 601.

[94]Moltmann, *Theology of Hope*, p. 21.

[95]Bultmann, *Theology of the New Testament*, I, p. 320.

[96]*Ibid.*, p. 321.

[97]"Faith" in *The Interpreter's Dictionary of the Bible*, ed. Buttrick, II, pp. 226-227.

[98]Bultmann, *Theology of the New Testament*, I, p. 322.

[99]*Church, Faith, Consummation*, p. 238.

[100]Johannes B. Bauer and Heinrich Zimmerman, "Faith" in *Bauer Enclopedia of Biblical Theology*, ed. Johannes B. Bauer (London: Sheed and Ward, 1970), p. 255.

Chapter Three Endnotes

[101]Warfield, "Faith" in *Dictionary of the Bible*, ed. Hastings, I, p. 831.

[102]"On the Study of Religious Commitment" *Religious Education, Research Supplement* (July-August, 1962), S98-S110. Also Charles Glock and Rodney Stark, *Religion and Society in Tension* (Chicago: Rand-McNally, 1965). Both quoted and examined in James D. Davidson, "Glock's Model of Religious Commitment: Assessing Some Different Approaches and Results", *Review of Religious Research*, 16 (No. 2, Winter, 1975), pp. 83-93. Note also Joseph E. Faulkner and Gordon F. DeJong, "Religiosity in 5-D: An Empirical Analysis" *Social Forces* 45 (December, 1966), 246-254 reprinted in Joseph E. Faulkner ed., *Religious Influence in Contemporary Society* (Columbus, Ohio: Charles E. Merrill Publishing Company, 1972), pp. 57-70.

[103]For example, Richard A. Hunt and Morton King, "The Intrinsic-Extrinsic Concept: A Review and Evaluation", *Journal for the Scientific Study of Religion* 10 (1971), 339-356. Harold Himmelfarb, "Measuring Religious Involvement", *Social Forces* 53 (1975), 606-618. John M. Finney, "A Theory of Religious Commitment", *Sociological Analysis* 39 (1978), 19-35. David L. Klemmach and Jerry D. Cardwell, "Interfaith Comparisons of Multidimensional Measures of Religiosity", *Pacific Sociological Review* 16 (October, 1973), 495-507. Wade Clark Roof, "Concepts and Indicators of Religious Commitment: A Critical Review", in *The Religious Dimension: New Directions in Quantitative Research*, ed. Robert Wuthnow (USA: Academic Press, 1979), pp. 17-45.

[104]Colin Campbell discusses the point that the "definition through absence approach" requires a careful statement of what constitutes religious commitment in order that its absence can be established. *Toward a Sociology of Irreligion* (London: Macmillan, 1971), pp. 26-27.

[105]N. J. Demerath III defines irreligion from his sociological perspective as "'unbelief in the elemental religious doctrine that is culturally relevant to the individual.' Note that I use the term 'unbelief' rather than 'disbelief' so as to include those whose beliefs have slowly eroded in either substance or saliency without any single act of rejection or final disavowal. Note too the phrase 'elemental religious doctrine' so as to emphasize doctrinal common denominators rather than the interpretation of the theological sophisticate, on the one hand, or the fundamentalist on the other. Finally, the definition stresses unbelief in doctrine that is 'culturally relevant to the individual.' One would hardly term a Christian irreligious for rejecting Hindu or Judaic tenets. Nor would one deem an upper-class Episcopalian irreligious for finding little meaning in a doctrine peculiar to the lower-class Pentecostalite, or vice versa. The point is simply that 'unbelief' is meaningless unless it refers to a belief that is at least potentially meaningful and accessible." "Program and Prolegomena for a Sociology of Irreligion" in *Actes de la X Conference Internationale*, Rome 18-22 Aout, 1969 (Rome: Conference Internationale de Sociologie Religieuse), pp. 162-163. Although not specifically studying irreligion, we have mainly followed similar patterns.

[106]Bultmann, *Theology of the New Testament*, I, p. 320.

Chapter Three Endnotes

[107]Moltmann, *Theology of Hope*, p. 22.

[108]*Dogmatics*, Vol. 3: *The Christian Doctrine of the Church, Faith, and the Consummation*, trans. David Cairns (London: Lutterworth Press, 1960), p. 146.

[109]*God, Revelation and Authority*, Vol. 2: *God Who Speaks and Shows* (Waco, Texas: Word Books, 1976), p. 167.

[110]"Faith, Hope, and Decision Making", p. 104, 106.

[111]*Ibid.*, p. 121.

[112]Tyrrell, *Man: Believer and Unbeliever*, p. 287.

[113]Translated and introduced by Garret Barden (Dublin: Gill and Son, 1965), p. 57. Note also Os Guinness's section on the value of understanding doubt in *In Two Minds*, pp. 15-18.

[114]*Church, Faith, Consummation*, pp. 265-266.

ENDNOTES FOR CHAPTER FOUR

[1]"Response to Glock", in *The Culture of Unbelief*, ed. Rocco Caporale and Antonio Grumelli (Berkeley: The University of California Press, 1971), p. 125.

[2]*Ibid.*, p. 126.

[3]"Unbelief as an Object of Research", in *The Culture of Unbelief*, ed. Caporale and Grumelli, p. 248.

[4]*Ibid.*, p. 249.

[5]"The Study of Unbelief: Perspectives on Research", *The Culture of Unbelief*, ed. Caporale and Grumelli, p. 61.

[6]Note especially these works on introductory sociological methods: John B. Williamson, David A. Karp, and John R. Dalphin, *The Research Craft: An Introduction to Social Science Methods* (Boston: Little, Brown, and Company, 1977). Norman K. Denzin, *The Research Act in Sociology: A Theoretical Introduction to Sociological Methods* (London: Butterworths, 1970). William J. Filstead, ed., *Qualitative Methodology: Firsthand Involvement with the Social World* (Chicago: Markham Publishing Company, 1970). William H. Banaka, *Training In Depth Interviewing* (London: Harper and Row, 1971). Stephen A. Richardson, Barbara Snell Dohrenwend, and David Klein, *Interviewing: It's Forms and Functions* (New York: Basic Books, Inc., 1965). A. N. Oppenheim, *Questionnaire Design and Attitude Measurement* (London: Heinemann, 1966). C. A. Moser and G. Katton, *Survey Methods In Social Investigation* (London: Heinemann, 1958, 1971).

[7]In the sample there were twenty-eight home owners (56 percent), including a number who had bought their own council houses, twenty who lived in council houses (40 percent), including two who were in pensioners' bungalows, and two (4 percent) who lived in privately rented accomodation (one a house and one a flat). All of the housing in the sample could be considered houses with the exception of the one flat and perhaps the two in pensioners' bungalows.

[8]Note Charles Y. Glock's statement in "The Study of Unbelief" in *The Culture of Unbelief*, ed. Caporale and Grumelli, p.60: "Precision can be improved without sacrificing a common instrument by narrowing the conception of belief and unbelief and/or by limiting to more homogeneous populations. For example, belief and unbelief studied only from the perspective of Christian doctrine among persons who had been reared in the faith could be accomplished with considerable precision using a common measurement." This study has narrowed both the conception of belief/unbelief as well as limiting the population in a very broad sense to those with a generally British (including Irish) background.

[9]Compare studies by Leslie J. Francis. *Teenagers and the Church* (London: Collins, 1984); The Bible Societies' *National Survey on Religious Attitudes of Young People, 1978*; David Martin in *Prospects For The Eighties: From A Census of the Churches in*

Chapter Four Endnotes

1979 undertaken by the Nationwide Initiative in Evangelism
(London: MARC Europe, 1983), p. 13; Bernice Martin and Ronald
Pluck.   *Young People's Beliefs* (London, General Synod Board of
Education, 1977).

The European Value Systems Study Group revealed about
Britain: "In this area the average endorsement of traditional
values indicated a slightly more positive attitude among women,
but with considerable differences between the sexes on particular
items.   On five of them the level of endorsement by women was
much greater than that of men; they were: regular weekly church
attendance (18 per cent women, 10 per cent men), membership of a
religious organisation (28 per cent women, 16 per cent men),
great confidence in the church (24 per cent women, 14 per cent
men), derives great comfort from religion (55 per cent women, 35
per cent men), parents should encourage religious faith in their
children (16 per cent women, 11 per cent men)."   Mark Abrams,
"Demographic Correlates of Values" in *Values and Social Change in
Britain* ed. Mark Abrams, David Gerard, Noel Timms (London:
Macmillan, forthcoming).

Note also C. Daniel Batson and W. Larry Ventis in *The
Religious Experience: A Social-Psychological Perspective* (Oxford
and New York: Oxford University Press, 1982), pp.36-40.   He
lists several American studies and gives two biological and two
social explanations for the fact that women are more likely to be
interested and involved in religion than men.   Also regarding the
USA is Joseph E. Faulkner and Gordon F. DeJong. "Religiosity in
5-D: An Empirical Analysis" in *Religious Influence in Contemporary Society*, ed. Joseph E. Faulkner (Columbus, Ohio: Charles
E. Merrill Publishing Co., 1972), p. 64.

[10]E. S. Pearson, ed., *Tracts For Computers*. (Cambridge:
The University Press, 1939), No. 24: *Tables of Random Sampling
Numbers*, by M. G. Kendall and B. Babinton Smith, p. 39.

[11]John B. Williamson, David A. Karp, and John R. Dalphin,
The Research Craft (Boston: Little, Brown and Company, 1977), p.
188.

[12]Cf. *Prospects for the Eighties*, (London: MARC Europe,
1983), p.13.

[13]C. A. Moser and G. Kalton, *Survey Methods in Social
Investigation* (New York: Basic Books, Inc., 1958,1972), p. 175.

[14]Gallup, conducting a one-hour interview for the European Value Systems Study Group in Britain, "reported a response
rate of 60 per cent on the active sample (largely due to the need
to make prior appointments and to indicate both the length and
the detail of the interview), . . ."   Abrams, Gerard, Timms,
ed., *Values and Social Change in Britain*, general appendix.

[15]John B. Williamson, David A. Karp, and John R. Dalphin,
The Research Craft (Boston: Little, Brown and Company, 1977),
pp.177-9.

[16]R. Bucher, C. E. Fritz, and E. L. Quarantelli, "Tape
Recorded Interviews in Social Research", *American Sociological
Review* 21 (1956), 359-364.

Chapter Four Endnotes

[17]*The Unchurched* (New York: Harper and Row, 1980), p.32.

ENDNOTES FOR CHAPTER FIVE

[1]Oliver R. Barclay, *Reasons For Faith* (London: Inter-Varsity Press, 1974), p. 7.

[2]Leo Tolstoy in *Anna Karenin* creates an interesting experience for comparison:
"'Christ stands invisible before you to receive your confession,' he said, pointing to the crucifix. 'Do you believe in the doctrines of the Holy Apostolic Church?' the priest went on, turning his eyes away from Levin's face and folding his hands under his stole.
"'I have doubted, I doubt everything,' replied Levin in a voice that jarred on his own ears, and stopped.
"The priest waited a few seconds to see if he would add anything further, and then, closing his eyes, said quickly with a strong provincial accent:
"'To doubt is a natural human weakness, but we must pray to our merciful Lord to strengthen us. What are your special sins?' he added without the slightest pause, as though anxious not to waste time.
"'My chief sin is doubt. I doubt everything: most of the while I am in doubt.'
"'To doubt is a natural human weakness,' repeated the priest. 'What do you doubt in particular?'
"'Everything. I sometimes even have doubts of the existence of God,' replied Levin in spite of himself, and was horrified at the unseemliness of what he was saying. But the words appeared to have no effect on the priest."
(London: Penguin Books, 1954).

[3]It is interesting to compare these reasons with the following section of the documents of Vatican II on atheism:
"Many, unduly transgressing the limits of the positive sciences, contend that everything can be explained by this kind of scientific reasoning alone, or by contrast, they altogether disallow that there is any absolute truth.
"Some laud man so extravagantly that their faith in God lapses into a kind of anemia, though they seem more inclined to affirm man than to deny God.
"Moreover, atheism results not rarely from a violent protest against the evil in this world, or from the absolute character with which certain human values are unduly invested, and which thereby already accords them the stature of God.
"Modern atheism often takes a systematic expression, which, in addition to other arguments against God, stretches the desire for human independence to such a point that it finds difficulties with any kind of dependence on God. Those who profess atheism of this sort maintain that it gives man freedom to be an end unto himself, the sole artisan and creator of his own history. They claim that this freedom cannot be reconciled with the affirmation of a Lord who is author and purpose of all things, or at least that this freedom makes such an affirmation altogether superfluous. The sense of power which modern technical progress generates in man can give color to such a doctrine.
"Not to be overlooked among the forms of modern atheism is that which anticipates the liberation of man especially through his economic and social emancipation. This form argues

218

Chapter Five Endnotes

that by its nature religion thwarts such liberation by arousing
man's hope for a deceptive future life, thereby diverting him
from the constructing of an earthly city. Consequently, when the
proponents of this doctrine gain governmental power they vigor-
ously fight against religion. They promote atheism by using
those means of pressure which public power has at its disposal.
Such is especially the case in the work of educating the young."
Walter M. Abbott, ed., *The Documents of Vatican II* (New York:
Guild Press, 1966), pp. 215-19 quoted in Shane Womack, "Encounters with Atheists at a State University: Personal Interviews and
Theological Reflections" (M.A. thesis, Emmanuel School of Religion, 1983), p.29.

ENDNOTES FOR CHAPTER SIX

[1]Leslie J. Francis' study shows that 16-20 year olds who go to church have these views: "Again, three out of five (60%) of the young people in the sample come down strongly on the side of saying that they think abortion is wrong. One in four (24%) takes the other view that abortion is not wrong, and the remaining 16% had not really made up their minds. This time, the responses of the boys and girls are almost identical." *Teenagers and the Church* (London, Collins, 1984), p. 82.

The *National Survey on Religious Attitudes of Young People 1978* found this: "Attitudes to this moral issue were less well defined. Over half (54%) thought abortion should be allowed only if there is a possibility of the child being born abnormal, or for other reasons. 18% thought that abortion should never be allowed, a viewpoint mainly influenced by conscience, parents and religious belief. 31% thought abortion should be allowed for anybody who wants it, again mainly decided by listening to conscience. These were the views of the Schools Sample.

"In summary, the data shows that the majority of young people are *not* prepared to commit themselves to moral absolutes, either definitely right or definitely wrong. Also, the most important reason given for coming to views on the various moral issues was 'listening to conscience'." (Sponsored by "Buzz" Magazine, The Bible Society, The Scripture Union, n.d.), p. 7.

The European Value Systems Study Group reported a 4.14 mean score on abortion. The sliding scale of agreeing with with abortion was:

Never									Always
1	2	3	4	5	6	7	8	9	10
30%	7%	8%	7%	21%	6%	5%	7%	2%	6%

Table 4.1 in Mark Abrams, David Gerard, Noel Timms, ed., *Values and Social Change in Britain* (London: Macmillan, forthcoming).

[2] Note D. Gerard, "In so far as membership of a moral community is necessary to sustain shared standards, and membership of a community of faith is necessary to sustain Christian belief, then uncertainty and doubt are increasingly likely to prevail. This is particularly so in the absence of an alternative moral scheme--as opposed to a position based on rejection of prevailing standards--and in the face of relatively high levels of indifference to religious values exhibited by young people. Nearly two-thirds of those aged under 25 years fell into the two lowest categories on the composite religious commitment scale." "Religious Attitudes and Values" in Abrams, Gerard, Timms, ed., *Values and Social Change in Britain*, (forthcoming).

[3]The European Value Systems Study Group concluded, "Overall the poll shows the British to be unsure of their moral values, unsure of their religious beliefs, but sure of their institutions and very proud of their country." BBC-TV, "Everyman", 13 December, 1981. The *National Survey on Religious Attitudes of Young People 1978* concurred with this conclusion, "There is the general impression of uncertainty about belief and even definite belief does not presuppose traditional religious practice . . .", p. 10.

Chapter Six Endnotes

[4]The European Value Systems Study Group found that in Britain 21% of the people agreed that there was only one true religion while 65% believed that there was no one true religion. BBC-TV, "Everyman", 13 December, 1981. It is not clear, however, whether the respondents in the sample viewed, for example, all the Christian denominations as one religion or as many.

[5]Tracey Early comments on a 1978 Gallup poll on the unchurched in the USA: "Gallup found even most of the 'churched' agree--51 percent strongly, 25 percent moderately, compared with the 'unchurched' 65 and 21--that 'an individual should arrive at his or her own religious beliefs independent of any churches or synagogues.' Since nobody arrives at belief in the Resurrection or other Christian doctrines apart from a faith community, there is a potential here for a move to open agnosticism." "Gallup Polls the 'Unchurched'", *Christianity and Crisis*, 38 (17 July, 1978), 183.

[6]"Luckmann argues that society no longer requires religious legitimation and that religion has become transformed into a subjective, private, reality. This reality is, he suggests, characterised by autonomy, choice and personal preference and an emphasis on: self-realisation; mobility; self-expression; sexuality and familism. It does not conform to the demands of the specialised institutional form of religion with its defined doctrine, specialised ministry and ecclesiastical organisation. The latter is consequently undermined. Such a private religious reality depends on restricted kin and friendship networks to support it and enables the individual to "manage" his own relationship to God and to choose with whom he will worship." Gerard, "Religious Attitudes and Values", in *Values and Social Change in Britain*, ed. Abrams, Gerard, Timms (forthcoming). Note also Robert Bellah's thoughts on the privitisation of belief in "Historical Background of Belief" in *The Culture of Unbelief*, ed. Caporale and Grumelli, pp. 46ff.

[7]Note here Tilman Winkler's thought that religion is hidden in everyday discussion through humour and cursing, discussed later in our chapter seven. "Latentes religiöses Bewusstsein in der Arbeiterschaft", *Texte* 4 (Hanover: EKD, [October, 1982]), pp. 13-17.

[8]Dietrich Bonhoeffer, *Letters and Papers from Prison* (London: Fontana Books, 1953), pp. 106-107.

[9]L. Feuerback, *Notwendigkeit einer Reform der Philosophie* (1841), Sämtliche Werke, eds. (Stuttgart: Bolin and Jodl, 1904), Vol. II, pp. 218-219 quoted in Hans Küng, *Does God Exist?* (London: Collins, 1980), p. 207.

[10]I am indebted to Dan Beeby for these thoughts.

[11]*The New Demons* (London: Mowbrays, 1973), p. 65.

[12]*Ibid.*, p. 71.

Chapter Six Endnotes

[13]*Ibid.*, p. 73. Note also Walter J. Hollenweger, "Religiöse Standortbestimmung im Rahmen einer Einführung in eine moderne Mythologie", *Texte* 4 (Hanover: EKD, [October,1982]), pp. 2-8.

[14]Quoted in Alan Gilbert, *The Making of Post-Christian Britain: A History of the Secularization of Modern Society*, (London: Longman, 1980), p. xi.

[15]*A Rumour of Angels* (New York: Anchor Books, 1970), p. 10.

[16]*Letters and Papers*, pp. 111-112.

[17]Ellul, *Demons*, p. 64.

[18]In Leslie J. Francis' profile of church-going youth in the 1980's, he finds that 43 percent pray every day, 47 percent pray irregularly and very infrequently, and 10 percent never pray. *Teenagers and the Church*, p. 66.

[19](New Haven: Yale University Press, 1952), pp. 41, 42.

[20]15 percent of the European Value Systems Study Group sample reported often thinking about death. Table 3.1. in Abrams, Gerard, Timms, ed., *Values and Social Change in Britain* (forthcoming).

[21]Bonhoeffer, *Letters and Papers*, p. 85.

[22]8 percent of the European Value Systems Study Group sample often regretted doing wrong. Table 3.1 in Abrams, Gerard, Timms, ed., *Values and Social Change in Britain* (forthcoming).

[23]Gerard, "Religious Attitudes and Values", in *Values and Social Change in Britain*, ed. Abrams, Gerard, Timms (forthcoming).

[24]Our 22 per cent compares with 19 percent of the European Value Systems Study Group sample who reported that they have had a spiritual experience. Table 3.1 in Abrams, Gerard, Timms, ed., *Values and Social Change in Britain* (forthcoming).

[25]Compare Lesslie Newbigin's discussion on explanation, framework, and enlightenment in *The Other Side of 1984* (Geneva: World Council of Churches, 1983), pp. 8ff.

[26]"Polanyi writes: 'Our fundamental beliefs are continuously reconsidered . . . but only within the scope of their own basic premises.'" Newbigin, *1984*, p. 30.

[27]Leslie J. Francis' study of church-going youth gives us this comparison: "About half of the sample feel that they might have had something which they would describe as a 'religious experience'. The nature of this experience can be very different from one person to another, but the important point is that half of the teenagers feel that they can look back in their lives and possibly point to something which spoke to them in a peculiar way of God's presence or activity.

Chapter Six Endnotes

"51% of the sample are quite clear that they have never experienced anything they would call a religious experience. 22% are very tentative about it all, but feel that they might have had a religious experience, although they are not really sure whether that is the right description or not. A further 11% are more sure than this, but not completely certain. This leaves one in six (16%) of the teenagers who are quite clear that they have had a religious experience at sometime or other.", p. 68.

[28]Compare John Paul Sartre's experience: "I was led to disbelief not by the conflict of dogmas, but by my parents' indifference. Nevertheless, I believed. In my nightshirt, kneeling on the bed, with my hands together, I said my prayers every day, but I thought of God less and less often. . . . For several years more, I maintained public relations with the Almighty. But privately, I ceased to associate with him. Only once did I have the feeling that He existed. I had been playing with matches and burned a small rug. I was in the process of covering up my crime when suddenly God saw me. I felt his gaze inside my head and on my hands. I whirled about in the bathroom, horribly visible, a live target. Indignation saved me. I flew into a rage against so crude an indiscretion, I blasphemed, I muttered like my grandfather: 'God damn it, God damn it.' He never looked at me again." from *The Words*, trans. Bernard Frechtman (New York: G. Brazliller, 1964), pp. 100-102 quoted in Shane Womack "Encounters With Atheists at a State University: Personal Interviews and Theological Reflections" (M.A.R. thesis, Emmanuel School of Religion, 1983), p. 76.

[29]This coincides with 1979 statistics showing that 11 percent of the total adult population attends church on a given Sunday in all England and 9 percent in the West Midlands. *Prospects For The Eighties*, (London: MARC Europe, 1983), pp. 23, 92. Note also older statistics and comments by Joan Brothers in her chapter on "Participation in Religious Institutions", in *Religious Institutions*, (London: Longman, 1971), pp. 26-39.

[30]David Martin shows that "'You don't need to go to church to be a good Christian' is the nearest thing to a fundamental creed amongst working-class people." *A Sociology of English Religion* (London: SCM Press, 1967), p. 69.

[31]*The Religious and the Secular* (London: Routledge and Kegan Paul, 1969), p. 121.

[32]The European Value Systems Study Group found similarly, "More than two-thirds of those who define themselves as not religious, and three-fifths of non-believers, identify with the established churches, as do two-fifths of the small group of atheists. Further, those who identify with established church are much less likely to attend church frequently than those from other denominations. They also score significantly lower on the scale of overall religious commitment than either non-conformists or Roman Catholics." Gerard, "Religious Attitudes and Values", in *Values and Social Change in Britain*, ed. Abrams, Gerard, Timms (forthcoming).

[33]*Toward a Sociology of Irreligion* (London: Macmillan, 1971), p. 33.

Chapter Six Endnotes

[34]David Martin maintains that "'Hypocrisy' is the main epithet applied to those with church affiliation and it is almost universally maintained that those who do not attend church are as good as those who do." *A Sociology of English Religion*, p. 69. Although certainly present, neither statements were made as often as one might have expected in the interviews.

[35]David Martin concurs, "The vast majority of English people identify themselves with the word 'Christian'." *The Religious and the Secular*, p. 106.

[36]Note here C. S. Lewis, *Mere Christianity* (New York: The Macmillan Company, 1943, 1960), pp. 10-11.

[37]The European Value Systems Study Group asked which specific commandments still applied to their interviewees and to others. The chairman, Prof. Jan Kerkoffs commented on the BBC television series, "Everyman", 13 December, 1981: "The interesting thing about the British is they are lower than European norms on the religious commandments and higher than the European norms on the social commandments. . . . This means that the Judea-Christian underpinnings of our value system seem, at least for me, these seem to be stronger in England than in the rest of Europe."

[38]Berger points out with regard to scholars what is sometimes true of these men, who relativize the primitive ages, but have a hidden double standard, "The *past*, out of which the tradition comes, is relativized in terms of this or that socio-historical analysis. The *present*, however, remains strangely immune from relativization." *A Rumour of Angels* (London: The Penguin Press, 1970), p. 58.

[39]The European Value Systems Study Group discovered: "Those who identified themselves as convinced atheists (Q.158) comprised only 4 per cent of the population. Indeed, an examination of the responses of the 45 self-confessed atheists reveals that twenty of them claimed some form of denominational attachment, ten believed in the existence of some sort of spirit or life force, ten believed in life after death, one actually believed in a personal God, eight asserted a belief in God (Q.163) and seven were agnostic. The true figure for convinced atheists is therefore nearer 2 per cent." Gerard, "Religious Attitudes and Values", in Abrams, Gerard, Timms, ed., *Values and Social Change in Britain* (forthcoming).

[40]*The Secularisation of the European Mind in the Nineteeth Century* (Cambridge: Cambridge University Press, 1975), pp. 100-101 quoted in "Man's Search for Meaning", *The Month* 237 (May, 1976), pp. 160-164.

ENDNOTES FOR CHAPTER SEVEN

[1](Oxford: Oxford University Press, 1982), p. 699.

[2]Barrett, p. 699, as does the Anglican profession of 56.8 percent (compared with 54 percent in this research). The predominance of Roman Catholic adherents in this research population brought a difference to Barrett's 13.1 percent (22 percent) and in Protestants, 15 percent (6 percent). Compare also Joan Brothers, *Religious Institutions*, (London: Longman, 1971), pp. 11-25.

[3]Mark Abrams, David Gerard, Noel Timms, ed., *Values and Social Change in Britain* (London: Macmillan, forthcoming).

[4]Gerhard Szczesny, *The Future of Unbelief*, trans. Edward B. Garside (London: Heinemann, 1961), pp. 312-214.

[5]Bernice Martin and Ronald Pluck, *Young People's Beliefs* (London: General Synod Board of Education, n.d.), p. 1.

[6]*Ibid.*, p. 6.

[7]*Ibid.*, pp. 20-26.

[8]Although this is a popular conception, Gerard points out that "Empirical studies, however, indicate that social class differences contribute little by way of explanation of patterns of church involvement." "Religious Attitudes and Values", in *Values and Social Change in Britain*, ed. Abrams, Gerard, Timms (forthcoming).

[9]Abrams, Gerard, Timms, ed., *Values and Social Change in Britain*, (forthcoming).

[10]David Martin, *A Sociology of English Religion* (London: SCM Press, 1967), p. 68.

[11]Tilman Winkler, "Latentes religiöses Bewusstsein in der Arbeiterschaft", *Texte* 4 (Hanover:EKD, [October, 1982]), 13-17.

[12]"Gallup Polls the 'Unchurched'", *Christianity and Crisis* 38 (17 July 1978), 184.

[13]Martin, *A Sociology of English Religion*, p. 105.

[14]*Ibid.*, p.69.

[15]*Ibid.*, p. 104.

[16]*Ibid.*

[17]"Towards a Reappraisal of Christian Apologetics: Peter L. Berger's Sociology of Knowledge as the Sociological Prolegomenon to Christian Apologetics" (D.Phil. thesis, University of Oxford, 1981), p. 321.

Chapter Seven Endnotes

[18]J. Russell Hale, *The Unchurched: Who They Are and Why They Stay Away* (New York: Harper and Row, 1980), part three.

[19]Abrams, Gerard, Timms, ed., *Values and Social Change in Britain* (forthcoming).

ENDNOTES FOR CHAPTER EIGHT

[1] Jan M. Lochman sketches some of "the history of the encounters of the church with atheism [which] is a history encrusted with prejudices and caricatures. It is replete with fixed battle lines and battle cries and marked by a mutual 'demonizing' of the other side." "Gospel for Atheists", *Theology Today* 26 (Oct., 1969), 300-302.

[2] Lesslie Newbigin, *The Other Side of 1984* (Geneva: World Council of Churches, 1983), p. 11.

[3] *Man: Believer and Unbeliever* (New York: Alba House, 1974), p. 282.

[4] James D. G. Dunn, *Unity and Diversity in the New Testament* (London: SCM Press, 1977), p. 58.

[5] Charles Y. Glock and Rodney Stark, *Christian Beliefs and Anti-Semitism* (New York: Harper and Row, 1966), p. 11.

[6] Dunn, *Unity and Diversity*, pp. 31-32.

[7] *Dogmatics*, Vol. 3: *The Christian Doctrine of the Church, Faith, and the Consummation*, trans. David Cairns (London: Lutterworth Press, 1960), p. 140.

[8] *Christ and Culture* (New York: Harper Torchbooks, 1951), p. 11.

[9] *A Strategy for the Church's Ministry*, (London: CIO, 1983), p. 16 quoted by John Mahoney, "Theological and Pastoral Reflections" in *Values and Social Change in Britain*, ed. Mark Abrams, David Gerard, Noel Timms (London: Macmillan, forthcoming).

[10] Translated by Bernard Murchland, (New York: The Macmillan Company, 1963), p. 158.

[11] Tyrrell, *Man: Believer and Unbeliever*, p. 285.

[12] Duplicated Report, (London: General Synod Board of Education, n.d.), p. 11.

[13] Abrams, Gerard, Timms, ed., *Values and Social Change in Britain* (forthcoming).

[14] *Ibid.*

ENDNOTES FOR CHAPTER NINE

[1] "The Case Against God", BBC Radio 4, 18 November, 1984.

[2] N. J. Demerath III, *Actes de la Conference Internationale* (Rome: Conference Internationale de Sociologie Religieuse, 1969), p. 175.

[3] Cornelio Fabro, *God in Exile: Modern Atheism*, trans. and ed. Arthur Gibson (New York: Newman Press, 1968), p. 241.

[4] *Toward A Sociology of Irreligion* (London: Macmillan, 1971), p. 25.

[5] *The Secularist Heresy: The Erosion of the Gospel in the Twentieth Century* (London: SPCK, 1956,1981), pp. 13-14.

[6] *Ibid.*, pp.15-16.

[7] *The Natural and the Supernatural Jew* (New York: Pantheon, 1962), pp. 252f. quoted in Martin E. Marty, *Varieties of Unbelief* (New York: Holt, Rinehart and Winston, 1964), pp. 29-30.

[8] Blamires, *The Secularist Heresy*, p. 19.

[9] *Christianity and the Social Order* (London: Chapman and Hall, 1912), p. 8 quoted in Donald R. Robertson, "The Relationship Between Church and Social Class in Scotland" (Ph.D. thesis, University of Edinburgh, 1966). Robertson also says, "Much of what has so far been brought to light in this chapter tellingly suggests that the church is an 'accepted' part of life not often viewed with rancour; but she often seems to be quite remote and vague. This is not, in the main, an age of inflamed religious passion, or bitter doctrinal controversy or of intensity or feeling about the church. The word, church, elicits few concrete images; people tend to be very mild in their expressions". p. 253.

[10] "On Methods and Morals", in *Values and Social Change in Britain*, ed. Mark Abrams, David Gerard, Noel Timms (London: Macmillan, forthcoming).

[11] *The Gravedigger File* (Downer's Grove, IL: InterVarsity Press, 1983), p. 103.

[12] Leo N. Tolstoy (London: Penguin Books, 1954), p. 463-464.

[13] "On the Development of Unbelief", in *The Culture of Unbelief*, ed. Rocco Caporale and Antonio Grumelli (Berkeley: The University of California Press, 1971), p. 180.

[14] "Gallup Polls the 'Unchurched.'" *Christianity and Crisis* 38 (17 July, 1978), p. 185.

Chapter Nine Endnotes

[15]John Mahoney, "Theological and Pastoral Reflections" in *Values and Social Change in Britain*, ed. Mark Abrams, David Gerard, Noel Timms (London: Macmillan, forthcoming).

[16]Dietrich Bonhoeffer, *The Cost of Discipleship* (New York: The Macmillan Company, 1937, 1959), p. 38.

[17]Charles H. Kraft, "The Limits of Indigenization in Theology", in *Readings in Dynamic Indigeneity*, ed. Charles H. Kraft and Tom N. Wisley (Pasadena: William Carey Library, 1979), pp.386-387.

[18]Mahoney, "Theological and Pastoral Relfections" in *Values and Social Change in Britain*, ed. Abrams, Gerard, Timms (forthcoming).

[19]Emil Brunner, *Dogmatics*, Vol. 1: *The Chritian Doctrine of God*, trans. Olive Wyon (London: Lutterworth Press, 1949), p. 101-102.

[20]Walter Hollenweger, unpublished lecture notes.

[21]Berger explains: "By a cognitive minority I mean a group of people whose view of the world differs significantly from the one generally taken for granted in their society. Put differently, a cognitive minority is a group formed around a body of deviant 'knowledge' (in the sense of) what is taken to be or believed as knowledge." *A Rumour of Angels* (London: Allen Lane, The Penguin Press, 1970), p. 15.

[22]*The Future of Unbelief*, trans. Edward B. Garside (London: Heinemann, 1961), p. 14.

[23]Colin Campbell notes, "As sociologists define religion as a social and not merely as a cultural phenomenon, so too must they define irreligion as a social phenomenon." *Toward a Sociology of Irreligion*, p. 28).

[24]*Between Belief and Unbelief* (New York: Harper and Row, 1974), p. 54.

[25]*The Future of Unbelief*, p. 79.

[26]Os Guinness, *The Gravedigger File* (Downer's Grove, Illinois: Inter Varsity Press, 1983), p. 35.

[27]*Ibid.*, p. 36. Note also the same author's D.Phil. thesis, "Towards A Reappraisal of Christian Apologetics: Peter L. Berger's Sociology of Knowledge as the Sociological Prolegomenon to Christian Apologetics" (University of Oxford, 1981), pp. 174-176, 295-298.

[28]Guinness, *Gravedigger*, p. 103. Note also Martin Marty, *Varieties of Unbelief* (New York: Holt, Rinehard and Winston, 1964), pp. 103-111.

[29]Official statistics from the Birmingham office of *Mission: England*.

Chapter Nine Endnotes

[30] For a discussion of liturgical dance, note J. G. Davies, *Liturgical Dance* (London: SCM Press, 1984).

[31] Jacque Ellul's *Prayer and Modern Man* is an important analysis of the modern dilemma of prayer. Trans. C. Edward Hopkin (New York: Seabury Press, 1973).

[32] *Letters and Papers from Prison* (London: Collins/Fontana Books, 1953), p. 67.

[33] Note J. G. Davies, *New Perspectives in Worship Today* (London: SCM Press, 1978), pp. 47-51.

[34] Dietrich Bonhoeffer, *Life Together*, trans. John W. Doberstein (New York: Harper and Brothers, 1954), pp. 97-99 quoted in J. Russell Hale, *Who Are the Unchurched?* (Washington: Glenmary Research Center, 1977), p. 91.

[35] Emil Brunner, *Dogmatics*, Vol. 1: *The Christian Doctrine of God*, trans. Olive Wyon (London: Lutterworth Press, 1949), p. 103.

[36] Note Lesslie Newbigin, *The Other Side of 1984* (Geneva: World Council of Churches, 1983), pp. 29-30.

[37] Note Os Guinness' notion of "creative persuasion" which includes Peter Berger's "cognitive respect" and "cognitive participation" in "Towards a Reappraisal of Christian Apologetics", pp. 327-372.

[38] Leo Tolstoy gives an insightful story illustrating how men give up their meaningless liturgies: "A clever and truthful man, once told me the story of how he ceased to believe. On a hunting expedition, when he was already 26, he once, at the place where they put up for the night, knelt down in the evening to pray--a habit retained from childhood. His elder brother, who was at the hunt with him, was lying on some hay and watching him. When S. had finished and was settling down for the night, his brother said to him: 'So you still do that?'
"They said nothing more to one another. But from that day S. ceased to say his prayers or go to church. And now he has not prayed or received communion for thirty years. And this not because he knows his brother's convictions and has joined him in them, nor because he has decided anything in his own soul, but simply because a word spoken by his brother was like the push of a finger on a wall that was ready to fall by its own weight. The word only showed that where he thought there was faith, in reality there had long been an empty space, and that therefore the utterance of words and the making of signs of the cross and genuflections while praying were quite senseless actions. Becoming conscious of their senselessness he could not continue them." *A Confession in a Confession: The Gospel in Brief and What I Believe* (Oxford: Oxford University Press, 1954), p. 5.

[39] In J. G. Davies, ed., *A Dictionary of Liturgy and Worship* (London: SCM Press, 1972), pp. 177.

[40] "Latentes religiöses Bewusstsein in der Arbeiterschaft", *Texte* 4 (Hanover: EKD [October, 1982]), 13-17.

Chapter Nine Endnotes

[41]Michael Green, *You Must Be Joking?* (London: Hodder and Stoughton, 1976), chapter 5.

[42]"Dynamic Equivalence Theologizing" in *Readings in Dynamic Indigeneity*, ed. Charles H. Kraft and Tom N. Wisley (Pasadena: William Carey Library, 1979), p. 264.

[43]*Life Together*, pp. 105-106 quoted in J. Russell Hale. *The Unchurched* (San Francisco: Harper and Row, 1980), p. 187.

[44]*The Unchurched* (San Francisco: Harper and Row, 1980), p. 191.

[45]"Towards a Reappraisal of Christian Apologetics", pp. 329-330.

[46]*The Religious and the Secular* (London: Routledge and Kegan Paul, 1969), p. 111.

[47]*Ibid.*, p. 112.

[48]Mahoney, "Theological and Pastoral Reflections" in *Values and Social Change in Britain*, ed. Abrams, Gerard, Timms (forthcoming).

[49]F. J. Foakes-Jackson in *Cambridge Theological Essays*, p. 474, quoted in *Christianity is Christ* (Chicago: Moody Press, 1965), p. 5.

[50]*Mere Christianity* (New York: The Macmillan Company, 1952,1960), pp. 38-39.

[51]"The Biblical Basis of Evangelism" in *Let the Earth Hear His Voice*, ed. J. D. Douglas (Minneapolis: World Wide Publications, 1975), p. 70.

[52]"Ancient Voices: The Message Looks for a Medium". Lincoln, Illinois: Lincoln Christian Seminary Lectureship, 6 April, 1976.

[53]*Christ and Culture* (New York: Harper Torchbooks, 1951), pp. 39-40.

[54]*Ibid.*, pp. 116-117.

[55]*Ibid.*, p. 45.

[56]*Ibid.*, p. 83.

[57]*Ibid.*, p. 85.

[58]*Ibid.*, p. 42.

[59]*Ibid.*, pp. 149-151.

[60]*Ibid.*, p. 43.

[61]*Ibid.*, p. 231.

Chapter Nine Endnotes

[62]"The Limits of Indigenization in Theology" in *Readings in Dynamic Indigeneity*, ed. Kraft and Wisely, p. 374.

[63]*Christ and Culture*, p. 5.

[64]*Ibid.*

[65]*Ibid.*, p. 6.

[66]*Ibid.*, p. 7.

[67]*Ibid.*, p. 10.

[68]D. Gerard, "Religious Attitudes and Values", in *Values and Social Change in Britain*, ed. Abrams, Gerard, Timms (forthcoming).

[69]"Towards a Reappraisal of Christian Apologetics", p. 79.

[70]Quoted in Kraft, "Dynamic Equivalence Theologizing", in *Readings in Dynamic Indigeneity*, ed. Kraft and Wisely, p. 264.

[71]The Limits of Indigenization in Theology", in *Readings in Dynamic Indigeneity*, ed. Kraft and Wisely, p. 378.

[72]*Christ and Culture*, p. 11.

[73]"Dynamic-Equivalence Theologizing", in *Readings in Dynamic Indigeneity*, ed. Kraft and Wisely, p. 284.

[74]"The Limits of Indigenization in Theology", in *Readings in Dynamic Indigeneity*, ed. Kraft and Wisely, p. 375.

BIBLIOGRAPHIES

MAIN LIST OF

SOURCES CONSULTED

ABBOTT, WALTER M., ed. *The Documents of Vatican II*. New York: Guild Press, 1966.

ABRAMS, MARK; GERARD, DAVID; and TIMMS, NOEL, eds. *Values and Social Change in Britain*. London: Macmillan, forthcoming.

BARRETT, DAVID A. *World Christian Encyclopedia*. Oxford: Oxford University Press, 1982.

BARCLAY, OLIVER R. *Reasons for Faith*. London: InterVarsity Press, 1974.

BATSON, C. DANIEL, and VENTIS, W. LARRY. *The Religious Experience: A Social-Psychological Perspective*. Oxford: Oxford University Press, 1982.

BAUER, JOHANNES B., and ZIMMERMANN, HEINRICH. "Faith". In *Bauer Encyclopdia of Biblical Theology*, pp. 343-355. Edited by Johannes B. Bauer. London: Sheed and Ward, 1970.

BECKER, O., AND MICHEL, O. "Faith". In *The New International Dictionary of New Testament Theology*. Edited by Colin Brown. Grand Rapids: Zondervan Publishing House, 1975. I, pp. 587-606.

BEHM, JOHANNES. "καρδία". In *Theological Dictionary of the New Testament*. Edited by Gerhard Kittel. Translated and edited by Geoffrey W. Bromiley. Grand Rapids: William B. Eerdmans Publishing Company, 1968. III, pp. 605-614.

BELLAH, ROBERT. *Beyond Belief: Essays on Religion in a Post-Traditional World*. New York: Harper and Row, 1970.

BERGER, PETER L. *A Rumour of Angels*. London: The Penguin Press, 1970.

BLACK, WILLARD M. "America's Fourth Religion", *Christian Standard* (September 30, 1984), 880-882.

BLACKMAN, E. C. "Faith". In *The Interpreter's Dictionary of the Bible*, II, pp. 222-234. Edited by George Arthur Buttrick. Nashville: Abingdon Press, 1962.

Main Source List

BLAMIRES, HARRY. *The Secularist Heresy: The Erosion of the Gospel in the Twentieth Century.* London: SPCK, 1956, 1981.

BONHOEFFER, DIETRICH. *Letters and Papers from Prison.* London: Collins/Fontanta, 1953.

_____. *Life Together.* Translated by John W. Doberstein. New York: Harper and Brothers, 1954.

_____. *The Cost of Discipleship.* 2nd Edition. New York: The Macmillan Company, 1959, 1963.

BORNE, ETIENNE. *Atheism.* Translated by S. J. Tester. London: Burns and Oates, 1961.

BRIERLEY, PETER, ed. *Beyond the Churches.* London: MARC Europe and Evangelical Alliance, 1984.

BROTHERS, JOAN, ed. *Readings in the Sociology of Religion.* Oxford: Pergamon Press, 1967.

BRUNNER, EMIL. *Dogmatics.* Vol. 1: The Christian Doctrine of God. Translated by Olive Wyon. London: Lutterworth Press, 1949.

_____. *Dogmatics.* Vol. 3: The Christian Doctrine of the Church, Faith, and the Consummation. Translated by David Cairns. London: Lutterworth Press, 1960.

BUDD, SUSAN. *Varieties of Unbelief: Atheists and Agnostics in English Society 1850-1960.* London: Heinemann, 1977.

BULTMANN, RUDOLF. *Jesus and the Word.* Translated by Louise Pettibone Smith and Erminie Huntress Lantero. London: Collins/Fontana, 1934, 1958.

_____. *The Theology of the New Testament.* Translated by Kendrick Grobel. 2 Vols. New York: Charles Scribner's Sons, 1951.

_____. " πείθω κτλ. " In *Theological Dictionary of the New Testament.* Edited by Gerhard Friedrich. Translated and edited by Geoffrey W. Bromiley. Grand Rapids: William B. Eerdmans Publishing, 1968. VI, pp. 1-11.

BULTMANN, RUDOLF, and WEISER, ARTUR. " πιστεύω κτλ. " In *Theological Dictionary of the New Testament,* Edited by Gerhard Friedrich. Translated and edited by Geoffrey W. Bromiley. Grand Rapids: William B. Eerdmans Publishing Company, 1968. VI, pp. 186-228.

CALVIN, JOHN. *Calvin's Institutes.* Reprint ed., MacDill AFB, Florida: MacDonald Publishing Company, n.d.

CAMPBELL, COLIN. *Towards A Sociology of Irreligion.* London: Macmillan, 1971.

Main Source List

CAMPBELL, R. J. *Christianity and the Social Order*. London: Chapman and Hall, 1912. Quoted in Donald R. Robertson, "The Relationshp Between Church and Social Class in Scotland". Ph.D. thesis, University of Edinburgh, 1966.

CAPORALE, ROCCO, and GRUMELLI, ANTONIO, ed. *The Culture of Unbelief* Berkeley: The University of California Press, 1971.

COHEN, ARTHUR A. *The Natural and the Supernatural Jew*. New York: Pantheon, 1962. Quoted in Martin E. Marty, *Varieties of Unbelief*, pp. 29-30. New York: Holt, Rinehart and Winston, 1964.

CONN, WALTER E., ed. *Conversion: Perspectives on Personal and Social Transformation*. Staten Island, New York: Alba House, 1978.

COVENTRY, JOHN. "Faith and a Modern Presentation of Traditional Beliefs", *The Month* 237 (May 1976), pp. 148-152.

CUPITT, DON. "The Case Against God", BBC Radio 4, 18 November, 1984.

DAVIES, J. G. *Liturgical Dance*. London: SCM Press, 1984.

_____. *New Perspectives in Worship Today*. London: SCM Press, 1978.

DEMERATH, N. J. III. "Program and Prolegomena for a Sociology of Irreligion". In *Actes de la X Conference Internationale*. Rome: Conference Internationale de Sociologie Religieuse, 1969.

DIXON, KEITH. *The Sociology of Belief: Fallacy and Foundation*. London: Routledge and Kegan Paul, 1980.

DUKE, MICHAEL HARE, and WHITTON, ERIC. *A Kind of Believing*. London: General Synod Board of Education, 1977.

DUNN, JAMES D. G. *Baptism in the Holy Spirit*. Studies in Biblical Theology, Second Series, no. 15. London: SCM Press, 1970.

_____. *Unity and Diversity in the New Testament*. London: SCM Press, 1977.

DURKHEIM, EMILE. *The Elementary Forms of the Religious Life*. Translated by Joseph Ward Swain. London: George Allen and Unwin, 1915, 1976.

EARLY, TRACY. "Gallup Polls the 'Unchurched'", *Christianity and Crisis* 38 (1978), 182-185.

ELLUL, JACQUES. *Prayer and Modern Man*. Translated by C. Edward Hopkin. New York: The Seabury Press, 1970.

_____. *The New Demons*. London: Mowbrays, 1973.

Main Source List

FABRO, CORNELIO. *God in Exile: Modern Atheism*. New York: Newman Press, 1965.

FANT, CLYDE. "Ancient Voices: The Message Looks for a Medium", Lincoln Christian Seminary Lectureship, Lincoln, Illinois, 6 April, 1976.

FEUERBACK, L. *Notwendigkeit einer Reform der Philosophie* (1841). Edited by Sämtliche Werke. Stuttgart: Bolin and Jodl, 1904. Quoted in Hans Küng, *Does God Exist?*, p. 207. London: Collins, 1980.

FLINT, ROBERT. *Anti-Theistic Theories*. Edinburgh: Blackwood and Sons, 1885.

FOAKES-JACKSON, F. J. *Cambridge Theological Essays*. Quoted in W. H. Griffith Thomas, *Christianity is Christ*, p. 5. Chicago: Moody Press, 1965.

FRANCIS, LESLIE J. *Teenagers and the Church*. London: Collins, 1984.

_____. *Youth in Transit*. London: Gower, 1982.

GAINE, JOHN J. "Young Adults Today and the Future of the Faith: A Report for a Meeting of the Secretariat for Non-Believers", Ushaw College, Durham, n.d. (duplicated).

GALLAGHER, MICHAEL PAUL. "Atheism Irish Style", *The Furrow* 25 (April 1974), 183-192.

GALLUP OPINION INDEX. *Survey of the Unchurched American*. Princeton, New Jersey: American Institute of Public Opinion, 1978.

GILBERT, ALAN D. *The Making of Post-Christian Britain*. London: Longman Group, 1980.

GREEN, MICHAEL. *Evangelism in the Early Church*. London: Hodder and Stoughton, 1970.

_____. *You Must Be Joking?* London: Hodder and Stoughton, 1976.

GUINNESS, OS. *In Two Minds*. Downers Grove, Illinois: InterVarsity Press, 1976.

_____. *The Gravedigger File*. Downer's Grove, Illinois: InterVarsity Press, 1983.

_____. "Towards a Reappraisal of Christian Apologetics: Peter L. Berger's Sociology of Knowledge as the Sociological Prolegomenon to Christian Apologetics". D.Phil. thesis, University of Oxford, 1981.

GUYAU, M. *The Non-Religion of the Future: A Sociological Study*. New York: Schocken Books, 1897, 1962.

Main Source List

HALE, J. RUSSELL. *The Unchurched: Who They Are and Why They Stay Away*. San Francisco: Harper and Row, 1980.

_____. *Who Are the Unchurched?* Washington D.C.: Glenmary Research Center, 1977.

HEBBLETHWAITE, PETER. "Man's Search for Meaning", *The Month* 237 (May 1976), 160-164.

HENRY, CARL F. H. *God, Revelation and Authority*. Vol. 2: *God Who Speaks and Shows*. Waco, Texas: Word Books, 1976.

HOLLENWEGER, WALTER J. "Experimental Worship". In *A Dictionary of Liturgy and Worship*. Edited by J. G. Davies. London: SCM Press, 1972.

_____. "Religiöse Standortbestimmung im Rahmen einer Einführung in eine modern Mythologie", *Texte* 4 (Hanover: EKD, [October 1982]), 2-8.

_____. "The 'What' and the 'How': Content and Communication of the One Message", *The Expository Times* 76 (11), pp. 322-328.

HUDDLESTON, TREVOR. "Christian Outreach to Unbelief", *The Month* 238 (July 1977), 221-226.

JEPSEN, ALFRED. " ﾂﾂﾂ ". In *Theological Dictionary of the Old Testament*, I, pp. 292-323. Edited by G. Johannes Botterweck and Helmer Riggren. Translated by John T. Willis. Grand Rapids: Eerdmans, 1974.

KÖNIG, CARDINAL FRANZ. "The Dialogue with Non-Believers in France", *Herder Correspondence* 6 (June 1969), 170-174.

_____. "The Second Vatican Council and the Secretariat for Non-Believers", *Concurrence* 1 (Spring 1969).

KÖNIG, CARDINAL FRANZ, and MIANO, VINCENZO. "Dialogue with Non-Believers", *Herder Correspondence* 5 (December 1968), pp. 367-372.

KRAFT, CHARLES H., and WISLEY, TOM N., ed. *Readings in Dynamic Indigeneity*, Pasadena: William Carey Library, 1979.

KÜNG, HANS. *Does God Exist?*. Translated by Edward Quinn. London: Collins, 1980.

LACROIS, JEAN. *The Meaning of Modern Atheism*. Translated by Garret Barden. Dublin: Gill and Son, 1965.

LAW, ROBERT A. *The Tests of Life*. Edinburgh: T & T Clark, 1909; reprint ed., Grand Rapids: Baker Book House, 1968.

LEPP, IGNACE. *Atheism in Our Time*. New York: The Macmillan Company, 1963.

LEWIS, C. S. *Mere Christianity*. New York: The Macmillan Company, 1943, 1960.

Main Source List

LOCHMAN, JAN. "Gospel for Atheists", *Theology Today* 26 (1969), 299-311.

MACINTYRE, ALASDAIR, and RICOEUR, PAUL. *The Religious Significance of Atheism*. New York: Columbia University Press, 1969.

MAGNO, JOSEPH A., and LAMOTTE, VICTOR S. *The Christian, The Atheist, and Freedom*. New York: Precedent Publishing, 1973.

MARSHALL, I. HOWARD. "Orthodoxy and Heresy in Earlier Christianity", *Themelios* 2 (September 1976), 5-14.

MARTIN, BERNICE, and PLUCK, RONALD. *Young People's Beliefs*. London: General Synod Board of Education, 1977.

MARTIN, DAVID. *A Sociology of English Religion*. London: SCM Press, 1967.

_____. *Religion in Secular Society*. London: Watts and Company, 1966.

_____. *The Religious and the Secular*. London: Routledge and Kegan Paul, 1969.

MARTY, MARTIN E. *Varieties of Unbelief*. New York: Holt, Rinehart and Winston, 1964.

MATCZAK, SEBASTIAN A. *God in Contempary Thought: A Philosophical Perspective*. New York: Learned Publications, 1977.

METZ, JOHANNES BAPTIST. "Unbelief as a Theological Problem", *Concilium* VI (June, 1965), 32-42.

MOLNAR, THOMAS. *Theists and Atheists: A Typology of Non-Belief*. The Hague: Mouton Publishers, 1980.

MOLTMANN, JÜRGEN. *Theology of Hope*. Translated by James W. Leitch. New York: Harper and Row, 1967.

NASH, HENRY S., and KIRN, O. "Faith". In *The New Schaff-Herzog Encyclopdia of Religious Knowledge*, IV, pp. 267-270. Edited by Samuel Macauley Jackson. London: Funk and Wagnalls Company, 1909.

National Survey on Religious Attitudes of Young People 1978. London: "Buzz" Magazine, The Bible Society, The Scripture Union, [1978].

NATIONWIDE INITIATIVE IN EVANGELISM. *Prospects for the Eighties*. London: MARC Europe, 1983.

NEWBIGIN, LESSLIE. *The Other Side of 1984*. Geneva: The World Council of Churches, 1983.

NIEBUHR, H. RICHARD. *Christ and Culture*. New York: Harper Torchbooks, 1951, 1956.

Main Source List

NOVAK, MICHAEL. *Belief and Unbelief*. London: Darton, Longman and Todd, 1966.

O'DEA, THOMAS F. *Alienation, Atheism, and the Religious Crisis*. New York: Sheed and Ward, 1969.

PANNENBERG, WOLFHART. *Basic Questions in Theology*. Volume 2. Philadelphia: Fortress Press, 1971.

PAUL, LESLIE. *Alternatives to Christian Belief*. London: Hodder and Stoughton, 1967.

PRESTON, GEOFFREY. "The Crisis of Faith in Adolescence", *The Clergy Review* 61 (August 1978), 299-304.

PRIESTLAND, GERALD. "The Case Against God", BBC Radio 4, 18 November, 1984.

PRUYSER, PAUL. *Between Belief and Unbelief*. New York: Harper and Row, 1974.

REUMANN, J. "Faith, Faithfulness in the New Testament". In *The Interpreter's Dictionary of the Bible*, Supplementary Volume, pp. 332-335. Edited by Keith Crin. Nashville: Abingdon Press, 1976.

REID, JOHN PATRICK. *The Anatomy of Atheism*. Washington, D.C.: Thomist Press, 1965.

ROBERTSON, DONALD R. "The Relationship Between Church and Social Class in Scotland". Ph.D. Thesis, University of Edinburgh, 1966.

ROOZEN, DAVID A. *The Church and the Unchurched in America: A Comparative Profile*. Washington, D.C.: Glenmary Research Center, 1978.

SARTRE, JOHN PAUL. *The Words*. Translated by Bernard Frechtman. New York: G. Brazliller, 1964. Quoted in Shane Womack "Encounters With Atheists at a State University", p. 76. M.A.R. thesis, Emmanuel School of Religion, 1983.

SCHILLEBEECKX, E. "Theological Reflections on Religo-Sociological Interpretations of Modern 'Irreligion'", *Social Compass* 10 (1963), 257-284.

"Secularization and Atheism", *Herder Correspondence* 5 (November 1968), 343-346.

SPIEGELBERG, FREDERIK. *The Religion of Non-Religion*. Stanford, California: James Ladd Delkin, 1953.

STOTT, JOHN R. W. "The Biblical Basis of Evangelism". In *Let the Earth Hear His Voice*. Edited by J. D. Douglas. Minneapolis: World Wide Publications, 1975.

STRINGFELLOW, WILLIAM. *A Private and Public Faith*. Grand Rapids: William B. Eerdmans Publishing Company, 1962.

240

Main Source List

SZCZESNY, GERHARD. *The Future of Unbelief.* Translated by Edward B. Garside. London: Heinemann, 1961.

TAYLOR, JOHN V. *The Go-Between God.* London: SCM, 1972.

THOMAS, W. H. GRIFFITH. *Christianity is Christ.* Chicago: Moody Press, 1965.

TILLER J. *A Strategy for the Church's Ministry.* London: CIO, 1983. Quoted by John Mahoney, "Theological and Pastoral Reflections" in *Values and Social Change in Britain.* Edited by Mark Abrams, David Gerard, Noel Timms. London: Macmillan, forthcoming.

TILLICH, PAUL. *The Courage to Be.* New Haven and London: Yale, 1952.

TOLSTOY, LEO. *A Confession in a Confession: The Gospel in Brief and What I Believe.* Oxford: Oxford University Press, 1954.

_____. *Anna Karenin.* London: Penguin Books, 1954.

TONKS, HAROLD. "Faith, Hope, and Decision Making". Ph.D. Thesis, University of Birmingham, 1981.

TOUCHET, FRANCIS H. "An Atheist Reconsiders Religion", *Perspectives in Religious Studies* 6 (1979), 243-253.

TYRRELL, FRANCIS M. *Man: Believer and Unbeliever.* New York: Alba House, 1974.

WARD, J. M. "Faith, Faithfulness in the Old Testament". In *The Interpreter's Dictionary of the Bible,* Supplementary Volume, pp. 329-332. Edited by Keith Crin. Nashville: Abingdon Press, 1976.

WARFIELD, B. B. "Faith". In *A Dictionary of the Bible.* Edited by James Hastings. Edinburgh: T. & T. Clark, 1898, I, pp. 827-838.

WETZEL, C. ROBERT, ed. *Essays on New Testament Christianity.* Cincinnati: Standard Publishing, 1978.

WILSON, BRYAN R. *Religion in Secular Society.* London: C. A. Watts and Company, 1966.

WINKLER, TILMAN. "Latentes religiöses Bewusstsein in der Arbeiterschaft", *Texte* 4 (Hanover: EKD, [October, 1982]), 13-17.

WOMACK, SHANE. "Encounters With Atheists at a State University: Personal Interviews and Theological Reflections". M.A.R. thesis, Emmanuel School of Religion, 1983.

WOOD, H. G. *Belief and Unbelief Since 1850.* Cambridge: Cambridge University Press, 1955.

Main Source List

SOURCES CONSULTED:

INTERVIEWING AND SOCIOLOGICAL METHOD

ADAMS, RICHARD N., and PREISS, JACK D., eds. Human Organization Research: Field Relations and Techniques. Homewood, Illinois: Dorsey, 1960.

BABBIE, EARL R. The Practice of Social Research. Belmont, California: Wadsworth Publishing Company, 1975.

BACKSTROM, CHARLES H., and HURSH, GERALD D. Survey Research. Chicago: Northwestern University Press, 1963.

BANAKA, WILLIAM H. Training in Depth Interviewing. New York: Harper and Row, 1971.

BELSON, W. A. "Research on Question Design", Business Review (Australia) 7 (1964b), 14-19.

BLUNDEN, R. M. "Sampling Frames", Commentary: Journal of the Market Research Society 8 (1966), 101-112.

BUCHER, R., FRITZ, C. E. and QUARANTELLI, E. L. "Tape Recorded Interviews in Social Research", American Sociological Review 21 (1956), 359-364.

CARTWRIGHT, A., and TUCKER, W. "An Attempt to Reduce the Number of Calls on an Interview Inquiry", Public Opinion Quarterly 31 (1967), 299-302.

COCHRAN, W. G. Sampling Techniques. 2nd ed. New York: Wiley, 1963.

DAVIDSON, JAMES. "Glock's Model of Religious Commitment: Assessing Some Different Approaches and Results", Review of Religious Research 16 (1975), 83-93.

DEAN, JOHN P., and WHYTE, WILLIAM FOOTE. "How Do You Know if the Informant is Telling the Truth?", Human Organization 17 (1958), 34-38.

DENZIN, NORMAN K. The Research Act in Sociology: A Theoretical Introduction to Sociological Methods. London: Butterworths, 1970.

DITTES, J. E. "Secular Religion: Dilemma of Churches and Researchers", Review of Religious Research 10 (1969), 65-80.

Interviewing Sources

DITTMAN, A. T. "The Relationship Between Body Movements and Moods in Interviews", *Journal of Consulting Psychology* 26 (1962), 480ff.

DURBIN, J. "Non-Response and Call-Backs in Surveys", *Bulletin of the International Statistical Institute* 34 (1954), 72-86.

FAULKNER, JOSEPH E., and DEJONG, GORDON F. "Religiosity in 5-D: An Empirical Analysis". In *Religious Influence in Contemporary Society*, pp. 57-70. Edited by Joseph E. Faulkner. Columbus, Ohio: Charles E. Merrill Publishing Company, 1972.

FILSTEAD, WILLIAM J., ed. *Qualitative Methodology: Firsthand Involvement with the Social World*. Chicago: Markham Publishing Company, 1970.

FINNEY, JOHN M. "A Theory of Religious Commitment", *Sociological Analysis* 39 (1978), 19-35.

GALLUP, G. H. "The Quintamensional Plan of Question Design", *Public Opinion Quarterly* 11 (1947), 385-393.

GANS, HERBERT T. *The Urban Villages*. New York: Free Press, 1962.

GLOCK, CHARLES Y. "On the Study of Religious Commitment", *Religious Education* Research Supplement (July-August 1962), S98-S110.

GLOCK, CHARLES Y., and STARK, RODNEY. *Christian Beliefs and Anti-Semitism*. New York: Harper and Row, 1966.

_____. *Religion and Society in Tension*. Chicago: Rand McNally, 1965.

GORSUCH, RICHARD L., and MCFARLAND, SAM G. "Single Vs. Multiple-Item Scales for Measuring Religious Commitment", *Journal for the Scientific Study of Religion* 11 (1972), 53-64.

GRAY, DAVID B. "Measuring Attitudes Toward the Church", *Journal for the Scientific Study of Religion* 9 (1970), 293-297.

GRAY, P. G.; CORLETT, T.; and FRANKLAND, P. "The Register of Electors as a Sampling Frame", *Government Social Survey* M59 (1950).

HANSEN, M. H., and HAUSER, P. M. "Area Sampling--Some Principles of Sample Design", *Public Opinion Quarterly* 9 (1945), 183-193.

HIMMELFARB, HAROLD. "Measuring Religious Involvement", *Social Forces* 53 (1975), 606-618.

HUNT, RICHARD A., and KING, MORTON. "The Intrinsic-Extrinsic Concept: A Review and Evaluation", *Journal for the Scientific Study of Religion* 10 (1971), 339-356.

Interviewing Sources

HYMAN, HERBERT HIRAM. *Interviewing in Social Research*. Chicago: The University of Chicago Press, 1975.

KAHN, R. L., and CANNELL, C. F. *The Dynamics of Interviewing: Theory, Technique and Cases*. New York: John Wiley, 1957.

_____. "Interviewing," *The Handbook of Social Psychology*. Vol. 2, pp. 526-595. Edited by G. Lindzey and E. Aronson. Reading, Massachusetts: Addison-Wesley, 1968.

KING, MORTON. "Measuring the Religious Variable: Nine Proposed Dimensions". In *The Social Meanings of Religion: An Integrated Anthology*. Edited by William M. Newman. Chicago: Rand McNally College Publishing Company, 1974.

KLAPP, ORRIN EDGAR. *Collective Search for Identity*. New York: Holt, Rinehart, and Winston, 1969.

KLEMMACH, D. L., and CARDWELL, J. D. "Interfaith Comparison of Multidimensional Measures of Religiosity", *Pacific Sociological Review* 16 (1973), 495-507.

LAZARSFELD, PAUL F. "The Art of Asking WHY in Marketing Research", *The National Marketing Review* 1 (1935), 26-38.

LEWIS, OSCAR. *The Children of Sanchez*. New York: Random House, 1961.

MACHALEK, RICHARD. "Definitional Strategies in the Study of Religion", *Journal for the Scientific Study of Religion* 16 (1977), 395-401.

MACHALEK, RICHARD, and MARTIN, MICHAEL. "'Invisible' Religions: Some Preliminary Evidence", *Journal for the Scientific Study of Religion* 15 (1976), 311-321.

MANNHEIMER, D. and HYMAN, H. "Interviewer Performance in Area Sampling", *Public Opinion Quarterly* 13 (1949), 83-92.

MICHIGAN UNIVERSITY SURVEY RESEARCH CENTER. *Interviewer's Manual*. Ann Arbor, Michigan: Institute for Social Research, University of Michigan, 1969.

MOSER, C. A. and KATTON, G. *Survey Methods in Social Investigation*. London: Heinemann Educational Books, 1958, 1971.

MOUW, RICHARD J. "Explaining Social Reality: Some Christian Reflections", *Themelios* 6 (January 1981), 7-12.

NELSON, HART M. et. al., "A Test of Yinger's Measure of Non-Doctrinal Religion: Implications for Invisible Religion as a Belief System", *Journal for the Scientific Study of Religion* 15 (1976), 263-267.

OPPENHEIM, A. N. *Questionnaire Design and Attitude Measurement*. London: Heinemann, 1966.

Interviewing Sources

PAYNE, S. L. *The Art of Asking Questions*. Princeton, New Jersey: Princeton University Press, 1951.

PEARSON, E.S., ed. *Tracts for Computers*. Cambridge: Cambridge University Press, 1939. No. 24: *Tables of Random Sampling Numbers*, by M. G. Kendall and B. Babinton-Smith.

POPE, BENJAMIN, and SIEGMAN, ARON W. "Interviewer Warmth and Verbal Communication in the Initial Interview", *Journal of Consulting and Clinical Psychology* 32 (1968), 588-595.

RICHARDSON, STEPHEN A.; DOHRENWIND, BARBARA SNELL; and KLEIN, DAVID. *Interviewing: Its Forms and Functions*. New York: Basic Books, 1965.

RIGNEY, DANIEL; MACHALEK, RICHARD; and GOODMAN, JERRY D. "Is Secularization a Discontinuous Process?", *Journal for the Scientific Study of Religion* 17 (1978), 381-387.

ROOF, WADE CLARK et al. "Yinger's Measure of Non-Doctrinal Religion: A Northeastern Test", *Journal for the Scientific Study of Religion* 16 (1977), 403-408.

SHAPIRO, S., and EBERHART, J. C. "Interviewer Differences in an Intensive Interview Survey", *International Journal of Opinion and Attitude Research* 1 (1947), 1-17.

SMITH, H. L., and HYMAN, H. "The Biasing Effect of Interviewer Expectations on Survey Results", *Public Opinion Quarterly* 14 (1950), 491-506.

SNOW, DAVID A., and MACHALEK, RICHARD. "On the Presumed Fragility of Unconventional Beliefs", *Journal for the Scientific Study of Religion* (March 1982).

STARK, RODNEY, and GLOCK, CHARLES Y. *American Piety: The Nature of Religious Commitment*. Berkeley: University of California Press, 1968.

STEBBINS, ROBERT A. "The Unstructured Research Interview as Incipient Interpersonal Relationship", *Sociology and Social Research* 56 (1972), 164-179.

STROMMEN, M. P. *Research on Religious Development*. New York: Hawthorne, 1971.

SUCHMAN, E. A., and GUTTMAN, L. "A Solution to the Problem of Question 'Bias'", *Public Opinion Quarterly* 11 (1947), 445-455.

TAPP, ROBERT B. "Dimensions of Religiosity in a Post-Traditional Group", *Journal for the Scientific Study of Religion* 10 (1971), 41-47.

VOGT, E. "Objectivity in Research", in *Readings in the Sociology of Religion*. Edited by Joan Brothers. Oxford: Pergamon Press, 1967.

Interviewing Sources

WEBB, E. J. et. al. *Unobtrusive Measure: Non-reactive Research in the Social Sciences.* Chicago: Rand McNally, 1966.

WILLIAMSON, JOHN B.; KARP, DAVID A.; and DALPHIN, JOHN R. *The Research Craft: An Introduction to Social Science Methods.* Boston: Little, Brown, and Company, 1977.

WUTHNOW, ROBERT, ed. *The Religious Dimension: New Directions in Quantitative Research.* New York: Academic Press, 1979.

STUDIEN ZUR INTERKULTURELLEN GESCHICHTE DES CHRISTENTUMS
ETUDES D'HISTOIRE INTERCULTURELLE DU CHRISTIANISME
STUDIES IN THE INTERCULTURAL HISTORY OF CHRISTIANITY

Begründet von/fondé par/founded by
Hans Jochen Margull † , Hamburg

Herausgegeben von/edité par/edited by

Richard Friedli   Walter J. Hollenweger   Theo Sundermeier
Université de Fribourg   University of Birmingham   Universität Heidelberg

Band 1   Wolfram Weiße: Südafrika und das Antirassismusprogramm. Kirchen im Spannungsfeld einer Rassengesellschaft.

Band 2   Ingo Lembke: Christentum unter den Bedingungen Latienamerikas. Die katholische Kirche vor den Problemen der Abhängigkeit und Unterentwicklung.

Band 3   Gerd Uwe Kliewer: Das neue Volk der Pfingstler. Religion, Unterentwicklung und sozialer Wandel in Lateinamerika.

Band 4   Joachim Wietzke: Theologie im modernen Indien - Paul David Devanandan.

Band 5   Werner Ustorf: Afrikanische Initiative. Das aktive Leiden des Propheten Simon Kimbangu.

Band 6   Erhard Kamphausen: Anfänge der kirchlichen Unabhängigkeitsbewegung in Südafrika. Geschichte und Theologie der äthiopischen Bewegung. 1880-1910.

Band 7   Lothar Engel: Kolonialismus und Nationalismus im deutschen Protestantismus in Namibia 1907-1945. Beiträge zur Geschichte der deutschen evangelischen Mission und Kirche im ehemaligen Kolonial- und Mandatsgebiet Südwestafrika.

Band 8   Pamela M. Binyon: The Concepts of "Spirit" and "Demon". A Study in the use of different languages describing the same phenomena.

Band 9   Neville Richardson: The World Council of Churches and Race Relations: 1960 to 1969.

Band 10   Jörg Müller: Uppsala II. Erneuerung in der Mission. Eine redaktionsgeschichtliche Studie und Dokumentation zu Sektion II der 4. Vollversammlung des Ökumenischen Rates der Kirchen, Uppsala 1968.

Band 11   Hans Schöpfer: Theologie und Gesellschaft. Interdisziplinäre Grundlagenbibliographie zur Einführung in die befreiungs- und polittheologische Problematik: 1960-1975.

Band 12   Werner Hoerschelmann: Christliche Gurus. Darstellung von Selbstverständnis und Funktion indigenen Christseins durch unabhängige charismatisch geführte Gruppen in Südindien.

Band 13   Claude Schaller. L'Eglise en quête de dialogue. Vergriffen.

Band 14   Theo Tschuy: Hundert Jahre kubanischer Protestantismus (1868-1961). Versuch einer kirchengeschichtlichen Darstellung.

Band 15   Werner Korte: Wir sind die Kirchen der unteren Klassen. Entstehung, Organisation und gesellschaftliche Funktionen unabhängiger Kirchen in Afrika.

Band 16   Arnold Bittlinger: Papst und Pfingstler. Der römisch katholisch-pfingstliche Dialog und seine ökumenische Relevanz.

Band 17   Ingemar Lindén: The Last Trump. An historico-genetical study of some important chapters in the making and development of the Seventh-day Adventist Church.

Band 18   Zwinglio Dias: Krisen und Aufgaben im brasilianischen Protestantismus. Eine Studie zu den sozialgeschichtlichen Bedingungen und volkspädagogischen Möglichkeiten der Evangelisation.

Band 19   Mary Hall: A quest for the liberated Christian, Examined on the basis of a mission, a man and a movement as agents of liberation.